Betty Williams
5444 N Maroa Ave Apt 101
Fresno CA 93704-2003

D1008778

# DO-GOODERS

Also by Mona Charen

*Useful Idiots: How Liberals Got It Wrong in the Cold War and Still Blame America First*

# DO-GOODERS

How Liberals Hurt Those They Claim
to Help—and the Rest of Us

## Mona Charen

Sentinel

SENTINEL
Published by the Penguin Group
Penguin Group (USA) Inc., 375 Hudson Street, New York, New York 10014, U.S.A.
Penguin Group (Canada), 10 Alcorn Avenue, Toronto, Ontario, Canada M4V 3B2
(a division of Pearson Penguin Canada Inc.)
Penguin Books Ltd, 80 Strand, London WC2R 0RL, England
Penguin Ireland, 25 St. Stephen's Green, Dublin 2, Ireland
(a division of Penguin Books Ltd)
Penguin Books Australia Ltd, 250 Camberwell Road, Camberwell,
Victoria 3124, Australia
(a division of Pearson Australia Group Pty Ltd)
Penguin Books India Pvt Ltd, 11 Community Centre, Panchsheel Park,
New Delhi – 110 017, India
Penguin Group (NZ), Cnr Airborne and Rosedale Roads, Albany,
Auckland, New Zealand
(a division of Pearson New Zealand Ltd) ·
Penguin Books (South Africa) (Pty) Ltd, 24 Sturdee Avenue,
Rosebank, Johannesburg 2196, South Africa

Penguin Books Ltd, Registered Offices:
80 Strand, London WC2R 0RL, England

First published in 2004 by Sentinel,
a member of Penguin Group (USA) Inc.

10  9  8  7  6  5  4  3  2  1

LIBRARY OF CONGRESS CATALOGING-IN-PUBLICATION DATA

Charen, Mona.
    Do-gooders : how liberals hurt those they claim to help—and the rest of us / Mona
Charen.
        p. cm.
    Includes bibliographical references and index.
    ISBN 1-59523-003-3
    1. Social problems—United States. 2. Liberalism—United States. 3. United States—
Social policy. I. Title.

HN65.C463 2004
361.973–dc22          2004059238

This book is printed on acid-free paper. ∞

Printed in the United States of America
Set in Bodoni Twelve
Designed by Daniel Lagin

*In memory of my parents:*

*George Charen (1913–1993)*
*and*
*Claire Charen (1923–1989)*

*And in gratitude for their love of learning, family, and America*

# Acknowledgments

One of the pleasures of book writing (and there are many pains) is the generous help that brilliant and wonderful friends and colleagues offer.

Karlyn Bowman of the American Enterprise Institute was unfailingly helpful with survey numbers. If she couldn't find it in the data, it didn't exist. Tom Atwood, president of the National Council for Adoption, directed me to valuable research about family welfare. Brent Baker and Jessica Anderson of the Media Research Center were fonts of information. Mary Schwarz of the Institute on American Values devoted herself to finding just the right essays on family structure. Jeannie Allen of the Center for Education Reform knew where to find the numbers I thought I knew on education but couldn't quite place. Sheri Annis recalled her work on Proposition 227 in California. I am also grateful to Pat Fagan, Kelly Hobbs, John Fund, C. Todd Jones, Barbara Ledeen, Barbara Comstock, Kate O'Beirne, Stephen and Abigail Thernstrom, and Robert Bork for a variety of suggestions.

I have relied on the work of many outstanding academics, journalists, and intellectuals for this work, but five deserve special mention. Heather MacDonald of the Manhattan Institute has brought her sharp eye and keen intelligence to many of the most vexing social issues of our time. She is liberally quoted in these pages. Michael Fumento has made a career of debunking conventional wisdom and his research has been invaluable. Byron York of *National Review* has a way of producing the indispensable article at just the right time. And Stuart Taylor brings his superb radar and eminent fairness to every issue he tackles. Finally, I'd like to acknowledge a debt to the late Michael Kelly, who was tragically killed while embedded with U.S. forces in Iraq. I did not know him personally, but his great spirit and superb writing have inspired me in the writing of this book.

My thanks also go to Rick Newcombe, president of Creators Syndicate, who was most patient and understanding when I had to take a one-month leave of absence from column writing to complete this work and who has long provided moral support and encouragement.

Hugo and Meghan Gurdon were kind enough to read much of the manuscript in draft form and offered trenchant comments. It's a measure of our friendship that I was willing to let them see the thing in such a primitive state. It's a little like appearing in public first thing in the morning before you've combed your hair or applied make-up. And Priscilla Buckley has once again taken the time to read an entire manuscript when she could have been working on her own books. I'm afraid I couldn't submit a draft to a publisher without her imprimatur. I'm also grateful for the advice and suggestions of David Frum and Danielle Crittenden, who helped me to keep my sanity.

My agent, Carole Mann, is the midwife of this project. I've relied on her unfailing expertise and friendship throughout. Adrian Zackheim, creator of Sentinel, helped to shape an amorphous idea into a real book and was patient through a series of early delays. Bernadette Malone is a wonderful editor.

On the home front, Laura Johnson helped to keep children and household running smoothly and ensured that everything was labeled, filed, and in its place. Gipper and Teddy owe her a lot too. The "dive coach" was of course invaluable in a thousand ways. This book would never have crossed the finish line without her. Clara Magram was a delightful, bright, and diligent research assistant.

My children have seen less of me than they would have liked for the past five months, but they've borne up very well and I'm extremely proud of them for their fortitude. It won't be long before I turn the writing franchise over to them. Finally, my husband, Bob, has, as always, been a source of sound advice, life-enhancing humor, and loving companionship. I regularly draw upon his wide knowledge and am fortunate to share my life with such a buoyant soul.

# Contents

# Introduction

In the late 1970s, as a college student, I took a stroll down Riverside Drive in New York City. In upper Manhattan, Riverside Park slopes down a hill toward the Hudson River. Gazing up at the city from the river, I was struck by its faded beauty. Riverside Church's gothic bell tower rose majestically above the trees along the park. The apartment buildings along Riverside Drive were stately—if you could imagine them spruced up and sporting gloved doormen as in days of old. Someone had planted cherry trees in the park near the river and their blossoms strove valiantly to cheer the dirty and decayed surroundings. A playground was situated where there must once have been a lawn, with a lovely view of the water. But you had to use your imagination to see it as anything other than an eyesore in 1979. The swings were broken. The seesaw was covered with graffiti. The chain basketball net had been so badly damaged that just a few strings of metal hung sadly from the rim, giving it the look of a broken spiderweb.

This part of Manhattan was not a slum—far from it. But, like the rest of New York and like so many other cities, it had degenerated into a graffiti-stained, soiled, broken-down, dangerous shell of its former self. Only a couple of years before, during the blackout of 1977, the neighborhood around Columbia University had been overrun by looters. Working for a professor that summer, I sat outside my apartment with a lighted candle and listened to the sounds of breaking glass as storefronts were smashed.

Freshmen at Barnard College (Columbia University's Women's College) were offered safety instructions at orientation. Never walk without a buddy after dark. Never enter Morningside Park (the park that separates Columbia University's campus from Harlem) under any circumstances. A Barnard girl who ignored this advice had been raped and murdered a few years before. Never open your door to a stranger, and so forth. Riverside Park was considered safe during daylight hours. Nevertheless, my close friend was attacked and nearly raped there in our senior year. We students stepped carefully around homeless people camped on sidewalks and averted our eyes from the toughs who roamed the subways.

My parents had both attended college in New York City as well–my father in the 1930s and my mother in the 1940s. Street crime then was nearly nonexistent. My father told me that many Columbia students used to travel up to Harlem for good jazz–something that was simply out of the question for us. My mother's experience was similar. In the 1940s, the city certainly contained more noncon-formists and Bohemians than other parts of the country–but the atmosphere of disorder, threat, and overall incivility that greeted students and others of my generation were unknown to them.

What happened? Liberalism happened. Starting in the 1960s, liberal ideas on crime, welfare, education, mental illness, family structure, and race relations–among many other things–gained pre-eminence. Brimming with arrogant self-righteousness, liberals of the 1960s announced that they would eliminate poverty, reverse in-justice, abolish rote learning, introduce sexual liberation, free the mentally ill, and compensate for the sin of racism. They thought of themselves as do-gooders, but with only a few exceptions, their ideas have yielded harm. Lyndon Johnson, Gloria Steinem, Norman Lear, Marian Wright Edelman, Jesse Jackson, and legions of their allies on the Left took a wrecking ball to American education, family life, criminal justice, welfare policy, and more.

The results of their efforts made life in cities like New York nearly unendurable by the early 1980s. Things were scarcely better in smaller cities and towns and the suburbs. New York City was like a ca-nary in a coal mine, reacting first to the noxious ideas that would quickly spread throughout the nation. Today, thanks to a return to sensible conservatism, New York is much improved. But if this country is to avoid the mistakes of the past, we must be sure we understand what went wrong.

Liberals always look back upon the 1960s as the high-water mark of idealism and selflessness. I view it differently. The ideas that took root in the 1960s were uniformly self-indulgent, childish, antiintellectual, irresponsible, and destructive. They failed because they were completely inconsistent with human nature.

This book is a chronicle of failure–the failure of liberals to help those they set out to help. But it is also a moral challenge. Liberals must be called to account for the real havoc they have created in so many lives. They must be asked to offer something more than good intentions when their actions lead to disaster.

For as long as I can remember, conservatives have been on the defensive. We've been at pains to prove that we are not what the liberals say we are. George W. Bush was only the most recent Republican to package himself as a "compassionate conservative," the better to rebut the popular image of conservatives as Scrooge-like. Before him, Jack Kemp styled himself a "bleeding-heart conservative" and George H. W. Bush advertised his new administration in 1989 as "kinder and gentler" than his predecessor's. During a debate with Bill Clinton, Bob Dole "boasted" that his own parents had been on government assistance.

Conservatives tend to underestimate the worth of their own principles–freedom, self-reliance, tough-mindedness, empiricism–and seem to accept the idea that liberal values–compassion, softheartedness (soft-headedness?), and equality–are superior. The purpose of this book is to call into question that presumption of liberal virtue.

Are liberals truly more concerned about the poorest and weakest members of society than other Americans? Or are they simply in love with the idea of their own righteousness? When you demonstrate indifference to the harmful effects of your supposedly benevolent efforts, isn't it fair to call your motives into question? Besides, throughout the past four decades, liberals have caused real damage. If that is "compassion," then clearly we need a great deal less of it.

Liberal dominance of important areas of America's social and political life has undermined many of the virtues that have sustained this country. Though liberal ideas have suffered setbacks in recent years in the areas of crime control, welfare, and family life, the rout is far from complete. This book is a contribution to finishing the job.

# DO-GOODERS

Chapter One
# JUDGE NOT—HOW LIBERALISM CREATED THE CRIME WAVE

If you were inclined to assault your neighbor and steal his car in 1958, you would have to consider that neither the police nor the courts would cut you any slack because you had a deprived childhood. Nineteen fifties' America was hardly a police state, but there was none of the sentimentality toward criminals that would characterize the following two decades. The average robbery earned a sentence of 389 days.[1] If you were arrested, the police would be free to question you about your whereabouts at the time the crime was committed and establish your alibi (if any)—all without reading you your rights or permitting you first to phone a lawyer. If, in the course of questioning you about your activities, the police found the baseball bat with which you beat your neighbor over the head, they could use it as evidence against you even if they lacked a warrant when they discovered it.

Thanks to self-described do-gooders, America went on a compassion binge in the 1960s. The compassion was extended toward the poor and minorities; unfortunately, among the prime beneficiaries of this tenderness were violent criminals who would go on to terrorize the very poor neighborhoods whose well-being liberals supposedly sought. Things would improve 30 years later when conservative policy makers were finally able to reverse the liberal policies that had created so much chaos.

An early signal of the sixties' laxity could be found in the statistics on punishment. In 1950, the expected punishment for murder and negligent manslaughter was 2.3 years in prison. By 1970, this had dropped to 1.7 years. Liberal academics and public intellectuals persuaded the nation that we needed to address the "root causes" of crime such as poverty and injustice. The psychotherapeutic model was much in vogue, and notions of "guilt" and "sin" were starting to seem passé. Improve the ghettoes, we were told, and crime would decrease. Give people hope, and crime would evaporate. Certainly expected punishment declined. In 1950, the chance that a murderer would face the death penalty was 1 in 67. By 1997, it had declined to 1 in 246.[2]

Every kind of crime, property and personal, exploded during the decades of the 1960s and 1970s. At the same time, sentences plunged. The graphs are the inverse of each other. Between 1961 and 1968, while the population expanded and the crime rate rocketed upward, the total number of prison inmates declined.[3]

The Supreme Court threw its considerable weight into the liberalizing trend in criminal law. In 1949, the Court declared that retribution was "no longer the dominant objective of the criminal law." With naïve optimism, it declared that the goal of incarceration would henceforth be "reformation and rehabilitation."[4] In *Mapp v. Ohio* (1961), the Court ruled that evidence obtained without a warrant or otherwise in violation of the Fourth Amendment could not be used in state criminal trials (a federal exclusionary rule had been in effect since 1914).[5] Evidence obtained through improper searches would be considered, in legal parlance, fruit of the poisoned tree, and therefore inadmissible. The practical effect, as Justice John Harlan predicted in his dissent, was to vastly increase the number of convictions thrown out "on a technicality." Justice Benjamin Cardozo had warned presciently in 1926 against a rule that would allow the "criminal to go free because the constable had blundered."[6] But Harlan's and Cardozo's warnings were swept aside. Subsequent studies have suggested that the exclusionary rule does nothing to deter police misconduct.[7] A rule requiring that police be sanctioned for illegal searches might have, but that is water over the dam.

The exclusionary rule quickly became a career criminal's best friend. Examples abound. In Washington, D.C., police noticed a car circling a neighborhood repeatedly and became suspicious. They pulled the car over and discovered that the driver had an outstanding arrest warrant. Searching the car, police found a loaded revolver, bullets, a sawed-off shotgun, and ammunition. The defendant was convicted but appealed on grounds that the search of his car was unconstitutional. The Court of Appeals for the D.C. Circuit agreed, ruling in 1977 that however justified police suspicions turned out to be, they had no right to search the vehicle without a warrant.[8]

As Ernest van den Haag, a professor of jurisprudence at Fordham University, pointed out, the exclusionary rule offers no advantage to innocent defendants. It merely serves to exclude evidence of guilt. The innocent man arrested without probable cause derives no benefit.[9]

In *Miranda v. Arizona* (1966), the Court clapped handcuffs on the police, ruling that no confession would be admissible in court unless it were preceded by an elaborate overture of warnings and safeguards. It should be noted that it had long been the practice that a confession extracted by coercion or torture would be invalid. The Miranda ruling went far beyond that commonsense rule. Every television crime-show viewer knows that police are now required to recite a lengthy list of rights to any arrested suspect, including, "You have the right to remain silent . . . ," and to extend the government's obligation to provide a lawyer for each defendant if he cannot afford to hire one himself. It is not possible to measure how many confessions were lost due to the Miranda ruling, but the impact on plea bargains is plain. Criminologist Henry Pontell reports that in the pre-Miranda years, 60 percent of California defendants pleaded guilty to the original top charge. After 1966, that figure dropped to 42 percent.[10] Far from simply forbidding police to coerce confessions, Miranda discouraged criminals from cooperating with the police in any fashion.

More than two decades of liberal judging followed, giving rise to outcomes that only intellectuals could rationalize. The U.S. Court of Appeals for the Tenth Circuit (which covers Oklahoma, Kansas, New Mexico, Colorado, Wyoming, and Utah), overruled a district court decision in 1995 involving the Eighth Amendment to the Constitution. A prisoner, one Josephine Brown, who believed his inner self to be female but who required an expensive cocktail of hormones to produce an outer simulacrum of femininity, sued the state of Colorado for refusing to provide him/her with estrogen and other medical attention. The district court declined to find that this amounted to cruel and unusual punishment, but the Court of Appeals disagreed. The judge who wrote the opinion was a Clinton appointee.[11]

Another Clinton-appointed judge, Harold Baer, ruled that $4 million worth of confiscated cocaine and heroin as well as a forty-minute taped confession could not be used in evidence at a drug trial in New York. Baer reasoned that the five suspects in the case had been arrested illegally. Police had noticed one of the defendants double park her car in the Washington Heights neighborhood of New York. Four men then dropped large duffel bags into the trunk. When the men caught sight of the police, they fled. The driver was pulled over, her car searched, and seventy-five pounds of drugs were discovered in the duffel bags.[12] The state of New York argued that the police had probable cause to search the vehicle since flight is usually interpreted as evidence of wrongdoing. But Judge Baer's view was that fleeing from the police was a normal response for residents of Washington Heights. The police, he said, were viewed as "corrupt, abusive, and violent."[13] Such was the public disgust with this ruling that the judge soon reversed himself (though Judge Baer claimed that hearing additional testimony from another police officer is what changed his mind).

Some liberal judging stories became worthy of late-night comedy. One concerned Judge Bruce Wright of New York, who was so benevolent toward muggers, rapists, and thugs that he earned the nickname "Turn 'Em Loose Bruce." John Derbyshire of *National Review* Online related an account of Wright's troubles:

> One day, Judge Wright got mugged in the street near his home. He was off work for a few days. It was a big story in the tabloid newspapers, and a lot of people were making jokes

about it. When Judge Wright returned to the bench, he made
a point of starting off that day's session with an announcement: "As I'm sure you all know, I was the victim of a criminal assault the other day. I want to make it clear that this
experience will in no way change my sentencing policies on
this bench!" As he paused to let this sink in, someone called
out from the back of the courtroom: "Mug him again!"[14]

There is no question that a liberal approach to crime–leniency in
sentencing, greater procedural protections for the accused, rational-
izations (poverty, rage, or frustration) for criminal conduct, and a
tendency to blame society rather than the perpetrator for criminal
acts–created a climate in the 1960s and 1970s that helped to boost
the crime rate. Other liberal initiatives and ideas further weakened
restraints on lawlessness: the decline of the family, welfare dependency, and the overall withdrawal of respect for authority.

The irony is that liberal solicitude for the criminal class hurt the
poor, particularly the black poor who tend to live in central cities,
more severely than it affected anyone else. The rich and the middle
class have been able, as criminologist John J. DiIulio has characterized it, to "harden their targets."[15] They've invested billions in private security guards for businesses, home burglar alarms, special
lighting, and secure apartment buildings with doormen. They've had
the freedom, because they have the means, to move away from high-
crime areas. The poor, however, were not able to afford those kinds
of defenses. They had to rely on cops and the justice system. And yet,
when they turned to the police and the courts, what did they find? A
great many pin-striped and/or robed limousine liberals, comfortably
removed from urban violence themselves, who insisted, in the name
of doing good, that every last benefit of the doubt go to the thugs and
murderers who were making life utterly miserable for the poor. As we
have witnessed in the revival of cities that has accompanied falling
crime rates in the 1990s and beyond, crime more than any other factor has blighted poor neighborhoods.

This was clearly not the intention of liberal policy makers. But, as in the cases of homelessness, education, and family structure, the sin lies not so much in the original mistake as in the stubborn refusal to acknowledge unintended results.

## Crime as a Civil Rights Issue

Liberal leniency on crime was a direct outgrowth of the heady civil rights era. The paternalism nurtured in the hearts of idealistic liberals as they marched with Dr. Martin Luther King Jr. strongly affected liberal thinking about crime. To the average do-gooder pre-1960, a criminal was just a criminal. But after the civil rights era, criminals came to be seen as victims of society deserving at first pity, later understanding, and, toward the early 1970s, outright celebration. Leonard Bernstein's 1970 fund-raiser for the Black Panthers was Exhibit A in that sorry tale.

The civil rights movement, it must be acknowledged, was liberalism's glory. Rarely does a public policy question present itself in such stark relief as good versus evil. The scandal of racism had to be exposed; the sin of racial discrimination had to be expunged. Liberals deserved credit for making this cause their own. It was unquestionably one of the most important crusades of American history, and the leaders of the movement, black and white, were nearly all liberals.

They've been dining out on it ever since. Actually, if that were the whole story, it wouldn't rankle so. We might smile indulgently as Old Uncle Henry recounted his freedom riding days for the thirtieth time or Aunt Sally described the terrible faces of the white racists in Selma or Montgomery.

One can even understand, to a point, the nostalgia liberals feel for the 1950s and early 1960s, a time when all of the bad guys had white skins and most of the good guys were dark. Unsubtle minds adore tidy categories: big business bad, unions good; whites bad, blacks good; women truthful, men liars; Native Americans peaceful, European settlers cruel. If liberals had simply reveled in their past virtue, all might have been well. But righteousness has a nasty habit of becoming self-righteousness, and liberals developed a severe case from which they have yet to recover.

This self-righteousness, this endless pursuit of the elation they enjoyed during the civil rights era, has led liberals to the very opposite results they claim to desire. It has poisoned relations between the races unnecessarily and contributed to a series of social pathologies that were entirely avoidable.

Of course, no discussion of crime can begin without the acknowledgment that crimes against black Americans went completely unpunished in many parts of the United States until the middle of the twentieth century. As Swedish economist Gunnar Myrdal observed after visiting the American South in the 1930s:

> The Negro cannot claim the protection of the police or the courts, and personal vengeance on the part of the Negro usually results in organized retaliation in form of bodily injury (including lynching), home burning or banishment.[16]

While crimes blacks committed against whites were punished extremely harshly, sometimes even savagely, black on black crime was often ignored by police, prosecutors, and judges, who were uniformly white. In Mississippi, a newspaper editor opined that few blacks were ever prosecuted for killing other blacks because "It's like dog chewing on dog, and the white people are not interested in the matter. Only another dead nigger–that's all."[17]

For reasons that may have their roots in this history, blacks have always committed a disproportionate share of violent crimes in America. In 1890 Philadelphia, the murder rate among blacks was five and a half times higher than that among whites.[18] Other cities showed similar trends. Though rates of violent crime have always been higher in the United States than in Europe, it was not until the post–civil rights era that violent crime soared.

Between 1960 and 1999, the violent crime rate in the United States increased 226 percent.[19] The murder rate increased 122 percent between 1963 and 1980; forcible rape increased by 287 percent, robbery rose by 294 percent, and aggravated assault increased by 215 percent.[20] Property crime ballooned as well, with burglary increasing 189 percent, larceny up 159 percent, and auto theft rising by 128 percent during the same period.[21] This crime explosion coincided, as noted earlier, with a new leniency in punishment. While the number of violent crimes jumped from 1 million in 1960 to 2.9 million in 1970, the number of prison sentences meted out by the courts declined from 40,000 in 1960 to 37,000 in 1970.[22] In other words, for every 100 serious crimes committed in 1960, 3.6 were punished by prison terms in 1960. By 1970, even that paltry figure had declined–to 1.3 prison terms per 100 crimes committed.

Why were so many prosecutors, judges, and juries around the nation suddenly so soft on crime?

Race consciousness was decisive. In the middle 1960s, despite passage of "landmark" civil rights legislation and decisions like *Brown v. Board of Education* in the Supreme Court, as well as the introduction of affirmative action in hiring, contracting, and college admissions, and much more, black ghettoes in dozens of American cities ignited in the worst racial violence since the Civil War (when, of course, the violence had been directed against blacks by whites). In New York's Harlem on July 16, 1964, a white police officer shot and killed a black youth who had, the officer claimed, come at him with a knife. Two days later, a riot began that eventually would spread to the Brooklyn neighborhood of Bedford-Stuyvesant and then to Rochester, Philadelphia, and a suburb of Chicago. (In Philadelphia, the first officer attacked was black.)

Television made rioting particularly contagious. People saw the looting and lawlessness in their living rooms. For the criminally inclined, this served as an engraved invitation. In the Watts neighborhood in Los Angeles, a routine traffic stop on August 11, 1965, sparked a spree of looting, arson (the expression "Burn, baby, burn" originated here), and violence that lasted six days. Thirty-four people were killed and over a thousand were injured. Hundreds of buildings were razed. Violence rocked Chicago in 1966, and in July 1967, a five-day riot plunged Newark, New Jersey, into chaos. Twenty-six were killed and 1,200 wounded. Detroit endured even worse. The dead numbered forty-three and the wounded topped two thousand.[23] Hundreds of cities saw outbursts of rioting during the "long hot summers" of 1965-1967. Tanks patrolled the streets, and curfews were imposed.

## Riot Ideology

It was a frightening and unstable time. Many Americans feared that the country was on the verge of a race war. President Johnson appointed an eleven-member panel known as the National Advisory Commission on Civil Disorders, or the Kerner Commission. The commission's report placed blame squarely on white America for the violence in the ghettoes. "What white Americans have never fully understood–but what the Negro can never forget–is that white society is deeply implicated in the ghetto," the report declared. "White institutions created it, white institutions maintain it, and white society condones it."[24] The causes of the riots, the report continued, were three: racism, powerlessness, and poverty. Explaining the report to Congress, commission member Fred Harris, a senator from Oklahoma, elaborated on a theme that would become foundational to the liberal approach to all issues touching upon race, including crime:

> Some people have mistakenly assumed that when the Commission spoke of racism we had in mind just the intense personal animosity many whites express toward Negroes and members of other minority groups. Not at all. We were equally concerned with the sort of racism you cannot see very well if you are white but which Negroes experience every day of their lives–the racism built into the very institutions of American society, the racism which systematically and quite impersonally excludes most Negroes from a decent education, from a livable home, from a chance to set up and run a

business, and—more important of all—from a decent, digni-
fied job at a living wage.[25]

The concept of "institutional racism" was born. The commission
recommended huge new expenditures on housing, job training, and
education (all of which were forthcoming). Liberal editorialists and
others enthusiastically agreed that the riots were a political wake-up
call to a racist and callous society. Civil rights leader Bayard Rustin
described the riots as a message from Negroes that "they would no
longer quietly submit to the deprivation of slum life."[26] As Federal
Communications Commission member Nicholas Johnson put it, "A
riot is somebody talking. A riot is a man crying out, 'Listen to me,
Mister. There's something I've been trying to tell you and you're not
listening.' "[27] James Farmer, leader of the Congress for Racial Equality (CORE), claimed to deplore the rioters, but he immediately qualified his "unqualified" condemnation: "We must remember that the
outrage of unemployment and hopelessness that pervades the ghetto
remains a prelude to the outrage of the . . . gasoline bomb."[28] And
Martin Luther King said, "Congress has created the atmosphere for
these riots."[29]

The political interpretation of the riots was always problematic.
If the riots were truly an outburst of desperation about long-
simmering injustice, why did none of the major riots take place in
the South?

While a majority of African Americans would later tell pollsters
that they viewed the riots as "largely spontaneous protests against
unfair treatment, economic deprivation, or a combination of the
two,"[30] the initial response of most African Americans to the torch-
ing of their neighborhoods and looting of local businesses was distinctly negative. In response to the polling question, "What did you
most like about what was going on?" two-thirds of respondents
replied "Nothing."[31] Fifty-four percent of African Americans in
Detroit believed that the rioters were motivated by "the chance to
get things" or "opportunity, lack of sanctions." And more than two-

thirds of African Americans believed strongly that rioters who stole property were "criminals."[32]

Nor did African Americans express the bitterness toward America that so many liberals hastily ascribed to them. According to a 1964 survey by MIT professor Gary T. Marx, 81 percent believed life was improving for Negroes, 87 percent agreed that America was worth fighting for, 70 percent thought the day would come when whites would fully accept Negroes, and 59 percent said the police treated Negroes either "fairly well or very well."[33]

Still, sympathy and understanding for the lawless dominated America's liberal policy makers. Harry McPherson, an aide to Lyndon Johnson, recalled later that "too often the White House would issue a strong statement against rioters and then follow it with an apologetic 'Of course, we understand why you rioted.' . . . It was the ambivalence of the liberal."[34] A commission appointed by California governor Pat Brown came to the same conclusions after looking into the Watts riot. The riots, said the commission, were not the work of criminals or hoodlums but instead grew out of deeply ingrained societal injustice: the high jobless rate, poor housing, and inadequate schools.[35]

The rioters, meanwhile, were quick to absorb and exploit the new dispensation they detected from the elites. A young rioter in Watts told a reporter, "The white power structure looks on us as hoodlums when actually we are deprived people."[36] But the patterns of violence betrayed no racial or political agenda. Symbols of the "white power structure" like banks, schools, and government offices were left untouched, while plenty of black-owned businesses went up in smoke. African American store owners who tried to defend their property by posting signs like "Soul Brother" in the windows fared no better than other establishments. As a black shopkeeper in Detroit observed, "You were going to get looted no matter what color you were."[37]

Abigail and Stephen Thernstrom mapped the progress of Detroit's riot:

The first store under attack in Detroit did not belong to a white, nor to a proprietor regarded as unusually greedy or unpleasant. It was Hardy's Drug Store, which was both black-owned and known to be generous about filling prescriptions on credit. The best black restaurant in the city went up in flames, and the leading black-owned clothing store was looted. Unaccountably, the mob left untouched Azzam's Market, a grocery store owned by an Arab that had been picketed by CORE and other groups two years earlier after the owner's son had shot a black customer to death in a fight. And yet the rioters burned down a black-owned liquor store on the same corner.[38]

Nor was it accurate to suggest that rioters were motivated by poverty and hopelessness. Watts was not a traditional inner-city ghetto at all, but a neighborhood of individual family homes on suburban-style streets. While by no means affluent, the neighborhood bore no resemblance to the gritty, decaying buildings of other cities' black ghettoes. Jobs were plentiful in the mid-1960s and widely available to blacks. In a survey conducted a year before the riot, the National Urban League had analyzed sixty-eight American cities in terms of quality of life for African Americans. Los Angeles, which included Watts, was ranked in first place.[39] Detroit too was far from wretchedness in the 1960s. The economy was healthy, the police department was under enlightened leadership, and the city was integrated. In fact, the first six hours or so of its riot were a joint enterprise between black and white youths. One Detroit youngster was clear-eyed about the nature of the enterprise:

> This is not a riot. A lot of people have a misconception of it. This is nothing but . . . pure lawlessness. People was trying to get what they could get. The police was letting them take it. They wasn't stopping it, so I said it was time for me to get some of those diamonds and watches and rings. It wasn't that I was mad at anyone or angry or trying to get back at the

white man. They was having a good time, really enjoying themselves until them fools started shooting.[40]

Many participants and observers alike noted a "carnival atmosphere" at the start. Lack of police response was a key contributor to the riots' spread. The Detroit episode began early on a Sunday morning when police raided a speakeasy. The crowd began pelting the police with stones. As Edward Banfield observed, "This might not have led to a riot were it not for the fact that at that particular time very few policemen could be mustered."[41] Sunday morning was normally a low crime period and many police were off duty. The looters (and the initial arrests were all for looting, not for setting fires or violence) also knew that the police would not use their guns. Accordingly, the theft went on for several hours while the police were nowhere to be found. This emboldened more and more criminally inclined youths to join the melee. Television offered real-time pictures of looters making off with liquor, television sets, and other merchandise, along with exact street addresses, further advertising the absence of police.

The riots that followed the assassination of Martin Luther King Jr. must also be understood within the context of the time. The spark for those riots was clearly political—but they followed a period in which riots mostly for "fun and profit," to use Banfield's phrase, had already been embraced, justified, and excused. White liberal America had signaled that black people were expected to riot in order to express themselves. Who could blame them?

## Crime as Social Protest

Sympathy toward rioters soon spilled over into sympathy for criminals in general. If people had torched their neighborhoods to protest injustice and oppression, were not quotidian crimes like burglary and mugging also symptoms of the underlying "sickness" of our society? President Lyndon Johnson declared, "Warring on poverty, inadequate housing, and unemployment is warring on crime."[42] Liberal mayors like John V. Lindsay of New York City seemed to believe that criminals were engaged in a colorful form of political commentary. "If we are to eliminate the crime and violence in this country," he said, "we must eliminate the hopelessness, futility, and alienation from which they spring."[43] Lindsay also made no secret of his contempt for the police. When a police officer was shot and killed in a black neighborhood, Lindsay and his chief of police declined to attend the funeral.[44]

Lindsay's response to calls for law and order was dismissive:

> We cannot turn our ghettoes into armed camps and condone the wanton use of force. This will not ensure the safety of our citizens as they daily walk our cities' streets. But it would heighten tensions and increase the possibility of widespread social disruption. . . . What is dividing Americans so badly from one another is the diagnosis and remedy too many of us seem ready to apply . . . [calls for law and order asking us] to choose between the random terror of the criminal and the official terror of the state.[45]

Ramsay Clark, attorney general in the Johnson administration, declared that "punishment as an end in itself is itself a crime in our times. . . . Rehabilitation must be the goal of modern corrections. Every other consideration should be subordinated to it."[46] Clark further argued that "crime among poor blacks . . . flows clearly and directly from the brutalization and dehumanization of racism, poverty, and injustice. The slow destruction of human dignity caused by white racism is responsible."[47]

Political scientist Andrew Hacker was irritated by the public's fear of street crime:

> In all probability, muggers take much less from individuals than do corporate, syndicate, and white-collar criminals. Many executives swindle more on their taxes and expense accounts than the average addict steals in a year. Unfortu-

nately, concentrating on street crime provides yet another opportunity for picking on the poor.[48]

Even if Hacker is correct about the numbers, his view—also described as a focus on "crime in the suites instead of crime in the streets"—is little comfort to the street crime victim. When a stranger sneaks up behind you in a darkened parking lot, you are unlikely to worry that you've been ambushed by an insider trader.

James Vorenberg, a member of Lyndon Johnson's crime commission and a professor of law at Harvard, voiced the prevalent liberal view that crime and violence were not matters for which individuals could be held accountable. Moreover, he displayed the classic error of the liberal worldview—the tendency to perceive criminals as sympathetic representatives of minority and poor communities rather than as predators in those neighborhoods:

> To a considerable degree, law enforcement cannot deal with criminal behavior. The most important way in which any mayor could be held responsible for crime is the extent to which he failed to fight for job-training programs, better schools, and decent housing. . . . With the possible exception of how we treat first offenders, I have become convinced that improvements or changes in the police, the courts or correctional agencies are holding actions at best.[49]

White criminals born in America after 1945 got an incredibly lucky break. They benefited richly from the new softness on crime that was primarily designed for their black associates. And while blacks commit a very disproportionate share of violent crimes in the United States, it has always been the case that whites, with their huge majority of the population, commit more crimes in absolute numbers.

Some of the same policies that created homelessness also contributed to the rising crime rate. When laws regulating public order, such as vagrancy statutes, loitering laws, and indecency statutes, were jettisoned, the resulting atmosphere of disorder invited criminal behavior. James Q. Wilson and George Kelling, in their famous 1982 *Atlantic* magazine article entitled "Broken Windows," observed:

> If a window in a building is broken and left unrepaired, all the rest of the windows will soon be broken. One unrepaired broken window is a signal that no one cares, and so breaking more windows costs nothing. . . .
>
> The citizen who fears the ill-smelling drunk, the rowdy teenager, or the importunate beggar is not merely expressing his distaste for unseemly behavior; he is also giving voice to a bit of folk wisdom that happens to be a correct generalization—namely, that serious crime flourishes in areas in which disorderly behavior goes unchecked. The unchecked panhandler is, in effect, the first broken window.[50]

Graffiti first began to mar America's cities in the mid-1960s. It began with Magic Markers and then progressed to spray paint. By 1973, 63 percent of New York's subway cars, 46 percent of buses, and 50 percent of public housing were "heavily graffitied."[51] Though commuters often could not even see their stops due to graffiti-covered windows, graffiti was welcomed by New York's elites. *New York* magazine issued "Taki Awards," prizes for the best subway graffiti of the year. Vincent Cannato, in *The Ungovernable City*, described the mood:

> The award was named for one of the first recognized graffiti artists in the city, identified by his tag, "Taki 183." According to the magazine, the award was a "recognition of this grand graffiti conquest of the subways." The award for "station saturation" went to the Broadway and 103rd Street station, where graffiti nearly covered the entire tile wall of the station. Artists like Claes Oldenburg praised graffiti, while *New York* magazine enlightened its upscale readers as to the differences between "Bronx," "Manhattan," "Brooklyn," and "Combo"

styles of graffiti. Richard Goldstein wrote that the most significant thing about graffiti was that "it brought together a
whole generation of lower-class kids in an experience which is
affirmative and delinquent at the same time." . . . Perhaps
the most famous defense of graffiti came from the pen of
Norman Mailer, who wrote an essay in 1974 [calling graffiti]
"the expression of tropical peoples living in a monotonous
iron-gray and dull brown brick environment."[52]

A 1974 study confirmed what subway riders and ordinary New
Yorkers sensed: 40 percent of the fifteen-year-olds arrested for vandalizing public property with graffiti were arrested again within
three years for more serious crimes.[53]

Beginning in May 1965, crime began to be mentioned as among
the top issues facing the nation, and blacks were more likely than
whites to mention crime and juvenile delinquency as high priorities.
But liberal politicians would not alter their approach. James Q. Wilson
analyzed the psychology in a 1971 magazine article:

> If one grants that tactically a strong position on crime and dis-
> order was [politically] expedient, was there any such position
> to be taken that was reasonable, morally defensible, and co-
> herent? Or was the only position to take one that was blindly
> "pro-cop" and that played on sentiments of vengeance and re-
> pression? I think there was such a position, defensible by lib-
> eral standards, that would have addressed predatory crime,
> urban violence, and campus disorder; at the time, I found few
> people who agreed with me. Even to speak of these things, to
> say nothing of speaking of them critically, was to "turn
> right," to be a "backlasher," to "go after the Wallace vote,"
> and so on. It almost literally became a mark of one's accept-
> ability as a liberal that one would have nothing to do with any
> of these issues except to say that the "only" cure for rioting
> and crime was to "solve the underlying problems of poverty
> and racism." . . . [54]

Wilson considered himself a liberal at the time, but he was already uneasy about the trajectory of his intellectual confreres. He continued:

> Let me recount what I have typically heard as the . . . "liberal" position: The rise in crime is illusory or exaggerated; whites are using the crime issue as a way of expressing racist sentiments; if there is a real increase in crime, only remedying the underlying social causes with bigger expenditures on poverty programs will make any real difference; the overriding need in dealing with the criminal justice system is to make it fairer, not to make it more effective; and much so-called crime would be eliminated if we did not "over-criminalize" behavior by making public intoxication and the sale of marijuana illegal.[55]

## "A Bleak Landscape"

While liberal editorial boards and legislators were extending sympathy to the rioters and criminals, the majority of law-abiding African Americans and others who lived and worked in the cities paid a steep price. Many small mom and pop businesses serving ghetto neighborhoods closed their doors forever. Ordinary crime soared after the riots. While the crime rate was growing during the first half of the 1960s–it rose 25 percent between 1960 and 1965–it shot up much more steeply after the riots. Between 1965 and 1970, violent crime increased by 82 percent.[56] In cities that had experienced riots, shopkeepers reported sharply more shoplifting, vandalism, and burglary–part of a new standard of crime that would not subside until the 1990s.

The new normal for crime–it would be awkward to call elevated crime levels that lasted for three decades a "crime wave"–devastated the inner cities. Entrepreneurs found it difficult to lure workers into the area. Insurance rates climbed to keep pace with liability claims. When merchants passed along these higher costs to customers–a crime surcharge, as it were–customers felt abused. Ugly security gates, annoying buzzers on doors, and dilapidated facilities made shopping in these neighborhoods too unpleasant for any except local customers. The effect was magnified by shop owners who simply stopped repairing their windows after the third or fourth smashing. Plywood-boarded stores became commonplace in the ghetto. Jonathan Bean described the way Detroit's Twelfth Street, once a "bustling thriving community," became a "bleak landscape of public housing, vacant lots, and windowless 'party stores.' "[57] Many merchants–but more blacks than whites–began to purchase pistols.[58]

Why would a business owner choose to remain in a neighborhood in which he feared for his life? Even if the risk of property loss was tolerable, what of the risk of murder? Why would a merchant put up with sky-high theft and fire insurance costs? Only those who had no choice or those whose emotional attachment to their neighborhoods withstood the onslaught of the riots remained. The rest packed up and departed. In due course, they were replaced by immigrants, often Koreans, who were less likely than their white predecessors to hire local blacks.

Fear of crime undermined the trust essential for healthy civic life. People became afraid to spend time on the streets and elected to hide in their homes and apartments. Relations between merchants and customers tended to become more adversarial as grocers, dry cleaners, liquor store owners, and others had to keep a wary eye out for shoplifters and armed robbers. Outdoor concerts, street fairs, and other civic activities declined as fear of crime kept people indoors.

High rates of crime also arguably slowed the progress of black/white and black/Asian race relations. Fear of black crime became the shadow darkening an otherwise sunny picture of gradually diminishing antiblack feelings during the decades after the civil rights movement. Progress in white attitudes toward African Americans was dramatic and profound in the post–civil rights era. Only 20 percent of whites told pollsters that black people "lived in their neighborhood" in 1964. By 1994, that number had jumped to 61 percent. Only 18 percent of whites in 1964 said they had black friends;

and only 9 percent said they had "good friends" who were black. By 1989, 66 percent of whites claimed to have black friends, and by 1994, 73 percent said blacks were among their "good friends."[59]

Similarly, the number of whites who thought it was acceptable for whites and blacks to date rose from 10 percent in 1963 to 65 percent in 1994. And the black/white intermarriage rate, though hard to pin down precisely because of reporting differences among the states, seems to hover around 15 percent. It stood at 0.7 percent in 1963.[60]

## The Truth About Black Crime

But white fear of black crime has stalked the garden party. Just as whites were shedding their old prejudices about black inferiority and belief in the justice of a quasi-apartheid system, they were acquiring a fear of blacks—and fear is a poor companion to friendship.

The liberal response, particularly among liberal blacks, was to argue that white fear was invented, just an excuse to dislike the "other." Michael Moore, in his book *Stupid White Men*, argues that white fear of black crime is irrational: "Obviously, no matter how many times their fellow whites make it clear that the white man is the one to fear, it simply fails to register."[61] The data suggest otherwise. Glance at the violent crime arrest rates for 1992. Among every 100,000 white adults, 215.5 were arrested for a violent crime. Among blacks, the number was 1,360.5. Though they represent only 12 percent of the adult population, blacks account for 50 percent of state prison inmates.[62] Though a majority of the victims of black criminals are black (a subject that will get more attention in the next section), blacks victimize a fair number of whites as well. In 1993, whites committed 186,000 violent crimes against blacks, while blacks committed 1.29 million violent crimes against whites. If you factor in the sizes of the two populations, writes criminologist John DiIulio, you find that whites are 57.5 times as likely to be the victims of black criminals as blacks are to be the victims of white criminals.[63]

Abigail and Stephen Thernstrom come to a slightly lower ratio of 50:1.[64]

Fifty-six percent of all those arrested for murder in the United States in 1995 were black. Again, when you consider that blacks comprise just 12 percent of the population and that the overwhelming majority of murderers are male, you find that just 6 percent of the population is responsible for 56 percent of the murders. The number is actually even smaller than that, because only a portion of young black males are criminals. Blacks also accounted for 60 percent of those arrested for robbery, 42 percent of those arrested for rape, and nearly 40 percent of those arrested for assault.[65] In 1993, blacks comprised 44.2 percent of all inmates in jails and prisons and 48.2 percent of federal prisoners.[66]

These data cannot be wished away, nor are they figments of a racist "backlash" mentality against the civil rights movement. A study by the National Center for Institutions and Alternatives found that 42 percent of young black males in Washington, D.C., were either in prison, on probation, on parole, or otherwise entangled with the criminal justice system.[67] In nearby Baltimore, more than 80 percent of those arrested in 1991 were black–though it should be noted that 65 percent of the population in Baltimore is African American, many times higher than the national average.[68]

White discomfort and suspicion about young blacks are telegraphed in many ways–women crossing the street at the approach of African American males, the studious avoidance of eye contact in iffy neighborhoods, the reflexive locking of car doors in the same areas. All of this, and more, is noticed and resented by blacks. "Why am I constantly treated as if I were a drug addict, a thief, or a thug?" Ellis Cose quotes a young black man complaining in *The Rage of the Privileged Class*. Many also complain of excessive police attention and of the indignity of being taken for a criminal. It *is* humiliating for innocent black men to be hassled by police merely because they belong to a group that commits so much crime. But while liberals interpret this indignity to be yet one more insult inflicted by a racist society, a more reasonable interpretation is that people are merely playing the odds. Besides, had liberals not dismantled the criminal sanctions that kept civil peace, the explosion of crime would never have plagued America's cities nor impeded racial comity.

Political correctness cannot force people to unlearn what they know from personal experience. Even Jesse Jackson once acknowledged, in an unguarded moment, the reality that some dare not utter:

> There is nothing more painful to me at this stage in my life than to walk down the street and hear footsteps and start thinking about robbery–then look around and see somebody white and feel relieved.[69]

As the Jesse Jackson story demonstrates, there is nothing prejudiced about fear. It is merely rational. So is appreciation of and love for blacks who make huge contributions to society. Colin Powell, Bill Cosby, Oprah Winfrey, Michael Jordan, and the average black person who works as a nurse, or teacher, or FBI agent are neither feared nor hated by other Americans.

But fear of black crime does enter the picture when it comes to hailing a cab. Actor Danny Glover once filed a complaint with New York City's Taxi and Limousine Commission after attempting unsuccessfully to hail a cab in Harlem.[70] Though Glover has one of the world's sweetest faces (besides being a world-famous celebrity), cab drivers could not see that. They saw only a large black man and decided to err on the side of caution. Was it prejudice? Taxi drivers are among the populations most vulnerable to street crime. Many take race as well as neighborhood and time into account when picking up a fare. Many are also black themselves.

Still, so many black men complained of being pulled over by police in traffic stops that a new term entered the language in the 1990s–an "offense" known as DWB: driving while black. This was related to the controversy that also surfaced at the time over the practice of so-called "racial profiling"–a term that first came to national prominence in connection with New Jersey state troopers who were accused of stopping a disproportionate number of black drivers on the state's highways based solely on race. Then-governor Christine Todd Whitman accepted the verdict against the New Jersey troopers on the flimsiest of evidence, and the state's police were put under orders from the Clinton Justice Department to stop being racists. In 1999, the year before New Jersey entered into a consent decree with the Justice Department, troopers had made 440 "consent searches" on the New Jersey Turnpike. In the six months after the anti-racial profiling campaign heated up, troopers conducted only eleven consent searches. The murder rate in Newark, New Jersey, jumped 65 percent.[71] Only several years later did a serious study prove that black drivers were significantly more likely to speed on New Jersey's turnpike than were drivers of other races. Heather MacDonald explained in the *City Journal*:

> We . . . now know that the troopers were neither dumb nor racist; they were merely doing their jobs. According to the study commissioned by the New Jersey attorney general and leaked first to the *New York Times* . . . blacks made up 16 percent of the drivers on the turnpike, and 25 percent of the speeders in the 65-mile-per-hour zones, where profiling complaints are most common. (The study counted only those going more than 15 miles per hour over the speed limit as speeders.) Black drivers speed twice as much as white drivers, and speed at reckless levels even more. Blacks are actually stopped less than their speeding behavior would predict–they are 23 percent of those stopped.[72]

On the other hand, even some liberals had difficulty accepting the party line that high black arrest rates were the result of racial bias in police forces (all cities had integrated police forces by the 1990s and most large cities had African American mayors and chiefs of police as well), or that high conviction rates were due to the continuing racism of the courts and juries. Liberal columnist Richard Cohen of the *Washington Post* caused a pretty substantial uproar with a 1986 column titled "Closing the Door on Crime."

> In order to be admitted to certain Washington jewelry stores, customers have to ring a bell. The ring back that opens the door is almost perfunctory. According to the owner of one store, only one type of person does not get admitted: Young black males. The owner says they are the ones who stick him up.
>
> Nearby is a men's clothing shop–upscale, but not really expensive. When young black males enter this store, the sales help are instructed to leave their customers and, in the manner of defensive backs in football, "collapse" on the blacks. Politely, but firmly, they are sort of shooed out of the store. The owner's explanation for this? Young blacks are his shoplifters.
>
> Are these examples of racism? The shopkeepers . . . are loath to talk about their policies and quick to assert their liberalism, but business, as they say, is business.
>
> As for me, I'm with the store owners. . . . Of course all policies based on generalities have their injustices. A storekeeper might not know that the youths he has refused to admit are theology students–rich ones at that. But then insurance companies had no way of knowing I was not a typical teenage driver. I paid through the nose anyway.[73]

## Who Suffers Most?

As much as black crime hurts whites and damages relations between blacks and whites, it hurts blacks more–particularly poor urban blacks. Because of the influence of race hustlers like Al Sharpton, Rep. Maxine Waters, and former D.C. mayor Marion Barry, the law-abiding black majority is often forgotten in discussions of race and crime. Measures that crack down on black criminals benefit everyone in society, but most of all those closest to them.

Crime in America is mostly an intraracial, not an interracial, matter. Ninety-three percent of black murder victims are killed by other blacks, and 85 percent of the murders committed by blacks are of other blacks.[74] Whites committed 66 percent of crimes against other whites between 1993–1998, while blacks were responsible for 17 percent.[75]

The Justice Department collects statistics about crime victimization. People are asked to report about their own experience with crime. In 1992, 82 percent of black victims identified their attackers as other blacks, and 71 percent of white victims reported that their attackers were also white.[76] In 2000, according to the FBI's Uniform Crime Reports, 49 percent of murder victims in America were black, 49 percent were white, and 2 percent were of other races.[77] Blacks were six times more likely than whites and eight times more likely than those of other races (excluding Native Americans) to be murdered in 1998.[78] Federal statistics also show that those earning less than $75,000 per year were robbed at a significantly higher rate than those with higher incomes. And according to the Bureau of Justice Statistics, "Persons of all other races experienced overall property crime, burglary and motor vehicle theft at rates lower than blacks."[79]

The crime rate differential was also reflected in surveys about fear. Between 1985 and 1991, the number of Americans who said crime was a major problem in their neighborhoods rose from 5 percent to 7 percent, but among African Americans living in cities, the number rose from 10 percent to 25 percent.[80] Twenty percent of black children reported that they feared being attacked going to and from school. Fifty-four percent of black children nationwide worry "a lot of the time" about becoming a crime victim, and 27 percent of black children (compared with 5 percent of white children) think it is "likely" that they will be shot.[81] In every survey since 1973, a majority of blacks have answered "yes" to the question, "Would you be afraid to walk alone at night in your neighborhood?"[82]

While the self-appointed spokesmen for the "black community" (if there is such a thing) rail against the police at every opportunity and stoke resentment of police tactics, black neighborhoods sink deeper into violence and misery. Though the racial provocateurs do their best to obscure it, African Americans do not suffer from too much policing; rather, the opposite is true. In one survey, black residents of central cities were twice as likely as whites to report that they had considered moving due to a lack of police presence in their neighborhoods.[83] Another poll found that 73 percent of black respondents favored "three strikes and you're out" laws.[84] Former drug czar William Bennett described what he saw of black attitudes toward law enforcement: "I visited more than 100 communities, many of which were located in the worst parts of urban America. And what I heard more than anything else from those in the firing line were pleas for *more* cops and for *more* prisons because they wanted *more* safety."[85]

George Kelling, one of the authors of the "broken window" theory of urban decline, met in the late 1990s with public housing residents in a large Midwestern city. William Bratton, former police commissioner of New York, described the session:

> Although Kelling preferred to meet in one of their homes, the citizens insisted on meeting in a nearby church. Later they explained that they feared meeting in the development because Kelling was white, and local hoodlums, assuming he represented government or police, would retaliate against them. These representatives were desperate: gang members had taken over the project and made life impossible for residents. The residents, all African-Americans, went on to express their anger with police—not about brutality or abuse, but about the lack of police presence and assertiveness. They believed the police had abandoned them.[86]

The next evening, Kelling was riding in a police cruiser with a young officer who had patrolled the neighborhood for three years. Gesturing toward the housing project, the officer commented, "Every citizen in that project hates us."[87]

Responding to the argument that black people are ambivalent about punishing black criminals, criminologist John J. DiIulio had this to say:

> That's not what I hear. I hear the anguished voices of innocent black crime victims in courts where I've listened to case after case involving black-on-black crime. I hear the frustrated black police sergeant tell me, as we cruise in a patrol car, that he can't get from one call to the next fast enough in the neighborhood where he grew up and where some of his elderly relatives live as virtual prisoners in their own homes. I hear the self-righteous black lifer who I'm interviewing in prison say that "the only reason I'm here is that I'm black and poor," and the black prison counselor snap back in reply, "The only reason you're here is because you killed a boy who was black and poor."[88]

In *There Are No Children Here*, Alex Kotlowitz described the ordinary terrors of life in central Chicago. He sketched the lives of two brothers, Pharoah, fifteen, and Lafayette, thirteen.[89] By their middle years, both had seen friends and relatives–including children–shot dead. Both knew what to do when they heard gunfire in their apartment: drop to the floor. If gunfire erupted when they were outside, they were to check which direction the shot came from and then run for cover. Lafayette told Kotlowitz, "If I grow up, I'd like to be a bus driver."

Elayne Bennett, who runs an abstinence program for inner-city girls called Best Friends, recalled that "all of my girls have been to funerals. None has ever been to a wedding."[90] Crime had made the lives of many inner-city African Americans a nightmare.

Yet do-gooders have consistently interfered with efforts to improve policing in dangerous neighborhoods. Vincent Lane, the former overseer of public housing in Chicago, sought to bring some order to the Robert Taylor Homes, a crime-infested public housing project. He proposed metal detectors to prevent gang members from bringing guns into the buildings, a photo ID system for visitors, and a policy that would have permitted guards and police to perform emergency searches without warrants in response to "barrages of gunfire." A democratically elected tenants' union supported all of these measures. But the American Civil Liberties Union (ACLU) brought suit—and succeeded in convincing a judge that the ACLU, and not the tenants' union, represented the interests of the 144,000 residents. The ACLU, naturally, opposed each of Lane's measures.[91]

New York's Legal Aid Society, along with other liberal groups, kept up a decades-long fight against measures that would make it possible to evict drug dealers from public housing. This amounted, they said, to denying the "rights" of accused drug dealers. What's next, a Legal Aid attorney asked in one such contest during the 1980s, "perhaps shooting them at dawn?"[92] Liberal judges put their oars in as well when the Bush I administration attempted to bypass the cumbersome eviction process, with its layers of appeals, and use civil asset forfeiture laws to remove drug dealers. In a 1992 decision, the Fourth Circuit Court of Appeals ruled that any such rule promulgated by the Department of Housing and Urban Development would violate the due process rights of the accused.[93]

## Crime Declines

Starting in the early 1990s, every category of crime in the United States began to drop sharply. It wasn't because America had successfully eliminated the so-called "root causes" of crime—poverty, joblessness, and racism. Something else had happened.

Starting in the 1980s, America's criminal justice system began to toughen up. Between 1960 and 1980, the probability that a criminal would face prison for his crime had declined by more than half. Between 1980 and 1997, that likelihood doubled. The average length of time served also began to edge upward after 1980. The National Center for Policy Analysis uses a datum called "expected punishment." It consists of the probability of arrest, the probability of conviction after an arrest, the probability of imprisonment after conviction and the average or median time served by those sentenced to prison. Using this index, expected punishment was a mere ten days in the early 1980s but rose to twenty-two days by 1995.

California tripled its prison population in the ten years after 1984, and saw its crime rate drop. By 1993, the state had reduced its murder rate by 10.4 percent, burglaries by 43 percent, and rapes by 36 percent. According to the Department of Justice, the tripling of prison inmates between 1975 and 1989 prevented 390,000 murders, rapes, robberies, and assaults in just the year 1989.[94]

Though intellectuals continued to believe in root causes, and liberal politicians continued to wage war on the police instead of on crime, states and localities began to back away from leniency. While experimenting with alternative sentencing like boot camp, house arrest, and community service, most American states simply got tough and built more prisons. The word on the street was, to paraphrase a movie of the 1970s, that Americans were mad as hell and were not going to take it anymore. Tolerance for the "abuse excuse" waned. The number of prison inmates quadrupled between 1975 and 2002.[95] The trend looks like a ski jump. The length of prison sentences also tripled between 1975 and 1989.[96] The federal government passed a "truth in sentencing" law requiring certain felons to serve at least 85 percent of their sentences. This too increased the average length of prison terms.

New York City under Mayor Rudolph Giuliani was the trendsetter, cracking down first on "quality of life" crimes. Giuliani appointed William Bratton as police commissioner in recognition of his outstanding work as chief of the transit police. New York's subways had become the most visible manifestation of the rot that had corroded public life. Every single car in the vast system was defaced, inside and out, by graffiti. The filthy stations, smelling of urine, were haunted by criminals and the homeless. Panhandlers were omnipresent. Wolf packs of young males would sometimes rampage through subway cars as they passed through tunnels, robbing and laughing. An estimated 180,000 scofflaws jumped the turnstiles yearly by 1990, costing the system $65 million in lost revenue and contributing to the Hobbesian atmosphere of the subway system.[97] This squalor was the harvest of thirty years of liberalism in one of the world's wealthiest cities.

Bratton put the "broken windows" theory to the test when he became chief of the 4,000-member transit police. He began by strategically stationing plainclothes transit officers where they could easily catch turnstile jumpers. After each crook was collared, he was searched. One in fourteen was found to be carrying an illegal weapon. One in seven had an outstanding warrant on another charge.[98] Within one year, apprehensions had increased by 60 percent.

Bratton also deterred subway crime by placing decoys–cops dressed as civilians–at various locations. Some dressed as homeless people, others were women. A former member of the decoy team testified to its success:

> Some guys were so afraid of the decoys that I overheard them picking out people they thought were decoy cops. Some of their picks were drunks just sleeping on the train or in the station. I heard guys say, "That's a decoy; leave him alone."[99]

The transit police also aggressively pursued graffiti vandals. (It was a sign of the new, more serious era that they were no longer called graffiti "artists.") Seventy-five of the most active vandals were caught and punished. The subway cars were scrubbed up, and the cleaner atmosphere boosted commuter morale. The loss of passengers that had become a hemorrhage during the 1980s slowed and then reversed. Subway crime declined by two-thirds in four years.[100]

Mayor Giuliani then offered Bratton the opportunity to implement the same policies on a citywide basis as chief of police. Giuliani's first move was to increase the size of the police force by 7,000 officers. Together with Bratton, he adopted a problem-solving, zero tolerance approach to law enforcement. Whereas other cities were adopting a grab bag of practices loosely described as "community policing," the New York police department targeted high crime areas. The emphasis on quality of life offenses was continued. Those who played their radios at blasting volumes, those who smoked marijuana or urinated in public, bicyclists who wove dangerously in and out of traffic–all were either ticketed or arrested. The police put an end to the careers of the "squeegee men," the hustlers who approached cars stopped at intersections, sprayed the windshields with dirty water, drew a rag across the glass, and then demanded payment. In high crime neighborhoods, special teams of officers stopped and frisked suspicious characters. Thousands of illegal guns were discovered and confiscated. And because police were specially trained in interrogation techniques for even casual stops, one thing led to another. Eugene Methvin described the links:

> "A topless dancer arrested for prostitution fingered the bouncer at her Brooklyn club in an unsolved murder. A car thief turned in a fence, who then turned in a father-son gun-dealing team. A parolee arrested for failing to report turned out to have been the only eyewitness to a drug-related murder."[101]

The crackdown on quality of life crimes, though it bore rich dividends in the feel and mood of the city, was only the beginning of Giuliani's aggressive anticrime strategy. The police also flooded high crime neighborhoods and dismantled the criminal infrastructure. They not only locked up more criminals, they also closed down chop shops, fences, and drug buying and prostitution rings.[102] New York's police department introduced the "Compstat" process, a twice-weekly meeting in which computerized crime maps were brought to bear on high crime areas. William Bratton repeats his comments from a typical departmental meeting:

> I want to know why those shootings are still happening in that housing project! What have we done to stop it? Did we

hand out fliers to everyone? . . . Did we run a warrant check
on every address at every project, and did we relentlessly pur-
sue those individuals? . . . What are we doing with parole vi-
olators? Of the 964 people on parole in the Seventy-fifth
Precinct, do we know the different administrative restric-
tions on each one, so when we interview them we can hold it
over their heads? If not, why?[103]

The results were stunning. Within five years, overall felonies had
declined by 50 percent and murder had decreased by 68 percent.
Where the city endured more than 2,600 murders per year in the
early 1990s, that number had dropped to fewer than 800 in 1997.[104]
The worst neighborhoods saw the most dramatic improvement. Between 1993 and 1997 crime fell by 39 percent in Harlem, 42 percent
in East New York, and 45 percent in the South Bronx.[105]

The *New York Times* was mystified. "Defying Gravity, Inmate
Population Climbs" noted a January 1998 headline. The story went
on: "The continued divergence between the shrinking crime rate
and the rising rate of incarceration raises a series of troublesome
questions, said criminologists and law enforcement experts. . . ."[106]
Troublesome to the *Times* perhaps. The explanation (as if any were
required) was within the article itself. Reporter Fox Butterfield acknowledged that more crimes were being punished and that inmates
were serving longer sentences. The *Times*'s confusion arose from
simple cause and effect. How could it be that prison populations
were increasing if fewer crimes were being committed? Were we
suddenly incarcerating jaywalkers and double parkers? Obviously
not. There were still, alas, in 1998, many many more crimes than
apprehensions or convictions. But as the prisons filled up, two
things happened: (1) those behind bars were completely incapaci-
tated from committing new crimes, and (2) word filtered out to the
criminal class that the likelihood of serious prison time for crimes
had dramatically increased–thus deterring some of those still on the
wrong side of the law.

The matter continued to befuddle the *New York Times* for years. Its pages were graced with half a dozen articles examining the "strange" phenomenon of larger prison populations and lower crime rates. In 2003, the paper editorialized:

> Our overflowing jails and prisons come at a high price, in dollars and in wasted lives. The number of men and women behind bars today is four times what it was in the mid-1970s, and it continues to grow. *This soaring incarceration rate is not tied to the violent crime rate, which is lower than it was in 1974* [emphasis added]. . . . When violent crime rates were higher, many politicians were afraid to be seen as soft on crime. But now that crime has receded and the public is more worried about taxes and budget deficits, it would not require extraordinary courage for elected officials to do the right thing and scale back our overuse of jails and prison cells.[107]

Meanwhile, back in the real world, New York's methods were widely copied, and even some cities that did not change tactics saw crime drop during the 1990s. Something was transmitted in the culture. In 2002, 21 million fewer Americans became crime victims than in 1973.[108] Half of the decline was attributable to New York alone.

But as a member of New York's Citizens' Crime Commission noted, "The experts will never forgive Bratton and Giuliani for proving them wrong. They want to believe that crime can only be reduced by sweeping social change. But they do have a fallback position: if the police did reduce crime, they did it by illegitimate means."[109]

## Damn the Police

Rather than celebrate the fact that previously written-off neighborhoods were experiencing a renaissance under Giuliani and that thousands of African American and other minority youngsters who would have been dead or maimed absent the crime drop were alive and well, liberal agitators took aim at the police and the mayor. Applying the principle that "no good deed goes unpunished," Mayor Giuliani's liberal detractors bore down on him in a multifaceted attack. The U.S. Civil Rights Commission, under the leadership of Mary Frances Berry—the same commission that would later issue a report on the 2000 election alleging, without evidence, that African Americans were prevented from voting in Florida—issued a report on police tactics that accused the department of "racial profiling" in its stop and frisk practices.[110] (Perhaps coincidentally, the report was issued during a campaign year in which Giuliani was widely expected to confront Hillary Rodham Clinton in a race for the United States Senate.)

Liberal critics objected that the New York police searched roughly 45,000 people, mostly in minority neighborhoods. Yet those stop and frisks netted thousands of illegal handguns and helped to reduce New York's gun homicides by 75 percent in the six years between 1993 and 1999.[111]

Mark Green, a former Naderite and Democratic candidate for various offices (he was defeated in the post-Giuliani race for mayor by Michael Bloomberg in 2001), held the post of public advocate in New York City during part of Giuliani's tenure. Not to be outdone by the Civil Rights Commission, he issued a report observing that while more police were being punished under Giuliani than under David Dinkins (Giuliani's predecessor), they were being punished less severely.[112]

While the Giuliani era was something of a miracle for New York City, there were two episodes that provided ammunition to enemies of the police. The first involved a Haitian immigrant named Abner Louima, who was arrested during a bar fight and taken into police custody, where he was horribly tortured. Officer Justin Volpe took him into a bathroom, beat him, and sodomized him with a plunger handle. He then forced the handle into Louima's mouth, breaking two teeth. Police waited ninety minutes before getting Louima to a hospital, where he was found to have a punctured colon and bladder.[113]

A more grotesque example of police misconduct would be hard to find, and there was universal disgust about the case throughout the nation. Mayor Giuliani immediately condemned the officers involved (Volpe is now serving a thirty-year sentence) and Louima received an $8.7 million settlement. But for some provocateurs, taking matters further was irresistible. Like a rotund moth to a flame, Reverend Al Sharpton fluttered to Louima's bedside while the latter was still recovering in the hospital. Sharpton encouraged Louima to add the detail that Volpe had shouted "Stupid nigger . . . learn to respect the police. It's Giuliani time," while attacking him. Louima later admitted that this part was not true—but not before it had become a bedrock belief in black neighborhoods.[114] When asked about this false and inflammatory language, Sharpton changed the subject: "Assault and sodomy is not based on verbiage."[115] No one was denying that the assault was a terrible crime, but by attempting to turn a crime into a racial spark, wasn't Sharpton committing a crime of his own? Not according to *Newsweek* magazine. The truth of the quotation was not important. "Louima later rescinded that part," the magazine reported in a story titled "A Mayor Under Siege," but "the false quote reflected a growing sense in minority neighborhoods that the mayor was responsible for the cops' anything-goes attitude."[116]

Two years later, four officers of New York's "street crimes unit" were patrolling a neighborhood that had recently experienced a rash of shootings. They were searching for an armed rapist thought to be responsible for fifty-one attacks. A few minutes past midnight, they spotted a man who fit the description they had been given. Heather MacDonald of *City Journal* described the scene:

> Officers Sean Carroll and Edward McMellon got out of the car, identified themselves as police, and asked the man to stop. Instead, 22-year-old Amadou Diallo, a peddler of bootlegged videos and tube socks on Manhattan's East 14th Street, continued into the vestibule and tried to get inside the building's inner door. Diallo had recently filed a wildly

false application for political asylum, claiming to be a Mauritanian victim of torture orphaned by the government security forces. In fact, he was a Guinean with two well-off and living parents. He had reason, therefore, not to welcome encounters with authorities.

The two cops ordered Diallo to come out and show them his hands. Turning away, Diallo reached into his pocket and pulled out what Carroll thought was a gun. "Gun!" Carroll shouted. "He's got a gun!" McMellon, who'd followed Diallo up the stairs, feared he was in point-blank danger and shot at Diallo three times before stepping backward, falling off the steps, and breaking his tailbone. Carroll, seeing McMellon down and thinking he'd been shot, opened fire.

As bullets ricocheted into the street, the other two cops concluded that a firefight was under way. They jumped out of the car and began shooting at the figure crouched in the vestibule. Diallo hadn't fallen prone, according to the cops' lawyers, because the nine-millimeter copper-jacketed bullets passed through him cleanly without bringing him down.

When the shooting stopped, eight to ten seconds later, the officers had fired a total of 41 rounds, 19 of which had hit Diallo, perforating his aorta, spinal cord, lungs, and other organs. Two of the officers had emptied their 16-bullet magazines. When they searched Diallo's body to retrieve his gun, they found only a black wallet and a shattered beeper in a pool of blood. Officer Carroll wept.[117]

As would any decent human being. It was a tragic mistake. All four officers were hospitalized that night for trauma. Witnesses said they were devastated to discover that they had killed an unarmed man.[118] But New York was home to a significant number of people, all liberals of one stripe or another, for whom the success of the city's conservative crime-fighting philosophy was an affront. The *New York Times*, which had been fighting a low-intensity battle against the crime crackdown, shifted avidly into overdrive, devoting an average of three stories per day to the case in the two months after the shooting and fanning the embers of racial distrust wherever possible.[119] The case, according to the *Times,* was not an example of a terrible mistake; it was the "dark underside" of the war on crime. Yes, the crime rate had dropped in the city, the *Times* reiterated again and again, but only at the expense of the civil liberties of all minority New Yorkers. "Minorities have sent City Hall a clear message," proclaimed a *Times* editorial, "that no one in their neighborhoods should be forced to exchange the fear of crime for a fear of police."[120]

The Reverend Al Sharpton staged daily demonstrations, and celebrities like Susan Sarandon, former mayor Ed Koch, and NAACP leader Kweisi Mfume lined up to be arrested for the cameras. Protesters carried signs comparing Giuliani to Hitler. Congressman John Conyers of Michigan decried New York "as way out in front in police brutality."[121] Jesse Jackson compared Diallo's shooting to the lynching of Emmett Till. (Till was the teenager who was lynched in Mississippi in 1955 for whistling at a white woman.) Ira Glasser of the ACLU chimed in that Diallo had been a victim of "Jim Crow justice."[122]

Never mind that shootings of civilians by police had declined during the 1990s to roughly half what they had been in 1985.[123] Miami, Philadelphia, and especially Washington, D.C. (whose police force is majority black), have much higher rates of fatal police shootings than does New York.[124]

The Louima and Diallo cases demonstrated that many liberals, though they claim to be do-gooders, are prepared to undermine the very progress that improves life for the poor and minorities. The reduction of crime in 1990s was the best thing to happen to poor people in this country in more than a generation. Not only were actual lives saved that would surely otherwise have been lost–mostly among young people–but whole neighborhoods that had been thought beyond saving began to blossom back to life. If the murder rate prevailing in 1993 had remained unchanged, 2,299 more black New Yorkers and 1,842 Hispanic New Yorkers would have died.[125] In the Buena-Clinton neighborhood in Garden Grove, California, once called "Orange County's worst slum," the crime rate fell by half during the

1990s. Whereas two decades ago, residents were sleeping on floors to avoid gunshots from rival gangs, today they can shop in new stores, enjoy a new park, and live in improved housing.[126] A similar pattern has been visible in cities around the nation.

But this improvement—so dramatic and so welcome for the poor—has been resisted and resented by liberals. It has upended their cherished idea that poverty causes crime. In fact, as the data from the past decade clarify, there is no evidence that poverty causes crime but a great deal of evidence that crime causes poverty. By aligning themselves against the police, against commonsense tactics like stop and frisk, against metal detectors in public housing, against swift and certain punishment, and for a broad array of legal protections for accused criminals, liberals helped to aggrieve the lives of the poor and society as a whole.

# Chapter Two
# STOKING FEAR AND HATRED IN THE NAME OF RACIAL SENSITIVITY

"African American voters were disenfranchised–period." So spoke Rep. Corinne Brown (D-FL) following the 2000 presidential election.[1] Jesse Jackson, who had jetted around the nation in a special plane chartered by the Democratic National Committee during the 2000 campaign, was his usual restrained and temperate self.[2] He denounced the Supreme Court decision that settled the election in Mr. Bush's favor as a new incarnation of the Dred Scott case. He accused the Bush campaign of "Nazi tactics." He saw a "clear pattern of voter suppression" and declared the existence of a "systematic plan to disenfranchise black voters." Kweisi Mfume, chairman of the NAACP, alleged that "police checkpoints were set up in and around polling places to intimidate black men." Al Gore's campaign manager, Donna Brazile, chimed in that the year 2000 had witnessed "a systematic disenfranchisement of people of color and poor people."[3] She then added for good measure that "in disproportionately black areas, people faced dogs, guns, and were required to have three forms of ID."[4] The chairman of the Democratic National Committee, Terry McAuliffe, accused Florida governor Jeb Bush and others of erecting police roadblocks to prevent African Americans from voting and of "tampering with the results in Florida."[5] At rallies across Florida in the days following the election, prominent liberal Democrats led choruses of "We Shall Overcome" and invoked the memory of Selma and Birmingham.

These were not the stray musings of crackpots or pamphleteers. These were leaders of the oldest political party in the United States.

There was not a particle of truth to any of these claims, but they were part of a pattern of racial exploitation and manipulation that Democrats have made their political signature in recent years. The party that claims to be the champion of African Americans is actually doing everything in its power to make America's second largest minority group paranoid, distrustful, and seething with anger at their fellow Americans.

Imagine, just for a moment, that any of these inflammatory charges were true. Consider how much shock and outrage there would have been if black Floridians had come forward with tales of intimidation by dogs and guns. Suppose even one barricade had been placed at a polling place in an African American neighborhood; the front pages of the nation's papers would have been bristling with fury—and justly so. The Justice Department would have brought prosecutions. The people whose civil rights were violated would have been flooded with offers from lawyers offering to take their cases pro bono. Politicians of both parties would have shoved past each other to reach microphones and denounce this terrible throwback to the days of Jim Crow. The *Today Show, Nightline*, the 24-hour news channels, and every other media outlet would have featured little else for months. But none of that happened because none of the allegations was true. No claims were filed. Not a single African American stepped forward with testimony concerning intimidation at a polling place. No lawsuits were initiated alleging voter intimidation. (There was a suit challenging Georgia's differing systems of voting in different counties—but it contained no suggestion that African Americans were prevented in any way from exercising their franchise).[6]

Nevertheless, the provocateurs who head the Democratic Party and lead the major "civil rights" groups, and some of their tame spaniels in the press, successfully planted the idea in the minds of many African Americans that large numbers of black voters had been "disenfranchised" in 2000. Thus Al Sharpton in 2003 declared:

What happened in 2000 is a disgrace and betrayal of everything this country should stand for. And the very next election after 2000 is 2004. That alone should mobilize and galvanize voters like we've never seen before. If someone breaks into your house, they steal something of value. Don't nobody break in your house and take something they can't use or can't sell. The only reason they steal a vote is it must be of value. We've got to redeem the robbery of 2000 in 2004.[7]

Charlie Gibson on *Good Morning America* offered much the same interpretation a couple of months after the 2000 election, telling viewers:

In African American precincts in Florida, more, far more, black votes were thrown out than white votes. A disproportionately high percentage of black voters show up at the polls and find their names aren't on the voting list. Many blacks are furious that if their votes had been counted, Al Gore would be president.[8]

Michael Moore, always reliable for thoughtful and measured commentary, said:

In what appears to be a mass fraud committed by the state of Florida, Bush, Harris and company not only removed thousands of black felons from the rolls, they also removed thousands of black citizens who had never committed a crime in their lives–along with thousands of eligible voters who had committed only misdemeanors.[9]

"Many Americans see Florida as a symbol of disenfranchisement and want to do something about it," Ralph Neas of People for the American Way told the *New York Times*. "The nature of the disenfranchisement has been an incentive and inspiration to people to get involved."[10]

Two reporters from the *Village Voice* blamed Gore's defeat on "a centuries-old national system of labor, education, and politics designed to keep African Americans from rising above the legacy of chattel slavery."[11]

And the American Civil Liberties Union concluded that:

> Today . . . the hard won gains of the civil rights movement and the Voting Rights Act are in danger of being extinguished. It is now abundantly clear, for instance, that this precious right was repeatedly violated in the much contested presidential election of 2000. In the state of Florida and at polling booths across the country, flaws in the voting system disproportionately affected people of color, effectively excluding them from the voting process.[12]

Four years later, this fiction is widely accepted as fact among African Americans–a misperception that has further embittered many toward the Republican Party and, more importantly, toward their country.

## Stoking Paranoia

In the aftermath of the Florida fiasco, the United States Civil Rights Commission weighed in with a report on voting irregularities. The Civil Rights Commission, created in 1957, had long since exhausted its original mandate and become a cheering section for racial quotas and affirmative action in all its guises. The commission's chairman, Mary Frances Berry, is a Jesse Jackson crony and was a contributor to the Hillary Clinton Senate campaign. Under her aggressive leadership, the commission "investigated" disenfranchisement claims and reported to the world that Florida was guilty as charged.

Couched in the ambiguous passive voice, the commission claimed that "black voters were nearly 10 times more likely than nonblack voters to have their ballots rejected."[13] The commission was widely quoted to the effect that 52 percent of all disqualified ballots were cast by black voters. "Countless Floridians," the report concluded, "were denied . . . their right to vote" and this "disenfranchisement fell most harshly on the shoulders of African-Americans."[14]

As Abigail Thernstrom and Russell Redenbaugh, Republican members of the U.S. Civil Rights Commission, noted in their dissenting report, "the Commission's report ha[d] little basis in fact" and was "prejudicial, divisive, and injurious to the cause of true democracy and justice in our society."

The dissenters point out that all of the overheated rhetoric notwithstanding, the commission found no examples of black Floridians who had been inhibited in any way from exercising the franchise. The inflamed accusations about police roadblocks and intimidation came down to this: one routine police traffic stop was set up *two miles* from the nearest polling place. Exactly one black voter complained of having been stopped at this police roadblock (police were checking for motor vehicle violations like burned out taillights and expired registrations). Roberta Tucker told the Civil Rights Commission that she "felt intimidated" when police stopped her. However, it is undisputed that after she had shown her driver's license to the officers, they sent her on her way and she proceeded directly to the polling place and voted.[15] The roadblock lasted ninety minutes, during which time police issued eighteen citations–twelve of them to white drivers.

Another black voter told the commission that he was disturbed to see a police cruiser parked near a polling place. But it turned out that the cruiser was parked there only so long as it took for the officer himself to vote.[16] The only colorable allegation of interference with voting came from one African American witness who claimed that she, but not a white man, was turned away from the polling place at closing time.

The commission's majority report also gave credence to the widely circulated notion that Florida's antifraud measure, intended to crack down on illegal voting by felons, was overinclusive and prevented many eligible voters–particularly eligible black voters–from exercising the franchise. In fact, as the Thernstrom/Redenbaugh dissent makes clear, "The Commission did not hear from a single witness who was actually prevented from voting as a result of being erroneously identified as a felon. Furthermore, whites were twice as likely as blacks to be placed on the list erroneously, not the other way around."[17] Nor did the commission grapple with the fact, reported by the *Palm Beach Post*, the *Miami Herald*, and other newspapers, that more than 6,500 ineligible Florida felons did vote in 2000.

The Civil Rights Commission and nearly all liberal commentary about the Florida vote muddied a crucial distinction—namely, that between voters being "disenfranchised" and voters having their ballots thrown out due to voter error. As the dissenting report noted:

> These pages [the commission's reports] are filled with references to the "disenfranchisement" of black voters, as if African Americans in Florida last year were faced with obstacles comparable to poll taxes, literacy tests, and other devices by which southern whites in the years before the Voting Rights Act of 1965 managed to suppress the black vote and keep political office safely in the hands of candidates committed to the preservation of white supremacy.[18]

In fact, about 180,000 ballots in Florida were not counted due to voter error: either undervoting (failing to make a selection for president), or overvoting (making more than one choice for president). It is impossible to know how many of the "spoiled" ballots were cast by African Americans since we have a secret ballot (even in Florida). Neither do the critics suggest how these ballots should have been included. How should an overvote or undervote be counted? Should election officials guess at the intentions of individual voters?

Finally, while stretching for the darkest possible interpretation of Florida's voting difficulties in 2000, liberal commentators and the Civil Rights Commission avoided the most obvious explanation. The NAACP had launched a huge "Operation Big Vote" campaign in 2000. It succeeded very well. Two-thirds more African Americans voted in 2000 than in 1996. Though blacks represented 13 percent of

Florida's population, they accounted for 15 percent of the total vote. Forty percent of these African Americans were voting for the first time. First-time voters make more mistakes than experienced voters. Further, the illiteracy rate is higher among African Americans than among whites, and a study undertaken by John Lott of Yale showed that the Florida county with the highest illiteracy rate also had the highest percentage of spoiled ballots.[19]

As the *National Journal*'s Stuart Taylor wrote in 2001, "Rarely have so many been so dishonestly inveigled into so utterly unfounded a sense of victimization."[20]

Why would prominent liberal Democrats want to make African Americans feel targeted and despised? Is it the act of a do-gooder to make someone feel hated? Hardly. It's like spreading false and malicious gossip. But it is a plain fact of American political life today that Democrats are completely dependent on black votes. The day African Americans stop casting 80 to 95 percent of their votes for Democrats is the day Democrats stop winning elections. That is the simple calculus that explains all of the divisive, mendacious, and inflammatory rhetoric Democrats employ on the subject of race.

In the year 2000, George W. Bush won 54 percent of the white vote and 31 percent of the Hispanic vote. But Al Gore won 90 percent of the black vote and thus topped Bush in the total popular vote.[21] In 1992, Bill Clinton won 39 percent of the white vote but 83 percent of the black vote. (In a three-way race, he became president with a plurality.) Similarly, in 1996, Clinton won 43 percent of the white vote and 84 percent of the black vote.[22] Blacks and Hispanics together contributed 24.4 percent of Clinton's total votes in 1996 and 28.5 percent of Gore's votes in 2000. In the U.S. Senate race in New York in 2000, Hillary Clinton won 46 percent of the white vote but 90 percent of the black vote.[23] The pattern was similar in New Jersey's gubernatorial race in 2001: Jim McGreevey, the Democrat, received 49 percent of the white vote and 88 percent of the black vote. Clearly, if Democrats cease to win huge majorities of the African American vote, they will be in serious trouble as a party.

Electoral necessity is an explanation, but it is not an excuse.

Democrats have chosen the lowest, most disreputable path to political success with black Americans–scare tactics, lies, and outright smears of Republicans.

Race baiting used to be a tactic used by politicians–both Democrats and Republicans, but mostly Southern Democrats–to gain white votes. George Wallace, a Democrat campaigning for Alabama governor in 1962, declared, "I draw the line in the dust and toss the gauntlet before the feet of tyranny, and I say, segregation now, segregation tomorrow, segregation forever."[24] Such appeals to racial feeling were discredited by the civil rights movement–or were they? That depends entirely on which race you are appealing to.

In the 2000 campaign, Vice President Al Gore scarcely let an opportunity pass to impugn George Bush's integrity on racial matters. In a speech before the NAACP, Gore said, "When my opponent, Governor Bush, says he'll appoint strict constructionists to the Supreme Court, I often think of the strictly constructionist meaning that was applied when the Constitution was written–how some people were considered three-fifths of a human being."[25] As Mr. Gore knows, there is absolutely no connection between the "three-fifths" rule and the term "strict constructionist." The first was a deal arrived at during the Constitutional convention. Southern delegates wanted their slaves counted in the census for the purposes of representation in Congress. Northerners resisted. Counting each slave as three-fifths of a person was the compromise position. It hardly need be added that slaves were not afforded three-fifths of a vote. They could not vote, nor could many of their descendents until well into the twentieth century.

Strict construction, also called original intent, has nothing whatever to do with this history. It is a lay term for a philosophy of judging that requires judges to evaluate Constitutional questions based upon what the Founders intended. It also has nothing to do with race. For Gore to suggest otherwise was a smear.

On another occasion, Gore used the same sleight of hand on the matter of the census. Because some Democrats believed that there had been an undercount of minority groups in the 1990 census, they backed a measure in 1999 that would have permitted the Census Bureau to conduct statistical sampling in minority neighborhoods instead of counting heads. Republicans argued that the Constitution requires an "actual enumeration" and opposed the change. In Vice President Gore's hands, this became, "The Republicans don't even want to count you in the census!"[26]

Gore's campaign manager, Donna Brazile, hinted to black audiences what the 2000 election was about by declaring that "I won't let the white boys win."[27] She went on to explain, "A white boy attitude is 'I must exclude, denigrate, and leave behind.' "[28]

The Gore campaign's sideswipes look positively benign, though, compared with the ads aired by the NAACP. A radio spot sponsored by the NAACP's National Voter Fund that ran on black radio stations said, "There are many ways intimidation was, and still is, used to keep African Americans from voting. Mobs, guns, and Jim Crow. Ropes, dogs, lies, and hoses."[29] NAACP chairman Julian Bond attempted to frighten African Americans about a potential Bush victory by suggesting that Clarence Thomas and Antonin Scalia, two Supreme Court justices for whom George W. Bush has expressed admiration, "have already pledged to eliminate the 1964 Civil Rights Act and the 1965 Voting Rights Act, and were they to get additional support, the civil rights that so many have fought and died for would vanish just like that."[30]

Bond did not offer any citations. Nor could he, since neither Scalia nor Thomas had ever said anything remotely like that. Imagine if a leading Republican figure, like Newt Gingrich, had said in 2000, "If Al Gore is elected, he will appoint justices like Ruth Bader Ginsburg and Stephen Breyer, who have already pledged to require homosexual studies in the public schools."

## George W. Bush and the KKK

Nothing so disgraced the 2000 campaign, though, as the radio and TV ads prepared by the NAACP about James Byrd. Byrd had been the victim of a vicious crime in 1998. Three white ex-cons with ties to a

KKK spin-off group had beaten Byrd and then dragged him by a chain behind their truck until he died and his body became dismembered. The crime outraged the Texas community of Jasper, which was 30 percent black. An interracial crowd of more than 800 showed up at the church for Byrd's funeral, including U.S. Senator Kay Bailey Hutchison. Flags flew at half-staff, and residents drove with their lights on to express grief and solidarity with Byrd's family. In due course, all three suspects were tried and convicted. Two were sentenced to the electric chair, one to life imprisonment. The response of the community was everything it should have been and stood in sharp contrast with the indifference or even malicious approval that might have greeted such a crime in 1940.

The NAACP television ad began with a grainy black and white video of a pickup truck with a chain extending from the rear bumper. Deep metallic sounds were heard in the background. Viewers then heard the voiceover of Renee Mullins, James Byrd's daughter:

> I'm Renee Mullins, James Byrd's daughter.
>
> On June 7, 1998, in Texas my father was killed. He was beaten, chained, and then dragged three miles to his death, all because he was black.
>
> So when Governor George W. Bush refused to support hate-crime legislation, it was like my father was killed all over again.
>
> Call Governor George W. Bush and tell him to support hate-crime legislation.
>
> We won't be dragged away from our future.[31]

The artificial language about phoning George Bush to ask him to support hate-crime legislation was inserted only to preserve the NAACP's status as a nonpartisan group and to abide by campaign finance laws that forbid some groups from explicitly saying "vote for" or "vote against" any candidate. But the meaning was clear. The ad was intended to horrify and enrage black voters and turn them out at the polls for Al Gore, not to effect hate-crimes legislation in Texas or any other state.

Actually, Texas already had a hate-crime statute on the books. It read as follows:

> In the punishment phase of the trial of an offense under the Penal Code, if the court determines that the defendant intentionally selected the victim primarily because of the defendant's bias or prejudice against a group, the court shall make an affirmative finding of that fact and enter the affirmative finding in the judgment of that case.[32]

Those found guilty of committing such bias crimes faced enhanced punishments. A proposed "Byrd Act" would have added a list of enumerated groups to be labeled as protected. George W. Bush's position was that the law should punish acts, not thoughts. It had clearly done so in the case of Byrd's killers. It's difficult to see how the existence of a different hate-crimes law would have enhanced the punishment beyond death. Still, the point of the NAACP campaign was not to argue the merits or demerits of hate-crimes legislation. It was only to reach down into voters' psyches and squeeze the chords of resentment and rage. The radio ad, which ran in eighteen markets starting in September 2000, was even more emotionally wrenching:

> I'm Renee Mullins. My father was James Byrd Jr.
>
> I still have nightmares thinking about him, the day three men chained him behind their pickup truck and dragged him three miles over pavement.
>
> I can see skin being torn away from his body.
>
> I can hear him gasping for air.
>
> I can feel the tears in his eyes, the struggle of his brain as images of his life painfully bang through his head as the links of a heavy chain clinched around his ankles dragging him bump by bump until he was decapitated.

On June 7, 1998, this happened to my father, all because he was black. I went to Governor George W. Bush and begged him to help pass a hate-crimes bill.

He just told me no.

I'm doing this commercial to ask you to call Governor Bush at——and tell him to introduce a hate-crimes bill in Texas. Let him know that our community won't be dragged down by hate crimes.[33]

Vice President Gore also appeared at a campaign event with Mr. Byrd's sister, Louvan Harris. Ms. Harris offered the following account while Gore stood at her side:

They spray-painted him black, chained him to a truck, dragged him three miles. His head came off, his arms–dismembered his whole body. We have a governor of Texas who doesn't think that's a hate crime. My question to him is: If that isn't hate, what is hate to George Bush? He had an opportunity to do something for our family. He did nothing.[34]

It would have required very little effort for Mr. Gore to pull himself over the bar of basic integrity. All he needed to say was, "Of course we're not suggesting that Governor Bush condoned this crime." He did not. And so the Gore campaign, together with the NAACP, implied that a vote for Bush was a vote for the KKK. At one point a journalist asked Jesse Jackson, "Is the NAACP going too far in suggesting that Governor Bush is someone who could support the murder of James Byrd?" Jackson said, "No."[35]

These ads were highly effective. Twenty-five percent of African Americans had voted for George W. Bush in his 1998 reelection campaign in Texas, but only 5 percent of black Texans voted for Bush for president in 2000.[36]

It became a staple of political commentary after the 2000 election to refer to states that voted for Bush as "red" and states that went for Gore as "blue," matching the colors many TV networks

used on their maps. The spirit of the Gore campaign was captured by
Paul Begala, who wrote:

> Yes, tens of millions of good people in Middle America voted
> Republican. But if you look closely at the map, you see a more
> complex picture. You see the state where James Byrd was
> lynched–dragged behind a pickup truck until his body came
> apart–it's red. You see the state where Matthew Shepard was
> crucified on a split-rail fence for the crime of being gay–it's
> red. The state where an Army private who was thought to be
> gay was bludgeoned to death with a baseball bat, and the
> state where neo-Nazi skinheads murdered two African-
> Americans because of their skin color, and the state where
> Bob Jones University spews its anti-Catholic bigotry, they're
> all red too.[37]

The Democrats are not always so heavy-handed. Bill Clinton was
more sly in his racial appeals. In 1998, for example, the Clinton
team got wind of a Republican suggestion to videotape certain voting booths in order to prevent voter fraud. Sensing an opportunity,
Clinton instructed his attorney general, Janet Reno, to send out letters condemning the idea as a threat to the 1965 Voting Rights Act.
"The Justice Department is committed to vigorously enforcing our
nation's voting laws," read the Justice Department announcement,
"and we will not tolerate harassment of minority voters."[38] In his
weekly radio address, President Clinton went further: "For the last
several elections there have been examples in various states of
Republicans either actually or threatening to try to intimidate or
try to invalidate the votes of African-Americans in precincts that
are overwhelmingly African-American–mostly places they think it
might change the outcome of elections."[39] Clinton demanded that
Republicans "stand up and put a stop" to this practice.

There was no such practice. Republican National Committee
chairman Jim Nicholson demanded an apology from Clinton for
"falsely and improperly" suggesting that Republicans wanted to

suppress the African American vote. But his protest became a mere footnote. The headline on the AP's story said it all: "GOP Accused of Planning to Harass Minorities at Polls."[40]

George W. Bush, ironically, did more to court the African American vote than any previous Republican presidential nominee. His campaign included so many stops at black churches and classrooms that reporters began to joke about it (they were doubtless skeptical about the possibility of a Republican winning African American support). His "No child left behind" education proposal was designed with poorly performing black and Hispanic kids in mind, and he addressed the NAACP to declare his belief that "reading is the new civil right."[41] The GOP spent $1 million on campaign ads that ran on black radio stations.[42] Bush reached out to groups like the Congress on Racial Equality and the NAACP. The very soul of the Bush appeal, that he was a "compassionate conservative," was intended to soften his image among traditionally hostile constituencies. He also dropped hints of his interest in appointing prominent African Americans to his cabinet and White House staff. Once elected he did appoint Condoleezza Rice to be the first African American woman to serve as National Security Adviser, selected Colin Powell as the first black secretary of state, and tapped Rod Paige as secretary of education. (Bush also speaks Spanish and reached out to Hispanic voters.)

Bush's reward was 8 percent of the black vote. As Tamar Jacoby noted with sadness about the 2000 campaign:

> In almost everything they did or said, Democrats encouraged blacks to think that whites were responsible for their problems.
>
> Gore played brazenly to the conventional black view that the politics of race are a matter of good and evil (the vice president actually used that language)—not a choice between two different visions of how to handle issues like poverty and opportunity, but rather a contest between people of goodwill (invariably liberals) and villainous racists (always conservative). Rather than spur black effort and black responsibility,

the campaign only encouraged blacks to believe that they always will be victims—encouraged them to go on flailing at white America and voting for Democrats to protect them from it.

In contrast, Bush and the Republican National Committee tried to appeal to blacks on the issues, addressing bread-and-butter problems and offering practical solutions. . . . Bush's education proposals and the passion with which he argued for them seemed tailor-made to appeal to poor black voters, who support school choice in overwhelming majorities. . . . But these Bush ideas fell on deaf ears in a community more interested in hearing the old Manichean catechism.[43]

Or perhaps a screaming lie is less avoidable than a quiet truth. The Democrats lost the election, but they won the battle for African American hearts and minds. They succeeded in making George W. Bush a bogeyman to many African Americans, and they succeeded in making millions of blacks feel victimized and oppressed over a phantom.

## It All Began with Bork

When Robert H. Bork was nominated to serve on the United States Supreme Court in 1987, the Left in America discovered the full value of the race card. A former solicitor general of the United States, Bork was among the country's most distinguished and brilliant jurists. At the time he was nominated, he was serving on the Court of Appeals for the D.C. Circuit, and had long been considered a natural for the high court. A former professor at Yale Law School, his record was pristine. No skeletons rattled in his closets. Witty and engaging, he would have been a formidable intellectual presence among the nine members of the Court.

Liberals were desperate to stop him. If there were no scandals in his past to discredit him, some would have to be invented. As Ann Lewis, a leader of one of the anti-Bork groups later acknowledged,

"This had to be fought beyond the walls of the Senate. If this were carried out as an internal Senate battle, we would have deep and thoughtful discussions about the Constitution, and then we would lose."[44] Thoughtful was not at all what the liberals had in mind. Instead, liberal advocacy groups and liberal senators teamed up for an utterly unprecedented public smear campaign against a Supreme Court nominee. Senator Teddy Kennedy kicked off the *auto da fe:*

> Robert Bork's America is a land in which women would be forced into back alley abortions, blacks would sit at segregated lunch counters, rogue police could break down citizens' doors in midnight raids, schoolchildren could not be taught about evolution, writers and artists could be censored at the whim of government, and the doors of the federal courts would be shut on the fingers of millions of citizens for whom the judiciary is—and is often the only—protector of the individual rights that are the heart of our democracy.
>
> President Reagan . . . should not be able to reach out from the muck of Irangate, reach into the muck of Watergate, and impose his reactionary vision of the Constitution on the Supreme Court and the next generation of Americans. No justice would be better than this injustice.[45]

This was a skein of lies and gross distortions indistinguishable from lies, and it set the tone for the weeks of vilification to come. Never before had a television campaign been aimed at defeating the nomination of a Supreme Court justice. But a consortium of liberal groups spent an estimated $15 million on the anti-Bork effort. People for the American Way (PFAW), the liberal lobbying group founded by TV producer Norman Lear, aired a particularly dishonest TV commercial starring Gregory Peck. The ad showed a typical American family on the steps of the Supreme Court. Peck's voiceover intoned, "There's a special feeling of awe people get when they visit the Supreme Court of the United States, the ultimate guardian of our liberties." Over images of the family gazing admiringly at the façade of the building, Peck urged that Bork did not belong there. "He defended poll taxes and literacy tests, which kept many Americans from voting. He opposed the civil rights law that ended 'whites only' signs at lunch counters. He doesn't believe the Constitution protects your right to privacy. And he thinks freedom of speech does not apply to literature and art and music."[46]

This was nonsense on stilts. Bork had never supported poll taxes or literacy tests to prevent African Americans from voting. He did not oppose civil rights. And his record on free speech had been more libertarian than that of many on the federal bench. Nor did he endorse forced sterilization or any of the other horrors in the catalogue presented by his enemies. Also, it is worth noting in passing that the liberal bromide about the Supreme Court as "the ultimate guardian of our liberties" is quite wrong. As Judge Learned Hand memorably put it, "Liberty lies in the hearts of men and women; if it dies there, no constitution, no law, no court can save it."[47]

Certainly any sense of fair play seemed to have died in the hearts of the NAACP, People for the American Way, the Alliance for Justice, and the liberal senators on the Senate Judiciary Committee. Though the opposition screamed that Bork did not believe in the right to privacy (a distortion), they invaded Bork's privacy by searching his video store rentals. (They were hoping to find pornography and were disappointed.)

There were exceptions. Some liberals showed courage and integrity in supporting Bork and defending his fitness to serve. Among these were Lloyd Cutler, who had served as Jimmy Carter's White House counsel; Griffin Bell, Jimmy Carter's attorney general; and former Supreme Court Justice John Paul Stevens.[48] In addition, former chief justice Warren Burger, former associate justice Byron White, and Thurgood Marshall all endorsed the Bork appointment. But they were steamrolled by the major interest groups. The campaign of vilification worked. Bork's nomination was defeated.

The beating heart of liberal opposition to Bork was not race but abortion. They knew that he would be an articulate voice against *Roe v. Wade* and it was that issue, above all others, that galvanized the opposition. But it is hard to make opposition to *Roe v. Wade* look like a scandal. That is why so much smoke was blown about "civil rights."

Having tasted of illicit success and warming to the raw power of the racism charge, it was easier for liberals to indulge in racism smears the next time around.

## "Handkerchief-Head"

When President George H. W. Bush nominated Clarence Thomas to the Supreme Court in 1991, a number of liberal pretensions were unveiled. Though liberals had always presented themselves as the advocates of blacks, Hispanics, and other minorities, their mask slipped when Thomas stood poised to join the Court. The liberal lynch mob quickly demonstrated that their loyalty lay not to progress or advancement for black Americans but to success for liberal Americans.

There is, of course, nothing immoral about cheering for one's own team. But the style of attack against Thomas revealed that another cherished liberal dogma—a belief in affirmative action—could easily be twisted to use as a club against a black nominee they detested. Finally, in their all-points-bulletin style of dirt seeking—a search that eventually unearthed the famous Anita Hill—they revealed the level to which the supposed heirs of Hubert Humphrey, Martin Luther King Jr., and Thurgood Marshall had fallen.

Clarence Thomas could not, obviously, be accused of racism in the traditional sense, but with the help of prominent black liberals, he could be presented as a racial traitor, mentally unbalanced, and—at the last moment—as a sexual predator. That the final insult played upon hoary racist stereotypes did not trouble the sleep of liberals—their sense of moral superiority is impregnable.

Long before Anita Hill had been heard of, a string of prominent black liberals took turns heaping scorn on Clarence Thomas. Democratic congresswoman Eleanor Holmes Norton, the delegate from

the District of Columbia, asked why the president had bothered to se-
lect a black man at all if he was going to sound like a white.[49] The liberal belief in affirmative action–supposedly intended to help blacks
advance–is thus revealed as something else: an effort to aid the advancement of liberal blacks.

Ronald Walters, chairman of Howard University's political science department, advanced the view that blackness "ultimately
means more than color; it also means a set of values from which
Thomas is apparently estranged."[50] Derrick Bell of Harvard Law
School let it be known that Thomas "doesn't think like a black," and
Judge Bruce Wright of New York described Thomas as "emotionally
white."[51] Thomas, then, who was born in poverty and worked his way
into national prominence, was not an authentic black man. Congressman Charles Rangel of New York grumbled that Thomas "goes
against the grain of everything black people believe in" and was
"completely against everything that is in the interests of minorities."

Worse, he was a traitor to his race. Major Owens, another member
of Congress from New York, called Thomas a "monstrous negative
role model." The response of black Americans, said Owens, is comparable to "how the French would have felt if the collaborative Marshal
Petain had been awarded a medal after World War II, or if in Norway,
Quisling had been made a high official in the government."[52]

Jack White, writing in *Time* magazine, seemed to offer the view
that Thomas might be suffering from a diagnosable mental condition–"Token Black Disorder"–in which the sufferer works too hard
to meet the demands of white society.[53] And Judge Leon Higgin-
botham offered that Thomas "was afflicted with racial self-hatred."[54]
Some black liberals arrogated to themselves the power of ex-
communication. Dr. Manning Marable, a professor at Columbia,
declared that Thomas had "ethnically ceased being an African-
American."[55] Columnist Carl Rowan snarled that "If you give
Thomas a little flour on his face, you'd think you had David Duke."[56]

Conservative opponents of affirmative action often point to its
inevitable stigmatization of beneficiaries. The person who has been
given a racial preference is often permanently tarred with the stigma

of inferiority: Did he or she achieve that job or that degree by meeting the same demands as the others, or is it an "affirmative action" hire or admission? Liberals have denied that stigma is a problem, yet in Thomas's case they wielded it like a rapier. Rangel noted that Thomas had attended Yale. Presuming that his admittance was part of an affirmative action program (which it may have been), Rangel sneered that Thomas had "dedicated his life to seeing to it that those benefits end with him." Congressman Louis Stokes of Ohio judged that the difference between "Judge Thomas and most black Americans who have achieved in spite of poverty, adversity, and racism is that most of them have not forgotten from whence they have come."[57] Even as late as 2003, *New York Times* columnist Maureen Dowd returned to this theme, calling Thomas "a clinical study of a man who has been driven barking mad by the beneficial treatment he has received. It's poignant really. It drives him crazy that people think he is where he is because of his race, but he is where he is because of his race."[58]

Movie maker Spike Lee demonstrated exquisite sensitivity to racial stereotyping by branding Thomas "A handkerchief-head, chicken-and-biscuit-eating Uncle Tom."[59] And *USA Today* columnist Barbara Reynolds let fly at the man she regarded as a turncoat:

> It may sound bigoted; well, this is a bigoted world and why can't black people be allowed a little Archie Bunker mentality? . . . Here's a man who's going to decide crucial issues for the country and he has already said no to blacks; he has already said if he can't paint himself white he'll think white and marry a white woman.[60]

When all of this was not enough to sink Thomas's nomination, they brought Anita Hill forward with her lurid tales of sexual harassment. Sexual harassment, all of the senators recited like obedient automatons, was a terribly serious offense and if true would certainly be enough to keep Thomas off the Court. But Hill's tale was full of holes, inconsistencies, and contradictions. She was overwhelmingly outnumbered by former staffers who testified that Thomas had always behaved as a perfect gentleman.

The national press cooperated in the "Get Thomas" campaign. For weeks, the newspapers and television programs became plastered with the Left's newest "civil rights" battle–the fight against sexual harassment. Anita Hill was dubbed the new movement's "Rosa Parks," and Catherine MacKinnon, the radical feminist theoretician of sexual harassment law, became a favorite on the talk show circuit.

Though decked out in the civil rights finery liberals always dress their causes in, the Anita Hill phase of the Thomas confirmation hearings must go down in history as among the tawdriest spectacles in American history. Before the full glare of the world press, senators and lawyers talked of pornographic movies, pubic hairs, and body parts. They recited passages from *The Exorcist*. The Democrats and the liberal press were ready to declare Thomas a social outcast as well as an unfit nominee based on the word of one shaky witness.

Thanks to the liberal Democrats, the nomination hearings for the second African American to serve on the U.S. Supreme Court became a forum for scurrilous charges and debased language. It was a true kangaroo court. They hoped to strip Thomas of his dignity and hold him up to ridicule. They succeeded instead in shaming themselves. Thomas himself called the charade a "high-tech lynching," and it is not too much to say that the liberals chained Thomas's reputation to a pickup truck and dragged it through the muck.

At the time, no one stopped to ask: Is this Democratic Party the champion of African Americans? Only later, when Bill Clinton was president and stood accused of far worse sexual harassment (by many more complainants) than Thomas, was the full measure of liberal hypocrisy revealed. Those who had painstakingly explained that any sexual advance on the part of a superior toward a subordinate in a work environment was per se sexual harassment were suddenly allowing that consenting adults ought to do whatever they please.

Clarence Thomas was not the first, nor was he the last, conservative black American to receive the full pariah treatment from liberal

America. There is a special venom reserved for African Americans who question the catechism of quotas, welfare, preferences, and abortion that liberals hold sacred. It has been suggested that this liberal fear of dissent is a confession of weakness. If they must impose a rigid orthodoxy and resort to character assassination against heretics, it is not because they are confident but because they are weak. Far from welcoming debate, they flee from it, firing stink bombs over their shoulders as they retreat. But as with playing the race card at election time, this is an explanation, not an excuse.

## Jelly Beans and "Niggers"—or Was It?

The average African American is fed a steady diet of negativity about race relations from self-styled "civil rights groups" (who would of course go out of business if white racism ceased to be a serious problem) and from liberal professors, journalists, clergymen, and politicians. Yet most of the examples of white racism that convulse the national press every three to four years turn out to be hoaxes, exaggerations, or malicious inventions. It is becoming predictable. Yet liberals persist in "discovering" white racists (usually lurking in Republican garb) because "standing up for minorities" or pretending to, gives them a flush of self-righteousness. There are other motives as well. Jesse Jackson has made a tidy living for himself and his friends by mau-mauing major corporations for contracts. In exchange for Jackson's promise not to make a stink about mergers and acquisitions, companies have ponied up handsomely for his organization and for those of his friends.

On November 4, 1996, the *New York Times* carried a front page story to the effect that Texaco executives had "bantered comfortably among themselves planning the destruction of documents demanded in a federal discrimination lawsuit and belittling the company's minority employees with racial epithets." The story continued:

> Unknown to almost everyone in the room, one executive was carrying a tape recorder. And it was on. . . .

> . . . The Texaco tapes offer an unfiltered, and perhaps
> unprecedented, glimpse into one company's senior levels,
> where important decisions–including promotion policies for
> minority employees–are made.

Note the implied lesson: This is what really goes in corporate America–
and this time we were lucky enough to catch them on tape!

> . . . The tapes, in which the executives are heard referring to
> black employees as "black jelly beans" and "niggers," raises
> the stakes in the discrimination suit brought against Texaco
> by six company employees on behalf of as many as 1,500
> other minority employees.[61]

There was a tremendous fuss. Texaco immediately issued a statement promising a full investigation and criminal prosecutions if required. The company's stock fell 2.6 percent on the day the story
appeared.[62] Richard T. Seymour, director of the Employment Discrimination Project of the Lawyer's Committee for Civil Rights Under Law pronounced that the revelations about Texaco "make the
case very strongly that there is a need for continued affirmative action programs. It also shows that corporate executives need instruction in ethics."[63]

On November 5, the Leadership Conference on Civil Rights
asked the Justice Department to join the suit. The next day the company announced that two of the executives caught on tape (both of
whom had recently retired) would have their retirement benefits denied and that two other employees who were present at the meeting
would be suspended. Jesse Jackson organized a boycott.

The *New York Times* editorial page too was quick on the trigger.
The tapes, the paper's editorial board argued, "emphatically" dis-
proved the theory that affirmative action was no longer necessary.
Never dreaming that its reporter might have gotten the story wrong,
the *Times* editorial concluded: "When its investigations are complete, Texaco will need to make an example of all those who uttered

racist comments at the meeting and make it clear that discrimination will no longer be tolerated. That is the only way to remove this ugly stain on Texaco's reputation."[64] And all say "Amen."

There was just one problem. The tape had been misinterpreted. When specialists hired by Texaco performed a digital analysis of the tape they discovered that the word the *New York Times* and plaintiff's lawyers were alleging was "nigger" was actually "St. Nicholas." As for the offensive term "jelly beans," it turns out to have been the terminology used by the "diversity trainers" Texaco had hired a few years before.

The *Times*, to its credit, did carry the corrected story on page one (though not in all editions),[65] yet–remarkably–the truth barely slowed the train set in motion by the accusation. Kweisi Mfume took no comfort from knowing that Texaco's executives had not used the word "nigger" after all: "The pain from these new words ought to run even deeper than before for those who feel it, because the intent runs even deeper. . . . The pain is still there, the intent is still there, even if the word 'nigger' is not."[66] The corporation still settled the discrimination case for $176 million. (Texaco may indeed have been guilty of discrimination or it may simply have wanted to cap the bad publicity.) And Mfume declared that "This is only a first step on a long path toward racial reconciliation."[67]

## Black Churches Are Burning

"Terror in the Night Down South," proclaimed *Newsweek* magazine in the spring of 1996.[68] "Flames of Hate: Racism Blamed in Shock Wave of Church Burnings," blared the *New York Daily News*. *USA Today* announced, "Arson at Black Churches Echoes Bigotry of the Past."[69] Mac Charles Jones, a board member of the Center for Democratic Rights (CDR), a group devoted to working with "progressive activists and organizations to build a movement to counter right-wing rhetoric and public-policy initiatives," described the arsons as the work of "a well-organized white-supremacist movement."[70] The CDR was widely quoted as the story gained momentum. Deval Patrick,

Clinton's assistant attorney general for civil rights called the arsons an "epidemic of terror."[71] As reporters leaped on the story, it quickly achieved the status of an urgent national problem. As *Newsweek* put it: "At least 21 predominantly black churches have been torched this year, and many African-Americans naturally believe these hate crimes are part of an orchestrated campaign of terror."[72]

Who said they were hate crimes? Well, just about the entire political, journalistic, and legal worlds. There were congressional hearings, federal investigations, and moving television coverage. No sooner had stories surfaced of a rash of arsons at black churches than President Clinton stepped forward to take command of the issue. He delivered a speech from the Oval Office:

> This morning I want to talk with you about a recent and disturbing rash of crimes that hearkens back to a dark era in our nation's history. Just two days ago, when the Matthews Markland Presbyterian Church in Charlotte, North Carolina, was burned to the ground, it became at least the thirtieth African-American church destroyed or damaged by suspicious fire in the South in the past 18 months. We do not now have evidence of a national conspiracy, but it is clear that racial hostility is the driving force behind a number of these incidents.[73]

Two days later, as the late Michael Kelly reported at the time, investigators released the name of the suspected arsonist in the Matthews Markland church fire. It was an emotionally disturbed thirteen-year-old girl. She was white, but there wasn't the slightest suggestion that she was motivated by racism.

Still, not to be outdone, Senator Bob Dole (R-KS), then a candidate for president, issued a statement saying, "I urge the Justice Department and all state and local law enforcement authorities to use every available resource to find and punish the cowards responsible for these vicious acts of hate."[74]

In fact, as some of the press stories acknowledged (usually on the jump page), investigators had found no evidence of a conspiracy of any sort, nor of racial motives in any but a handful of the fires. That did not slow the outrage machine. Deval Patrick said that while a conspiracy was a "chilling thing," the possibility that "these are separate acts of racism is even worse."[75] Al Gore chimed in that the "conspiracy is racism itself."[76] Jesse Jackson went further, describing the church burnings as "a kind of anti-black mania, a kind of white riot."[77] Congresswoman Maxine Waters (D-CA) said, "Never in my wildest dreams did I expect to be refocused on such outright tyranny."[78] Hugh Price, president of the National Urban League, declared, "The flames of bigotry and intolerance are soaring higher than they have in a generation."[79]

The *Washington Post* carried a story called "Trial by Fire" that concluded, "In the 1950s and 60s, homemade bombs destroyed hundreds of targets, especially black churches, homes of black ministers, synagogues and integrated schools. The current church burnings, devastating black churches and integrated ones, seem part of a similar effort to turn back the clock to Jim Crow time: blacks are warned to stay in their place, whites are warned not to mix."[80]

Al Sharpton expressed himself in *Essence* magazine:

> Nearly 40 black churches burning to the ground is the most satanic thing I've ever witnessed. . . . It is ironic that when an American military base was recently bombed in Saudi Arabia, the United States quickly responded by vowing to end terrorism. What about domestic terrorism? I ask. Why should our people, who are disproportionately represented in the armed forces, continue to protect America's interests abroad, when no one is committed to protecting our interests here?[81]

Sharpton has become quite a respected figure in the Democratic Party. All of the major Democratic candidates who ran for president in 2000 (and Hillary Clinton, in her run for the Senate) flattered and praised him—a clear demonstration of the liberals' ethical handicap.

If a Republican has a questionable club membership in his past, or wrote an article thirty years ago that seemed insufficiently integrationist, he will be subjected to peremptory justice by liberals. Even if the rest of his life makes St. Francis seem surly by comparison, he will be a moral pariah. However, the standard is a little different for liberals, and most especially for black liberals.

Sharpton had been instrumental in fomenting hatred toward Jews during the Crown Heights pogrom in 1991. At the time, he called Jews "diamond merchants" and taunted: "If the Jews want to get it on, tell them to pin their yarmulkes back and come over to my house."[82] Just imagine if those words had come from the lips of Rush Limbaugh. In 1992, when Sharpton ran for the U.S. Senate from New York, he described his primary opponents as "recycled white trash."[83] In 1995, he led a boycott of Freddy's Fashion Mart, calling its owner "some white interloper." Sharpton's gangs picketed the store, shouting, "This block for niggers only: no whites and Jews allowed." Some chanted, "Kill the Jew bastards and burn down the Jew store." One protester took the words literally and broke into the store with a gun. He shot four people and then set the store ablaze, killing seven.[84]

President Clinton flew down to South Carolina for the rededication of a church that had been burned. Traveling with him on Air Force One was Jesse Jackson, who warmed up the crowd first. The climate that made burning black churches possible, Jackson said, was not just the work of the Klan ("white robes") but also of conservatives on the Supreme Court ("black robes") and in the Congress ("blue suits"):

> It's easy to scapegoat the Klan . . . but the clouds have been seeded by forces far more powerful than they are. That's why the conspiracy may not be one or two or three individuals in a room saying "Let's burn churches." We have something worse than that. We have a cultural conspiracy, where if you light a match in a field, and little fires break out all over the field, it means that the land mines have been laid. . . .

Those in blue suits who use thinly coded, veiled race symbols when they say welfare and crime and three strikes and anti–affirmative action, they're sending signals, they're sending messages more profound than their language. . . . When these blue suits seed the clouds and black robes restrict our political districts, they're laying the groundwork for those . . . that burn churches.[85]

When the president added, "Every time you hear somebody use race or religion as an instrument of division and hatred, speak up against it"[86]–the crowd knew to whom he referred. "It is the cruelest of ironies," the president continued, "that an expression of bigotry in America that would sweep this country is one that involves trashing religious liberty."[87]

It was just too tempting for many commentators to resist linking the church fires with conservative policies. And they succumbed. Jack E. White of *Time* magazine wrote:

. . . All the conservative Republicans, from Newt Gingrich to Pete Wilson, who have sought political advantage by exploiting white resentment should come and stand in the charred ruins of the New Liberty Baptist Church in Tyler [Alabama] . . . and wonder if their coded phrases encouraged the arsonists. Over the past 18 months, while Republicans fulminated about welfare and affirmative action, more than 20 churches in Alabama and six other southern and border states have been torched.[88]

Politicians and religious figures of all political persuasions rushed to condemn the church arsons. The National Council of Churches established a fund to rebuild burned-out churches–and so did the Christian Coalition. Mary Frances Berry, chairwoman of the Civil Rights Commission, dismissed the latter, sneering, "You have the very people who created the context for the fires rushing over and saying 'Let us help you put them out.' "[89] The Hudson Institute's Michael Fumento reported that Americans (supposedly little changed from the dark days of Jim Crow) deluged the National Council of Churches with contributions of $100,000 per day at the height of the scare, creating a fund of more than $9 million. When this was combined with insurance money, there were enough funds to rebuild every burned church three times over.[90] Not that the money went for that purpose. As Fumento noted, at least a third and possibly more of the money raised by the NCC was overseen by a former Marxist named Don Rojas, who earmarked some of the funds for programs advocating "economic justice" and combating "interlocking oppressions from gender to homophobia."[91]

But even before Clinton traveled to South Carolina, doubt was creeping into the comfortable morality play. Try as they might, federal, state, and local officials saw no evidence of a white racist conspiracy to attack black churches. In fact, on closer examination, it turned out that only about half of the churches that had been torched in 1995 and 1996 were African American. Among these, a handful did appear to be the work of white racists, but the vast majority were not. Michael Fumento analyzed *USA Today*'s reporting. The paper had made waves by "discovering" the epidemic of black church fires—mostly by relying on the work of Left-leaning groups like the Center for Democratic Rights, the Southern Poverty Law Center, and the National Council of Churches. But months later, its reporters got to the true story. Though *USA Today* had reported that black churches were burning across the American South, more thorough analysis revealed that of 780 church fires in the United States in 1995, only 144 took place in the eleven Southern states.[92] Of these 144, only 64 were black churches. More revealing, the paper acknowledged that "Analysis of the 64 fires since 1995 shows only four can be conclusively shown to be racially motivated." Of the thirty people arrested in connection with the arsons, ten were black.[93]

Michael Kelly further reported that a review of the data by the

Bureau of Alcohol, Tobacco, and Firearms of forty-nine black church fires in the South concluded that ten had been the result of accidents:

> Of the thirty-nine fires that were connected to arson, arrests had been made in nine cases by the end of June. These are the only cases in which there is enough evidence to ascertain beyond guesswork the motives of the arsonists, and compelling evidence of a racial motive has been unearthed in only two of them, *involving the same two suspects* [emphasis added].[94]

Two or four—whichever number is correct—it hardly amounts to the kind of epidemic the nation had talked itself into over the previous several months. Some of the fires had been set by volunteer firefighters who set fires for the fun of putting them out (a not uncommon phenomenon). Others were the work of drunken louts. Many were never solved.

Naturally, the hysterics who had hurled curses at America for its racism and cruelty never recanted. But what is more disturbing is their rush to assume the worst about America's white majority. Any fair-minded person living in the USA in the mid-90s ought to have been skeptical about a wave of KKK-style terrorism sweeping the South. The America of the 1990s was a place where integration was the rule, not the exception; where people without friends of another race were the minority; where interracial marriage was commonplace; where African Americans were revered for their contributions to entertainment, the arts, the military, business, and sports. Equal opportunity and equal rights were (and are) matters of national doctrine.

The civil rights movement has achieved totemic status in American life—sometimes even eclipsing the rest of American history. Every American school child, for example, knows who Martin Luther King Jr. was but few can accurately identify James Madison. Black candidates easily win election in predominantly white districts. Carol Mosely Braun was elected to the Senate in Illinois. Douglas Wilder was elected governor of Virginia. Even after his majority/minority district in North Carolina was redrawn, making it only 36 percent black, Mel Watt was reelected with 56 percent of the vote.[95] Four other members of the Congressional Black Caucus–Cynthia McKinney of Georgia, Corrine Brown of Florida, Sanford Bishop of Georgia, and Eva Clayton of North Carolina–had similar experiences.[96] The most popular political figure in the nation in the 1990s, the one whose candidacy was considered a "dream" for the Republicans, was Colin Powell. This is not to say that old-fashioned white racism was utterly vanquished, but certainly white racism had become a fringe phenomenon.

Not so liberal nostalgia for our racist past. Liberals are prepared, on the flimsiest pretext, to declare that the Klan rides again. "St. Nicholas" becomes "nigger" because at some level "nigger" is what they expect and want to hear. Faced with old-fashioned white racism, they know what to do. Gin up the usual outrage. Round up the usual suspects. It's always easier to choose up sides when the battle is over and you know who was right and who was wrong–and perhaps, just as important, who lost and who won. It's a bit more challenging to make moral judgments in the here and now without benefit of hindsight. Liberals excelled at beating the dead horse of Nazism but fell considerably short on confronting the evil of communism.

Not only does this insult the honorable white people who have banished racism from polite society, it does incalculable damage to the morale of black Americans. The stoking of racial animus is evidence of the way liberals harm those they claim to want to help. It further undermines black progress by diverting attention away from the true problems of twenty-first-century America–problems such as disintegrating families, weak schools, and the multiculturalist assault on American identity–while do-gooder Don Quixotes ostentatiously swing at white racist windmills.

## Message to Blacks: Be Afraid

But demoralization has its uses—particularly at election time. During the 1998 election cycle, the Democratic Party ran ads on black radio stations in key districts with the following language:

> When you don't vote, you let another church explode.
> When you don't vote, you allow another cross to burn.
> When you don't vote, you let another assault wound a brother or sister.
> When you don't vote, you let the Republicans continue to cut school lunches and Head Start.
> When you don't vote, you allow the Republicans to give tax breaks to the wealthy while threatening Social Security and Medicare.
> On November 3, vote. Vote smart. Vote Democratic for Congress and the U.S. Senate.[97]

That same year, in the Texas district represented by Democrat Martin Frost, the Democratic Party sent flyers to every black household featuring a picture of Martin Luther King Jr. side by side with a beautiful little black girl. While King "had a dream for all children," the ad warned, voters should not "let Republicans take that dream away. . . . Republicans are so desperate, they are willing to resort to anything—even voter intimidation—to keep Democrats from passing laws that help our community."[98]

Republican Ellen Sauerbrey and Democrat Parris Glendening were in a dead heat in the race for governor of Maryland. Sauerbrey's strong showing was unusual for a Republican in that heavily Democratic state. But in the last three weeks of the campaign, as Matt Labash of the *Weekly Standard* reported, all of that changed.

> With an assist from adman Robert Shrum, himself no stranger to employing Klan imagery when taking on Republicans, Glendening carpetbombed Sauerbrey in TV ads that

claimed she voted against "the civil-rights act" and that she had "a civil rights record to be ashamed of."

The civil-rights act in question was a 1992 state bill that would have permitted sex-harassment suits to be brought in Maryland courts instead of federal courts. The bill was killed by a Democratic majority, and even Maryland's black House speaker voted it down. So over-the-top was Glendening's claim that he was even repudiated by his uneasy ally, Baltimore's black mayor Kurt Schmoke, who refused "to participate in a campaign to try to persuade people that she is a racist."[99]

Democrats claim that it is Republicans who resort to race baiting. They cite the "Willie Horton" commercial from 1988. It is true that a pro-Bush group (though not the Bush campaign) aired ads regarding Horton. It is not clear why this represents race baiting. Horton was a convicted murderer doing time in a Massachusetts prison. Under a furlough program staunchly defended by Governor Michael Dukakis as "rehabilitative," Horton received a weekend pass to leave the prison.[100] While on furlough he terrorized a couple in Maryland, pistol whipping and slashing the man and brutally raping the woman twice.

The first candidate to mention this political weakness was not Bush, but Senator Al Gore, who ran against Dukakis in the Democratic primaries. Gore mentioned the ill-advised furlough program in a debate. The pro-Bush ad purchased by a private group mentioned Horton by name (as Gore had not), and showed his picture. Because Horton was African American, liberals harshly denounced this spot as the lowest form of race baiting. Surely that is a reach. The point about the Horton ad was that Dukakis was soft on crime. Horton had been serving a life sentence for murder. Seventy-six other convicts listed as "escaped" from Massachusetts had actually walked away from just such furloughs as Horton enjoyed.[101] Had Horton been white, Hispanic, or Asian, his picture would have been seized just as greedily by Republicans hoping to make the political point sting.

The racism charge is also most useful at confirmation time. Its misuse since the 1990s has amounted to Leftist McCarthyism.

## The "Troubling" Judge Pickering

On March 14, 2002, the Senate Judiciary Committee voted down the nomination of Charles Pickering to serve on the Fifth Circuit Court of Appeals. It was a straight 10–8 party-line vote. The Democrats explained that they were saving the country from a man with a "troubling" record on civil rights, "reproductive rights," and other issues. The truth is that Pickering was pro-life. That alone was enough to get the character assassination squads geared up. Reaching into their well-worn bag of tricks, they pulled out the white sheet and threw it over Pickering's head. If such tactics will further frighten and alienate black Americans and encourage their belief that white racists are hidden under every bed, so be it. The important thing is to make sure that no judge who disapproves of abortion on demand is confirmed.

People for the American Way prepared the ground. In an e-mail circulated among the "activist network," a collection of like-minded advocacy groups as well as Democratic committee staffers, PFAW demanded a second hearing on Pickering's nomination. The justification, they claimed, was that Pickering had a large number of unpublished opinions in his judging history. In fact, Pickering had published ninety-five opinions in ten years—about average for a federal judge. Judges do not publish all of their opinions, only those that explore new legal ground or are otherwise interesting or noteworthy. Some of President Clinton's nominees had published even fewer opinions without attracting the interest of committee Democrats. But the Democrats were stalling for time, scheduling a second hearing so that activists and committee staff would have time to comb through Pickering's unpublished opinions searching for incriminating material.

At a press conference, PFAW's Ralph Neas presented the bill of particulars against Judge Pickering. Byron York summarized the gist of it in *National Review:*

> The report was a grab-bag of issues, all of which suggested that Pickering was an unreconstructed segregationist who was hostile to the rights of women, minorities, and the poor. The report criticized Pickering for a 1959 law review note on Mississippi's interracial marriage ban that Pickering wrote as a first-year law student; it accused Pickering of having had "contact" with Mississippi's racist Sovereignty Commission in the 1970s; it accused Pickering of being indifferent to equal voting rights; it said Pickering had a "troubling record of reversals in the Court of Appeals"; it said he was hostile to abortion rights; and it accused him of blurring the separation of church and state.[102]

Senator Tom Daschle obligingly echoed these themes when he was interviewed on ABC's *This Week* program. Pickering had displayed an "insensitivity to civil rights, to equal rights, especially to minorities," Daschle alleged. "This really lays bare the administration's real position of civil rights. This exposes the Southern strategy clearly. There is no doubt in my mind we now know from where they come."[103]

The Democrats, of course, can say the moon is a balloon. Without the echo chamber of the press, their words would scarcely ripple the capital's reflecting pool. But the liberal press amplifies and dignifies the Democrats' charges, giving the most partisan and unjustified attacks the patina of statesmanship. Thus, the *Detroit Free Press* editorialized, "With his nomination of Pickering, President George W. Bush is substantiating fears that he would attempt to turn the federal judiciary into a right-wing monster."[104] The *Atlanta Journal and Constitution* headlined its view with "Extremist Judge Unfit to Sit on Appeals Court."[105] And the *Los Angeles Times* said, "Say No to This Throwback."[106] The *New York Times* did not entirely regurgitate the PFAW

talking points but put its own pompous spin on the same idea. Following the scandal surrounding Trent Lott's unfortunate comments at
Strom Thurmond's birthday party (about which more in a moment),
the *Times* tried to wring every policy ounce out of the imbroglio:

> Going forward, the White House and the Senate must raise
> the bar. There has been talk that the Bush Administration
> may renominate Charles Pickering, a Trent Lott protégé, to
> the Louisiana-based Court of Appeals for the Fifth Circuit.
> Judge Pickering was rejected in March by the Senate Judi-
> ciary Committee, after concerns were raised about contacts
> he had, as a state legislator in the 1970s, with Mississippi's
> segregationist Sovereignty Commission, and his unusual ef-
> forts, as a trial judge, to persuade prosecutors to reduce the
> sentence of a man convicted of cross burning. The White
> House should not renominate him.[107]

So who is this Pickering who so shamed the Bush administration?
Pickering was a sixty-four-year-old federal judge from Laurel,
Mississippi. Not only was he not a racist, his record actually showed
an admirable degree of courage on the subject of civil rights. In
1967, Pickering was an elected prosecutor. He chose to testify
against the Imperial Wizard of the Ku Klux Klan, who was on trial
for firebombing the home of a civil rights worker. By taking the
stand, Pickering risked more than his reputation. He was defeated
in his bid for reelection as his friends had warned he would be.
Charles Evers, brother of the murdered civil rights campaigner
Medgar Evers, said:

> In 1967, many locally elected prosecutors in Mississippi
> looked the other way when faced with allegations of violence
> against African-Americans and those who supported our
> struggle for equal treatment under the law. Judge Pickering
> was a locally elected prosecutor who took the stand that year
> and testified in the criminal trial against the Imperial

Wizard. . . . Judge Pickering later lost his bid for reelection because he dared to defy the Klan, but he gained my respect and the respect of many others as a man who stands up for what is right.[108]

It wasn't enough, however, to gain the respect of Teddy Kennedy, Joseph Biden, John Edwards, Charles Schumer, and the other Democrats on the Senate Judiciary Committee who have probably never had to defy anything more frightening than a negative focus group.

Testifying against the KKK was in character for Pickering. He was also known for hiring black staffers at a time when few other Mississippians did. He urged the chancellor of the University of Mississippi to create the Institute of Racial Reconciliation and served on its board of directors. And he defended a young black man accused of stealing from a young white woman. Pickering remained with the defendant through two trials, finally winning an acquittal.[109] A reporter for the *New York Times* (whose editorial board thundered against Pickering), wrote of Pickering's hometown of Laurel, "The city's black establishment overwhelmingly supports his nomination. . . . they admire his efforts at racial reconciliation, which they describe as highly unusual for a white Republican in the state."[110] Stuart Taylor Jr. further reported that "Black leaders also praised Pickering for 'directing federal money to medical clinics in low-income areas when he was a state senator [and] persuading white-owned banks to lend money to black entrepreneurs.' The black president of the City Council, Thaddeus Edmonson, told [*New York Times* reporter David] Firestone, 'I can't believe the man they're describing in Washington is the same one I've known for years.' "[111]

The liberals' charge of racial "insensitivity" was based on four things: a law review article dating back forty years; "contact" with the segregationist Mississippi Sovereignty Commission; his decisions in cases involving minority employment; and Pickering's recommendation of leniency for a defendant in a cross-burning case.

The article in question was a law note Pickering had written in

1959, as a twenty-one-year-old first-year law student. At the suggestion of a law professor, he had authored an article describing a techni-
cal fix for the state's flawed antimiscegenation statute. At the time,
twenty-three states had such laws. It is true that it would have been
better if Pickering had condemned the law—but the law review article
must be viewed, as lawyers might say, in the context of all the facts and
circumstances. He was twenty-one. He didn't applaud the law. And
the rest of his career shows a high degree of respect for racial equality.
As a federal judge, he overturned a damage award in a civil case because he believed that the jury was biased against the plaintiffs, an interracial couple. He ordered that the matter of damages be retried.

During the course of his confirmation hearings, Pickering was
asked if he had ever had "contact" with the Mississippi Sovereignty
Commission. He said no. Committee staff then triumphantly produced evidence of a phone call Pickering had made in 1972 to someone who was a member of the Sovereignty Commission. Perhaps
Pickering ought to have remembered the call, but Democrats on the
committee ought to have taken into account the reason for the call.
Pickering was a state senator representing Jones County. At the
time, the Klan was involved in fomenting violence during a labor dis-
pute in Jones County. The call was an attempt to find out what was
happening—not a request for an application form.

In the rendering by PFAW and the committee Democrats, Pickering's decisions in two employment discrimination cases showed
"hostility" to civil rights. The first case concerned a grocery store
owned by two black brothers who were cut off by a supplier. They
sued, alleging a civil rights violation. Pickering granted the defendant's motion for summary judgment. What the Democrats and liberal activists never revealed about the case was that the brothers had
been behind in their payments and were under criminal indictment
at the time the supplier withdrew their credit.

The second case concerned a black fireman who alleged racial
discrimination after he was fired. Pickering gave summary judgment
to the defendant in this case as well, stating that "The fact that a

black employee is terminated does not automatically indicate discrimination."[112] The judge took account of the fact that the fireman was chronically late for work. This became, in the words of PFAW, "a disturbing hostility toward civil rights plaintiffs."[113]

The cross-burning case obviously offered the greatest scope for demagoguery and the Democrats played it like a Stradivarius. Senator John Edwards (D-NC) leaped on the case, accusing Pickering of being soft on a cross burner and unethical in his handling of the case as well.

As Byron York explained in *National Review*, the case came before Pickering in 1994:

> Three men—20-year-old Daniel Swan, 25-year-old Mickey Herbert Thomas, and a 17-year-old whose name was not released because he was a juvenile—were drinking together when one of them came up with the idea that they should construct a cross and burn it in front of a house in which a white man and his black wife lived in rural Walthall County. While it is not clear who originally suggested the plan, it is known that the 17-year-old appeared to harbor some sort of hostility toward the couple; on an earlier occasion, he had fired a gun into the house (no one was hit).[114]

Because the case involved a cross burning, local officials contacted the Justice Department in Washington, which dispatched investigators from the Office of Civil Rights. Justice Department prosecutors next struck plea-bargain deals with two of the three defendants. York explained:

> In a move that baffled and later angered Judge Pickering, Civil Rights Division prosecutors early on decided to make a plea bargain with two of the three suspects. The first, Mickey Thomas, had an unusually low IQ. . . . The second bargain was with the 17-year-old. Civil Rights Division lawyers

allowed both men to plead guilty to misdemeanors in the cross-burning case (the juvenile also pleaded guilty to felony charges in the shooting incident). The Civil Rights Division recommended no jail time for either man.

The situation was different for the third defendant, Daniel Swan, who, like the others, faced charges under the hate-crime statute. The law requires that the government prove the accused acted out of racial animus, and Swan, whose defense consisted mainly of the contention that he was very drunk on the night of the cross burning, maintained that he simply did not have the racial animus necessary to be guilty of a hate crime under federal law.

The case went to trial in Pickering's courtroom. During the course of testimony, it appears that Pickering came to suspect the Civil Rights Division had made a plea bargain with the wrong defendant.[115]

Referring to the seventeen-year-old, Pickering later wrote in a postverdict memorandum, "It was established to the satisfaction of this court that although the juvenile was younger than the defendant Daniel Swan, nevertheless the juvenile was the ringleader in the burning of the cross involved in this crime." Pickering was dismayed that the government had not asked for jail time for the seventeen-year-old, which would have been eminently possible considering the nature of the offense. "It was clearly established," Pickering continued, "that the juvenile had racial animus. . . . The court [i.e., Pickering] expressed both to the government and to the counsel for the juvenile serious reservations about not imposing time in the Bureau of Prisons for the juvenile defendant."[116]

Swan, meanwhile, was convicted. Though he had no criminal record and the testimony of seven witnesses suggested that he had no racial hostility toward blacks (there was one witness to the contrary but that was disputed), the government recommended seven and a half years in prison. Pickering balked. The more guilty defendant, the one who had shot up the home of this interracial couple, gotten into fights with black kids at school (resulting in suspension), bragged about shooting into the home of some "niggers," and the clear ringleader in the crime, received no jail time. Pickering wrote, "The recommendation of the government in this instance is clearly the most egregious instance of disproportionate sentencing recommended by the government in any case pending before this court."[117]

The Justice Department's insistence on seven and a half years was based on applying two different laws to the case. Pickering doubted that both were applicable. He asked the prosecutors to check with Washington as to whether the same sentencing standards were used in other circuits. They were late getting back to him. He had to delay the sentencing date. Growing exasperated, Pickering phoned a friend in the Justice Department's civil division (Al Gore's brother-in-law, as it happens) to express his frustration with the department. This is the call that Senator John Edwards would later absurdly characterize as a breach of ethics.

Eventually, the Civil Rights Division did get back to Judge Pickering. They decided to drop their insistence that Swan serve a minimum of five years under one of the statues. Pickering accordingly sentenced Swan to twenty-seven months in jail—a sentence he considered just under the circumstances. At sentencing he told Swan, "The type of conduct you exhibited cannot and will not be tolerated. . . . I would suggest to you that during the time you're in prison that you do some reading on race relations and maintaining good race relations and how that can be done."[118]

President Bush renominated Judge Pickering after Republicans achieved control of the Senate in 2002. This time, his nomination was approved by the Judiciary Committee, but Democrats swore to filibuster the nomination on the Senate floor. Rather than fight the Democrats over the confirmation issue, President Bush elected to give Pickering a recess appointment—a move that would install Pickering on the Appeals Court until the end of the next congressional session. Senator John Kerry (D-MA) was not above a little demagoguery in this case, declaring, "Here we are, on the weekend before a national holiday, when we celebrate Martin Luther King's birthday, and George W. Bush celebrates it by appointing Charles Pickering, *a known forceful advocate for a cross-burner in America* [emphasis added], to the federal court of the United States."[119] Paul Krugman, a columnist for the *New York Times*, offered another typically liberal interpretation of Bush's decision:

> The most sinister example [of Bush solidifying his base] was the recess appointment of Charles Pickering Sr., with his segregationist past and questionable record on voting rights, to the federal appeals court—the day after Martin Luther King's actual birthday. Was this careless timing? Don't be silly: it was a deliberate, if subtle, gesture of sympathy with a part of the Republican coalition that never gets mentioned in public.[120]

But is the secretly racist white Southern voting bloc really the base of the Republican Party? A thousand liberal attacks and insinuations would have it so. Unfortunately, Senate Majority Leader Trent Lott provided fodder for this particular liberal cannon when he offered a belated endorsement to the 1948 Dixiecrat ticket. Speaking at the one hundredth birthday celebration for Senator Strom Thurmond (R-SC), the Mississippi Republican said, "I want to say this about my state: When Strom Thurmond ran for president, we voted for him. We're proud of it. And if the rest of the country had followed our lead, we wouldn't have had all these problems over all these years."[121]

When the firestorm erupted, Lott sought to backpedal from this boneheaded statement. "A poor choice of words conveyed to some the impression that I embraced the discarded policies of the past. Nothing could be further from the truth, and I apologize to anyone who was offended by my statement."[122] Well, that "anyone" included pretty much the entire population of the United States. Conservative writers and opinion makers were first to condemn Senator Lott. His comment seemed to have been scripted by a Democrat hoping to make a Republican fit the unreconstructed segregationist model. It was as if the dearest wish of Robert Shrum, a Democratic operative who loves to portray Republicans as racists, had come true: One of the country's leading Republicans reveals a soft spot for segregation!

The ticket Strom Thurmond ran on in 1948 was the last gasp of white supremacy in America. When Harry Truman proposed a civil rights plank for the Democratic platform, thirty-five southern delegates walked out. They formed the State's Rights Party (popularly christened "Dixiecrats") and went on to hold their own convention in Birmingham, Alabama. The party nominated Strom Thurmond, then the governor of South Carolina, for president, and Mississippi governor J. Fielding Wright for vice president. The party received a million votes and won four states–Alabama, Mississippi, Louisiana, and South Carolina–giving the party thirty-nine electoral votes. So Lott was right: Mississippi had gone for Thurmond. Lott's memory of the episode must have been strong, since his roots were in the Democratic party; his first political job (1968–1972) was as administrative assistant to Democratic congressman William M. Colmer.

Lott's attempts to salvage his reputation revealed the dismaying lack of self-assurance that afflicts many Republicans. Appearing on Black Entertainment Television, Lott solemnly promised to support affirmative action "across the board" and to reconsider his support for Judge Pickering. Thus he proved willing to sell out reputable conservative positions to atone for his personal reactionary ones.

## The Fable

The Democrats have been remarkably successful at rewriting the history of the parties vis-à-vis the civil rights movement. Comedian and political commentator Al Franken, for example, in his book *Lies and the Lying Liars Who Tell Them*, wrote:

> When President Lyndon Johnson signed the Civil Rights Act, he is said to have turned to an aide and remarked, "We have just lost the South for a generation." The Republican Party became home to Southern bigots and still is today.

While the Democratic Party lost the South that year, they did gain my dad. A lifelong Republican who voted for Herbert Hoover and every GOP candidate through Nixon, Dad switched parties in 1964 because the Republican nominee, Barry Goldwater, voted against the Civil Rights Act. . . . [123]

In fact, if Franken's father was eager to distance himself from the party that failed to support the Civil Rights Act, he ought to have remained a Republican. According to the *Congressional Quarterly*, only 61 percent of Democrats in the House of Representatives supported the act, while 80 percent of Republicans voted in favor. In the Senate, 69 percent of Democrats and 82 percent of Republicans voted in favor.[124] Among the Democratic senators who voted against the legislation were J. William Fulbright (Bill Clinton's mentor), who was a racist, and Albert Gore Sr. Al Gore Jr. asserted several times during the campaign of 2000 that his father was defeated for reelection because he *supported* the Civil Rights Act. That is, not to put too fine a point on it, false. The former vice president belongs in Franken's book.[125]

It is true that Barry Goldwater was among those who voted against the bill, but it is a total distortion to imply that he opposed the bill because he was a segregationist. Goldwater was in fact a founding member of the Arizona chapter of the NAACP and remained a member throughout his life. He pushed to desegregate the Arizona National Guard and hired blacks in his family's business. He had been a strong supporter of both the 1957 and 1960 Civil Rights Acts, but he had philosophical objections to the 1964 act—specifically to certain provisions that he believed unconstitutionally extended the power of the federal government.[126]

But this history is conveniently forgotten in the thrill of defaming Republicans. The Democrats have so successfully tarred Republicans as "intolerant" or worse that they can now casually refer to the myth with confidence that voters will understand. Thus, Howard Dean in 2004 accused Republicans of "dividing Americans against each other, stirring up racial prejudices and bringing out the worst in people."[127] And political analyst Norman Ornstein intoned that "Republicans have been playing with fire on this issue for years and now it has turned on them."[128]

The fable goes as follows: When the Democratic Party endorsed civil rights and passed landmark legislation, white bigots decamped to the Republican party. But as Gerard Alexander of the University of Virginia has observed, the facts don't support this view:

> The myth that links the GOP with racism leads us to expect that the GOP should have advanced first and most strongly where the politics of white solidarity were most intense. The GOP should have entrenched itself first among Deep South whites and only later in the periphery. The GOP should have appealed at least as much, if not more, therefore, to the less educated, working-class whites who were not its natural voters elsewhere in the country but who were George Wallace's base. The GOP should have received more support from native white Southerners raised on the region's traditional racism than from white immigrants to the region from the Midwest and elsewhere. And as the Southern electorate aged over the ensuing decades, older voters should have identified as Republicans at higher rates than younger ones raised in a less racist era.
>
> Each prediction is wrong. The evidence suggests that the GOP advanced in the South because it attracted much the same upwardly mobile (and non-union) economic and religious conservatives that it did elsewhere in the country.[129]

Gerard points out that the realignment of Southern voters did not begin in the Deep South but rather in the "peripheral" states like Virginia, North Carolina, Tennessee, Texas, and Florida. Though Dwight Eisenhower did poorly among Deep South whites, he polled very well in the periphery, starting the realignment that would one day make the South a Republican stronghold. Peripheral Southern voters also preferred Nixon to Wallace in 1968. "In the 1960s and '70s," writes Alexander, "nearly three-quarters of GOP House victories were in the peripheral rather than the Deep South, with the GOP winning twice as often in urban as rural districts."[130] Additionally, the Republicans benefited from the immigration of millions of Midwestern, Northeastern, and other transplants who moved south starting in the 1950s. They tended to bring two things with them: more enlightened views on race and more openness to the Republican party. Alexander concludes:

> In sum, the GOP's Southern electorate was not rural, nativist, less educated, afraid of change, or concentrated in the most stagnant parts of the Deep South. It was disproportionately suburban, middle-class, educated, younger, non-native-Southern, and concentrated in the growth points that were, so to speak, the least "Southern" parts of the South. This is a very strange way to reincarnate George Wallace's movement.[131]

To be sure, there are Republicans who were racists in their youth, but there are just as many Democrats of whom the same can be said. Senator Robert Byrd (D-WV) was a member of the Ku Klux Klan as a young man. President Clinton awarded the Medal of Freedom to former senator William Fulbright, a signer of the "Southern Manifesto" condemning *Brown v. Board of Education*. Clinton said of him, "It doesn't take long to live a life. He made the best of his, and helped us to have a better chance to make the best of ours. . . . The American political system produced this remarkable man, and my state did, and I'm real proud of it."[132] Senator Ernest Hollings made the decision, when he was governor, to fly the confederate flag over the state capitol in South Carolina.

Neither party is pure on matters of race. It is high time Republican presidential candidates skipped Bob Jones University on the campaign trail. But the Democrats have resorted to the charge of racism so often and so illegitimately that it has become the modern bloody shirt. Should John Ashcroft, whose career has been spotless and whose wife teaches law at Howard University, be confirmed as attorney general? "Racist!" Shall Carol Ionnone, a scholar who had the temerity to critique Alice Walker, be confirmed for the National Endowment for the Humanities? "Racist!" Shall Priscilla Owen be confirmed for the Court of Appeals? "Insensitive."

Sowing distrust and paranoia is good for Democrats politically, but it harms the country, and it harms African Americans in particular. Polling shows strong and consistent disparities between whites and blacks on the subject of discrimination and racism. A 1999 ABC News/Lifetime poll asked, "Is there discrimination against blacks?" Twenty-two percent of whites said, "Yes, a lot," while 57 percent of blacks saw a lot. Forty-six percent of whites believed the answer was "Yes, somewhat," along with 25 percent of blacks. Thirty-two percent of whites and only 17 percent of blacks responded "Little/none." Most observers agree that with every passing year, American society becomes progressively less racist. Yet the number of black respondents who believe that there is "a lot" of discrimination against blacks increased by 13 points between 1996 and 1999.[133] A *Newsweek* poll conducted in 1999 found that 65 percent of black respondents thought the situation of blacks in America was worse or about the same as it was five years ago.[134] Asked whether blacks would ever be able to close the income gap with whites, 71 percent of whites said yes but only 42 percent of blacks agreed. Eighty percent of blacks thought racism in the workplace was either a "big problem" or "somewhat of a problem."[135] According to another poll, 81 percent of blacks agreed that there is a "strong tendency in American society to attack and silence strong black women such as attorney Anita Hill and Justice Department candidate Lani Guinier."[136]

Liberal Democrats bear a heavy burden of guilt for convincing blacks that little has changed in the secret hearts of whites–of white Republicans anyway. Clearly, African Americans can see for themselves that things have improved economically and socially. They don't rely on the Democratic Party or so-called civil rights leaders to tell them how things are going in their personal lives. And yet the spirit of pessimism and perceived oppression that liberals do so much to stoke obscures great progress.

Liberals often complain that blacks are portrayed unfairly on television and in movies as criminals or drug addicts (a doubtful proposition since Hollywood is famously fond of portraying white businessmen as villains and killers), but liberals themselves do African Americans and America itself an injustice by significantly understating black progress. Forty percent of blacks are now comfortably middle class, compared with only about 5 percent in 1940.[137] But black Americans don't seem to know this. A 1991 Gallup poll found that nearly half of black Americans thought that 75 percent of blacks lived in poverty. The true figure was 26.4 percent.[138]

Little attention goes to the good news. Only 37.7 percent of blacks were high school graduates in 1960. That figure had reached 86.5 by 1995.[139] The disparity between the median income of white and black families seems large—$42,646 for whites compared with $25,970 for blacks—until you control for marriage. The income gap between married white and black families was only $6,200 in 1995.[140] And this figure may even be misleading, since 56 percent of black families lived in the South in 1995, where wages are lower. In 130 cities and counties in 1994, John McWhorter reports, black married families actually earned more than white married families.[141] The percentage of black families living in the suburbs continues to rise rapidly. It has jumped from 31.5 percent of all black families in 1995 to 36 percent in 2002.[142]

If the Democrats have their way, African Americans will continue to feel oppressed, despised, and handicapped into the indefinite future. All progress will be downplayed and every setback amplified. In this way, Democrats can continue to rely on lopsided black support at the polls. If Republicans are smart, they will aggressively challenge the Democrats for black votes. They will get comfortable before black audiences and appear on black radio shows. They will expose the lies on which the Democrats have dined for so long. If they enjoy even moderate success, they will break the back of the Democratic Party.

## Chapter Three
# THE PROMISE OF COMPASSION; THE REALITY OF DEGRADATION THROUGH WELFARE

The easy, at-home test for liberalism is welfare: Are you pro or con? Until 1996 and even beyond, it was a perfect acid test because within the welfare debate lurked every cherished principle of the liberal worldview. It could illuminate the conservative side as well.

If you believed in welfare, you probably also believed in a series of propositions about American society, economics, human nature, and government. Every good liberal believed in welfare because he knew that (a) good jobs were difficult if not impossible to find; (b) racism made it particularly taxing for minorities to find work; (c) no one who could work would ever take welfare instead; (d) it is the duty of the government to take care of people who cannot or will not take care of themselves; and (e) it is excessively judgmental as well as being none of anyone's business why a woman might have a number of children by different (mostly absent) fathers while she collects welfare. To ask the question is to blame the victim. Finally, there was a private thought, rarely expressed, but nevertheless potent: If black people collect welfare in disproportionate numbers, well, it's the least society can do after centuries of slavery and discrimination.

ADC, Aid to Dependent Children, was a New Deal program originally designed for widows and orphans. Poverty in those days meant true want. In 1932, there were 13 million unemployed, nearly a third of the workforce. Historian William Leuchtenberg mapped some of the misery:

Many lived in the primitive conditions of a preindustrial society stricken by famine. In the coal fields of West Virginia and Kentucky, evicted families shivered in tents in midwinter; children went barefoot. In Los Angeles, people whose gas and electricity had been turned off were reduced to cooking over wood fires in back lots. Visiting nurses in New York found children famished; one episode, reported Lillian Wald, "might have come out of the tales of Old Russia." A Philadelphia storekeeper told a reporter of one family he was keeping going on credit: "Eleven children in that house. They've got no shoes, no pants. In the house, no chairs. My God, you go in there, you cry, that's all." . . . In Chicago, a crowd of some fifty hungry men fought over a barrel of garbage set outside the back door of a restaurant; in Stockton, California, men scoured the city dump near the San Joaquin River to retrieve half-rotted vegetables. The Commissioner of Charity in Salt Lake City disclosed that scores of people were slowly starving, because neither county nor private relief funds were adequate, and hundreds of children were kept out of school because they had nothing to wear.[1]

Added to the economic misery was a partially natural, partially man-made catastrophe that struck the Great Plains. Starting in the early 1930s, a drought spread across the region. The drought hit particularly hard because the land, which had once been covered by grasses, had been plowed and farmed to meet the increased demand for wheat during World War I. By 1935, the western third of Kansas, southeastern Colorado, the Oklahoma panhandle, the northern two-thirds of the Texas panhandle, and northeastern New Mexico had been dubbed "the Dust Bowl." "The land just blew away," recalled one Kansas preacher. "We had to go somewhere."[2] One out of four family farmers abandoned his land during the Dust Bowl years, creating the largest internal migration in American history to that date.[3]

Between 1929 and 1933, the gross national product of the United

States shrank by half.[4] Steel plants operated at just 12 percent of ca-pacity.[5] Between one and two million men wandered the country searching for work of any kind. Local public and private charities were overwhelmed. It was in that political and economic climate that Aid to Dependent Children, the nation's first federal welfare bill, was enacted.

While many of the other New Deal public works programs ex-pired after World War II, ADC grew. In 1950, it was amended and re-named Aid to Families with Dependent Children to include the mother or other adult caregiver in the home. While poverty declined dramatically in the late 1940s and 1950s, the number on the AFDC rolls continued to rise.

A federalized welfare system was a necessary corrective to the economic disaster of the Great Depression. And, if social mores had not changed, the program might have remained a relatively small-scale safety net for those whom fortune had abused. But mores did change—and with a vengeance.

There is always a certain tension in alms giving between reliev-ing poverty and encouraging dependence. The Victorians had distin-guished between the "deserving poor" and the "undeserving poor." For the former there would be temporary help and succor. For the latter, a stern lecture. Even among liberals in the New Deal era, the distinction between the deserving and undeserving poor was main-tained. Frances Perkins, FDR's secretary of labor, opposed giving ADC benefits to mothers of illegitimate children.[6] Additionally, New Dealers were frank in recognizing that charity itself can be corrupt-ing to the recipient. Even in the midst of the Great Depression, Franklin Roosevelt noted: "Continued dependence on relief induces a spiritual and moral disintegration fundamentally destructive to the national fiber. To dole out relief in this way is to administer a nar-cotic, a subtle destroyer of the human spirit."[7] John F. Kennedy agreed: "No lasting solution to the problem [of poverty] can be bought with a welfare check." And Robert Kennedy, in a rare mo-ment of clear-sightedness, was even more emphatic:

In our generosity we have created a system of hand-outs, a second-rate set of social services which damages and demeans its recipients, and destroys any semblance of human dignity that they have managed to retain through their adversity. In the long run, welfare payments solve nothing, for the giver or the receiver; free Americans deserve the chance to be fully self-supporting.[8]

One way to ensure that welfare remained a last resort instead of a way of life was the informal use of shame. If accepting charity from the state carried a stigma, people would resort to it only in extreme situations. No law needed to be passed; no policing was required. The stigma did its work pretty efficiently.

Throughout the 1950s, receipt of welfare carried a stigma. So did bearing a child out of wedlock. Welfare workers were encouraged to reject as many applicants as they accepted.[9] In many areas, unwed mothers had to promise not to receive "male callers . . . meeting me . . . under improper conditions."[10] In order to qualify for welfare, applicants were required to answer a long list of intrusive questions. They were also urged to identify the fathers of their babies.

## Goodbye Shame, Hello Entitlement

But the Great Disruption of the 1960s swept shame out the door. As Marvin Olasky described it in *The Tragedy of American Compassion*:

> Until the 1960s, the public dole was humiliation. Soon, young men would be told that shining shoes was demeaning, and that accepting government subsidy meant a person "could at least keep his dignity." This was the key change of the 1960s–not so much new benefit programs as a change in consciousness concerning established ones, with government officials approving and even advocating not only larger payouts but a war on shame.[11]

The sixties arrived like an earthquake, and all of the old standards, prejudices, habits, and beliefs that had kept welfare relatively contained and unwed childbearing to a bare minimum tumbled and crashed. The New Left arrived with its mixture of warmed-over Marxism and red-hot self-indulgence to ask: Why shouldn't women have sex outside of marriage? Who's to say that a baby born outside marriage is in any way "illegitimate"? Whose fault is it that so many people are poor? Shouldn't the wealthiest country on earth provide a basic standard of living for all of its people?

Along with changing mores came supercharged liberal politics. Lyndon Johnson's War on Poverty, he proclaimed, would mean the final end of privation. A new octopus of government programs–including the Economic Opportunity Act, the Neighborhood Youth Corps, VISTA, the Public Works and Economic Development Act, the Job Corps, and the Community Action Program–were created to take the place of the New Deal programs that had lapsed. In his State of the Union address in 1964, Johnson declared:

> Very often a lack of jobs and money is not the cause of poverty, but the symptom. The cause may lie deeper in our failure to give our fellow citizens a fair chance to develop their own capacities, in a lack of education and training, in a lack of medical care and housing, in a lack of decent communities in which to live and to bring up their children.[12]

Sargent Shriver, Johnson's War on Poverty czar, predicted that the Office of Economic Opportunity would end poverty by 1976.[13] The era of big government arrived with a crescendo.

The National Council of Churches signed on to the War on Poverty with a will, declaring that the Biblical reminder that the poor would always be with us was no longer operative. That sentiment was only a reflection of "the primitive status of human technology and the scarcity of developed resources." But modern life and leadership by the federal government would provide "adequate levels of living for all."[14] The answer to poverty, the sixties' liberals proclaimed, was not Maimonides' wisdom, "Give a man a fish and feed him for a day; teach a man to fish and feed him for life," but cash, credits, and programs, programs, programs.

Entitlement became the order of the day. The *New York Times* declared the birth of a "new philosophy of social welfare that seeks to establish the status of welfare benefits as rights, based on the notion that everyone is entitled to a share of the common wealth."[15] The mid-1960s saw the creation of the National Welfare Rights Organization, the brainchild of two professors at the Columbia University School of Social Work: Frances Fox Piven and Richard A. Cloward. Piven and Cloward believed not that too many, but rather too few, Americans were receiving government relief. Through sit-ins, demonstrations, and other street theater, they were determined to achieve their "rights." Beulah Sanders, NWRO's second president, testified before the Finance Committee of the U.S. Senate about the group's philosophy:

> I do not believe that we should be forced to work. I do not believe that we should be forced to take training if it is not meaningful. If you are going to give us something that we can hope for and advance in, possibilities to go on to higher salaries, then I would agree to do it. This is why we have had a disturbance in New York City and around the country. . . . [16]

"The overarching goal," recalls Felicia Kornbluh, who laments the passing of the NWRO, "was to establish welfare, or a minimum standard of living, as a citizenship right and a human right. This minimum was to be based neither on wage work nor on any other specific contribution to the state—but was conceived as a universal 'right to live' and an expression of equality among citizens of an abundantly affluent nation."[17] In essence, the group demanded "a right to live" off others. It was bankrolled by the Rockefeller Brothers Foundation.[18]

In *The Poorhouse State*, a 1966 critique of the welfare system, journalist Richard Elman denounced welfare caseworkers' intrusive questions as well as their attempts to get men to support their children (or their girlfriends' children). As Fred Siegel described it, Elman "was outraged by the way the system urged and cajoled clients to restore themselves to productive citizenship and break the cycle of dependency." Elman "argued that America needed to 'make dependency legitimate' so that the dependent could 'consume with integrity.' "[19]

*New York Times* columnist Tom Wicker was willing to admit that welfare payments were not necessarily temporary:

> Really compassionate and effective reforms to do something about poverty in America would have to recognize, first, that large numbers of the poor are always going to have to be helped. Whether for physical or mental reasons, because of environmental factors, or whatever, they cannot keep pace. . . . Thus the aim of getting everyone off welfare and into "participation in our affluent society" is unreal and a pipe dream. . . . [A] decent standard of living ought to be made available not just to an eligible few but to everyone, and without degrading restrictions and policelike investigations.[20]

New York was among the first cities to sign up for the new era. As Vincent Cannato details in *The Ungovernable City*, liberal Republican mayor John V. Lindsay appointed another Columbia University social work professor as his welfare commissioner. Mitchell Ginsberg instituted a number of liberal reforms. First, he outlawed so-called "midnight raids" on female welfare recipients to check whether they were living with a man. Next, he urged caseworkers to go out and find eligible applicants for public assistance who were not on the rolls. New York's government actually advertised for welfare "clients." Most significantly, he eliminated a number of eligibility steps, including the personal interview, investigation, and home visit. Instead, applicants had merely to submit a statement of need. The *Daily News* promptly dubbed the new welfare commissioner "Come-and-Get-It Ginsberg."[21]

Quite naturally, welfare enrollment ballooned during Lindsay's do-gooder tenure. There were 531,000 welfare recipients in New York when Lindsay took office in 1966. By 1972, there were 1.25 million (which historian Fred Siegel notes was more than the population of fifteen states). This growth coincided with a healthy economy. During the same period unemployment dropped from 6 to 3 percent.[22]

It did cross the minds of some politicians that this new army of government beneficiaries could be usefully employed. Senator Abraham Ribicoff, Democrat of Connecticut, offered a suggestion to Mayor Lindsay on one of his trips to Washington, D.C. Noting that New York was "unquestionably one of the filthiest cities anywhere," Ribicoff recommended that Lindsay ask able-bodied welfare recipients to "help make New York sparkle." After all, he continued, how much training do you need "to have a stick, a broomstick with a spike on it to pick up a piece of paper?"[23] Both Lindsay and Senator Robert Kennedy of New York were repulsed by the suggestion, reports Fred Siegel, in *The Future Once Happened Here*: "Kennedy compared the very limited work requirements of the 1967 federal legislation to the 'punitive attitude reminiscent of medieval poor law philosophy.' Lindsay thought that the 'coercion' of work requirements could 'alienate' the poor and might even lead to an 'explosion' of violence."[24]

The welfare rights movement received a huge assist from the U.S. Supreme Court. In 1968, the court found state rules denying benefits to mothers who had a man living in the house to be unconstitutional. Later in the same term, the Court ruled that mothers considered "employable" by welfare workers could not be denied benefits. In 1969, the Court struck down state residency requirements for welfare eligibility.[25] And in 1970, the Court ruled that welfare payments were a property right of the recipient, and that government could not discontinue payments until after a full evidentiary hearing. Justice Brennan, writing for the majority, noted that existing rules permitted a post-termination hearing, but this, he advised, was insufficient. In an opinion fully reflecting the spirit of the 1960s, Justice Brennan wrote:

> It may be realistic today to regard welfare entitlements as more like "property" than a "gratuity." Much of the existing wealth in this country takes the form of rights that do not fall within traditional common-law concepts of property. It has been aptly noted that "society today is built around entitlement." The automobile dealer has his franchise, the doctor and lawyer their professional licenses, the worker his union membership contract and pension rights, the executive his contract and stock options; all are devices to aid security and independence. Many of the most important of these entitlements flow from government: subsidies to farmers and businessmen, routes for airlines and channels for television stations; long-term contracts for defense, space, and education; social security pensions for individuals. Such sources of security, whether private or public, are no longer regarded as luxuries or gratuities; to the recipients they are essentials, fully deserved, and in no sense a form of charity. It is only the poor whose entitlements, although recognized by public policy, have not been effectively enforced.[26]

So real productivity was irrelevant. The entire economy was actually based on a series of entitlements flowing in some way or other from the federal government. The government just conjured goods and services, like Harry Potter. And there was more. Justice Brennan further opined that:

> From its founding the Nation's basic commitment has been to foster the dignity and well-being of all persons within its borders. We have come to recognize that forces not within the control of the poor contribute to their poverty. This perception, against the background of our traditions, has

significantly influenced the development of the contemporary public assistance system.[27]

Justice Hugo Black, in dissent, noted that the majority was simply legislating its policy preferences and dressing it up as Constitutional law: "I would have little, if any, objection to the majority's decision in this case if it were written as the report of the House Committee on Education and Labor, but as an opinion ostensibly resting on the language of the Constitution, I find it woefully deficient."[28] But such precision about the meaning of a written Constitution, then as now, was disregarded. By the logic of the majority's decision, everyone was a supplicant of some kind. Everyone was entitled to something, and the justices would find a way to say that the Constitution required what they preferred. Besides, the poor "we have come to recognize" are not poor for any reasons within their control, but are instead the victims of outside forces. This tendentiousness in thinking about the poor (are none poor because of unwise choices?) characterized liberal thinking for decades.

## The Safety Net Becomes a Hammock

Roosevelt's worry that the dole would become a narcotic was long forgotten as the "Great Society" powered up. If the poor had once been blamed for their condition, they were now to be recruited in a vast social engineering project. They would be empowered with government-funded lawyers, assisted by government-funded social workers, housed in government-provided apartments, fed with government-supplied food stamps, treated by government-paid physicians, and trained by a government-funded Job Corps. It is not too much to say that poverty chic took hold in some quarters. Even fashions began to incorporate the poor look. Faded blue jeans appeared on society ladies' slender legs. Suburban teenagers punched knee holes in their mall-purchased jeans. More than that, the poor became a political symbol. The persistence of poverty was proof of the failures of capitalism, the injustice of America, and the stain of racism. After all the poor had been through, the welfare activists seemed to say, it would be too onerous to ask them to work. Lawyer Edward Sparer of New York's Henry Street Settlement House argued in a series of court cases that "any insistence on work carried echoes of racial injustice in the South, where debt peonage and other forms of forced labor had lasted long into the twentieth century."[29]

This theme persisted for decades. A committee of Roman Catholic bishops released a pastoral letter in 1984 harshly critical of the U.S. economic system. The levels of poverty and unemployment in America constituted a "social and moral scandal," declared the bishops. Among their proposals was a major overhaul of the welfare system, which they called "woefully inadequate," and a "moratorium on rhetoric about welfare cheaters" to help eliminate the "stigma" associated with receiving relief.[30] Milwaukee archbishop Rembert Weakland added that "We find it a disgrace that 35 million Americans live below the poverty level and millions more hover just above it."[31]

*Time* magazine reported on the Catholic bishops' letter this way:

Feed the hungry. Clothe the naked. Shelter the homeless. With such biblical exhortations in mind, five U.S. Roman Catholic bishops have been examining American capitalism since 1981 to see how well it conforms to their church's social teaching. . . . In the first draft of the pastoral letter, the committee praised the "impressive strides" of the U.S. economy in providing goods and services, but condemned what it called the "massive and ugly" failures of the system.[32]

Just in case readers might be left in any doubt as to where *Time* magazine stood on the matter, the article was titled "Am I My Brother's Keeper?"[33]

Bill Moyers always knew where blame lay:

While Congress restored some of the cuts made in those first Reagan budgets, in the years since, the poor and the working

poor have borne the brunt of the cost of the Reagan Revolution. The hardest-hit programs have been welfare, housing,
and other anti-poverty measures. . . . Meanwhile, rich people got big tax breaks. . . . [34]

By the time that broadside was fired, welfare payments had already
exceeded the minimum wage in New York and other cities. Throughout the post–World War II years, the unemployment rate rose and fell
in tandem with the business cycle, but welfare caseloads rose and rose.
Between 1963 and 1973, caseloads increased by 230 percent, and the
upward trend continued until 1994, when 9 million children and three
million adults were receiving benefits.[35] In the Great Depression year
of 1936, 147,000 families, about 1 percent of the population, received
welfare. In 1994, a strong year economically and a world away from the
Depression, 15 percent of the population was on welfare.[36]

But the liberal press saw welfare through only one lens. Whatever largesse might do to the recipient, liberals knew one thing:
Handouts made the givers feel virtuous. And liberals reveled in their
own saintliness. Juan Williams protested, "When you look at the reality of cutting people off–of saying you can't have more benefits if
you have children while you are on welfare–you're talking about putting children on the street who are hungry and naked, and that's a
sin."[37] President Clinton, a year before he signed welfare reform legislation, promised, "We have no intention of abandoning the American people to unproven theories and extreme positions. We're the
people party and we're going to stick up for the people."[38] Marian
Wright Edelman, founder of the Children's Defense Fund (CDF) and
widely considered the grand dame of welfare advocacy, wrote in 1987
that "children are poor because we have lost our moral bearings."[39]
It was Edelman who hit upon the idea that cloaking the welfare state
in the mantle of "the children" would serve as excellent public relations. "When you talked about poor people or black people you faced
a shrinking audience," she argued. "I got the idea that children
might be a very effective way to broaden the base for change."[40] CDF

has since achieved almost totemic status among policy makers, especially Democrats, and its signature neckties and scarves featuring children have become a common sight on Capitol Hill. A CDF conference in 2000 caught the spirit of the organization. The *City Journal*'s Kay Hymowitz described the session she attended:

> The panel, consisting of William Spriggs of the National Urban League, Deepak Bhargava of the Center for Community Change, and Jacqueline Marte and Shana Turner, two young former welfare recipients, was asked: "Why do we have so many poor people even at a time of such prosperity?" Turner, now a student at the University of Massachusetts, was the star of the session. The problem, she announced, could be captured in one word: "greed." "Instead of giving money to an organization, the rich go on vacation for the third time in a year. . . . People with money don't care." The audience, which apparently did not include moneyed representatives from the many corporations underwriting the conference, applauded enthusiastically.[41]

That is the mantra. Liberals cling to the idea that critics of welfare are motivated by greed or callous disregard for the less fortunate. In fact, during the twenty-five years that followed Lyndon Johnson's declaration of war on poverty, U.S. taxpayers spent $3 trillion providing every conceivable support for the poor, the elderly, and the infirm. Private foundations spent scores of billions more, and private and religious charities even more. Nevertheless, as Ronald Reagan later quipped, "In the war on poverty, poverty won."

Even at the very early stages of the welfare explosion, some recognized that making welfare more and more attractive could corrupt those it was intended to help. Some actually intended this result. Frances Fox Piven and Richard Cloward predicted the breakdown of families. "From our perspective," they wrote, "the weakening of the family signified a weakening of social control, especially over the young, and it was the young who were most prominent in the disorders of the 1960s."[42]

## The Family Collapses

Others were less sanguine about what the Great Society and liberal sexual mores were unleashing. Daniel Patrick Moynihan, then a relatively obscure assistant secretary of labor in the Johnson Administration, prepared a report on the "Negro family" in 1965. It took note of the rising levels of welfare dependence among "Negroes" even as unemployment was falling. Moynihan was also the first prominent public figure to draw attention to the alarming rise in illegitimacy among blacks. The report was subtitled "The Case for Government Action," and good liberal that he was, Moynihan recommended more federal jobs programs and a family assistance plan (similar to what he would later recommend to President Nixon). But the reaction to the report in the black community was distinctly negative. Moynihan was accused of "blaming the victim" and worse, of racism. No one in the black community, and very few white liberals, were prepared to believe that welfare could be damaging the family structure of recipients. And having seen what happened to Moynihan, most observers shrank for decades from raising the subject again.

Not that all or even most welfare recipients were black, but for most of the postwar years, blacks comprised about 40 percent of welfare clients, a disproportionate share considering that they were only 12 percent of the total population.[43] The percentage of black households headed by women increased from 28 percent in 1970 to 40 percent in 1980. Divorce and unwed childbearing were the most common reasons for people to seek welfare. In the 1950s, blacks had been more likely than whites to be married.[44] Starting in the 1960s, marriage simply tanked in the black community. Whereas only 28 percent of black women were "never married" in 1960 (compared with 24 percent of whites), 56 percent of black women were never married in 1994 (compared with 34 percent of whites). But childbearing, particularly to young women and girls living in cities, did not drop off with the marriage decline. Instead, by 1994, fully 70 percent of all black births in the United States were to unmarried women.[45] In 1999, the total number of American children born out of wedlock reached 33 percent.[46]

Gallons of ink and millions of man-hours have been devoted to analyzing this sudden explosion of single-parent families and welfare dependence. Liberals have offered a number of theories about why poor and, particularly, black Americans stopped marrying in large numbers in the 1960s but did not stop bearing children. William Julius Wilson suggested that jobs disappeared in the inner cities–making young black men poor marriage prospects. But this failed to explain why Korean, south Asian, and Caribbean immigrants found jobs and started businesses in the cities. Nor did it account for why young women would choose to be single mothers. In the wake of the successful welfare reform of 1996, the answer seems clear.

The ready availability of welfare did not, by itself, induce single women to get pregnant, but the existence of welfare served as what the psychologists would call an "enabler." Young men have always wanted to have sex with young women. And vice-versa. In addition, young women have always wanted babies. They did not start to want babies in 1965. Babies are adorable and the desire to give birth is among the most powerful urges in human life. But, until the latter half of the twentieth century, most human societies were organized to prevent young men from freely indulging their sexual hunger. Fathers and brothers of young women, and women themselves, insisted upon marriage first. Young unmarried women were discouraged from satisfying their own sexual urges and their yearning for children before marriage by a powerful stigma attached to both.

In the 1960s, with a metaphorical pruning shear, American society–led by liberals–simultaneously cut the strands of the stigma attached to premarital sex and unwed childbearing *and* provided young women with the wherewithal (their own apartments and a monthly stipend) to make getting along without a husband possible, and to immature eyes, even desirable. Add to this the fact that the culture was sending messages to young blacks that welfare was a form of reparations for slavery and Jim Crow, and the recipe for social disaster was complete. Among all ethnic groups, illegitimacy rose steeply; among African Americans, it skyrocketed. In 1960, the white rate of illegitimacy was 2 percent. In 1999, the rate was 27 percent. Among blacks, the 1960 rate was 23 percent. By 1999, it had climbed to near 70 percent.[47] In some black neighborhoods, children can grow up without knowing anyone who is married.

## Cheerleading for the Dole

Liberalism thus baited what many conservatives would later call the "welfare trap." Though designed to provide for the needs of women and their children, welfare in too many cases proved the end of the road. Nearly half of all welfare recipients remained on the rolls–and thus remained poor–for ten years and more. And while the welfare package (including food stamps, housing allowances, medical care, and other benefits) kept millions of people from starvation and destitution, it also accustomed too many to a life of dependence and idleness. The safety net became a hammock. As the *City Journal*'s Sol Stern reported, between 1965 and 1974 the number of unmarried mother families on welfare swelled from 4.3 million to 10.8 million. By the early 1970s, "one person was on the welfare rolls in New York City for every two working in the city's private economy."[48]

The press did its best to present all of the poor as needy. On ABC's *World News Tonight*, Peter Jennings offered:

> When you get close to the poor, you recognize right away that very often the level of assistance which they get from government doesn't lift them up to the legal poverty line, let alone above it, which seems to say that your congressmen and your state legislators have failed to recognize that children and families in poverty are a national disaster. In your name, they often argue about other priorities and welfare cheats. Twelve million American children who cheat.[49]

And PBS's Ken Bode wondered whether public dissatisfaction with the welfare system wasn't a response to Republican propaganda:

> There is a broad public dissatisfaction with welfare policy in this country, but how much of this is a hangover of politicians who massaged the messages of welfare queens and welfare fraud, and produced a popular sense in the American population that undeserving people are getting something for nothing, particularly undeserving people of color?[50]

In 1992, *Time* senior editor Thomas Sancton was contemptuous of President George H. W. Bush's criticisms of the welfare system:

> [Bush] compared the dole to a "narcotic" in his State of the Union message and regularly peppers his speeches with vows to "change welfare and make the able-bodied work." This line is not surprising coming from a political heir of Ronald Reagan, who voiced his contempt for public assistance with apocryphal stories of "welfare queens" driving Cadillacs. . . . What's going on here? Has America's traditional compassion for the downtrodden worn thin? Is the country that paid billions to liberate a wealthy oil sheikdom on the other side of the globe suddenly unwilling to feed hungry kids at home?[51]

Sancton might profitably reread Franklin Roosevelt's identical warning about relief becoming a "narcotic."

Liberals frequently scoffed at the idea that welfare recipients drove Cadillacs or munched bonbons all day. Clearly, some welfare recipients were and are truly needy. Those with mental disabilities and illnesses that inhibit the capacity to seek help are especially vulnerable and in need, but by creating a system of benefits that asked no questions and demanded no accountability from recipients, liberals invited abuse. This they could never acknowledge. According to the Children's Defense Fund and its allies, there were no undeserving poor. There were no careless poor women or irresponsible poor men. All were victims.

Rachel Wildavsky and Daniel R. Levine profiled Marie A. of Germantown, Maryland, for *Reader's Digest* magazine. By the age of forty-three, Marie had had nine children by five different fathers. Her welfare package included rent-free housing, food stamps, Medicaid, and, "when any of her nine minor children are living with her," tax-free cash grants from AFDC. She lived in a comfortable, three-bedroom townhouse–complete with dining room, den, laundry room, dishwasher, and microwave–on a neat, peaceful block in Woodbridge, Virginia. "It was rent-free courtesy of a federal program that provides subsidized housing to welfare families in non-welfare neighborhoods," Wildavsky and Levine reported. In Marie's last two years in Woodbridge, "police officers were called to her home 72 times. By the time the family left, in August 1994, rubbish littered their yard, and the inside of their house was damaged and filmy with grime."[52]

Having babies without fathers–even with generous welfare allowances–is a recipe for poverty. More than two-thirds of children born out of wedlock are poor, compared with 33 percent of the children of divorce. Only 6.7 percent of children born to never-married mothers will reach their eighteenth birthdays without experiencing a single year of poverty.[53] The system designed to rescue people from poverty in fact served paradoxically to invite people into poverty and then to plump the pillows once they were settled. In the expanding economy of the 1980s and 1990s in particular, failure to marry and hold a job became the principal cause of persistent, generation-to-generation poverty. This was not lost on welfare recipients themselves, 62 percent of whom told one 1990s survey that "the system undermines the work ethic and encourages people to be lazy." Seven out of ten welfare recipients in the same poll admitted that they were not looking for work. Though the liberal establishment contemptuously dismissed the suggestion that welfare encouraged illegitimacy, 64 percent of the system's "clients" believed it did.[54]

The panoply of benefits and supports available to young women who got pregnant as teenagers made unwed childbearing practical. When the stigma was withdrawn, unwise girls were sure to do what came naturally–keep their illegitimate babies–rather than what was best for the child: place them for adoption. In 2000, the *Washington Post* chronicled the story of Nicole, a pretty sixteen-year-old from rural Maryland. Pregnant for the second time (she had undergone an abortion at fourteen), she was determined to keep her baby. The sixteen-year-old father tormented Nicole with serial infidelities. There was certainly no talk of marriage. But, though the boy was a jobless high school dropout, Nicole was sure he would be a "good father." Though both sets of grandparents urged Nicole to place the child for adoption, she resisted. She knew that she would have her own place and a monthly stipend once the baby was born. As soon as news of her pregnancy spread, she became something of a celebrity at school. Other girls begged to see her sonogram pictures. A state agency sent her a complete Thanksgiving meal and gifts at Christmas, as well as offering counseling on her legal rights and referrals for more state services after the birth. Her friends threw her a baby shower.[55]

Cindy K. fell into the welfare trap at the age of fifteen when she chose to have a baby "for someone to love me." Sixteen months later, she gave birth to another son by a different father. Without welfare, she told the *Reader's Digest*, she would not have attempted to raise either child, but would have placed them for adoption. Herself a child of a welfare-dependent single mother, Cindy knew little else. The fathers of each of the children came by from time to time, but the burden of the four-month-old and the twenty-month-old fell almost exclusively on the exhausted, immature teenager. "I wasn't alone when these kids were made," she softly complained, "but I'm here to do everything myself. Sometimes I just get real mad."[56]

Despite the accumulating evidence of welfare's corrupting influence–the rise of the permanent underclass, crime, illegitimacy, a culture of nonwork, and drug abuse–liberals maintained their

belief in generous welfare benefits and fiercely resisted all reform efforts. *Newsweek*'s Tom Morganthau, criticizing Michigan governor
Thomas Engler's welfare reform, wrote in 1991:

> Appealing as it may be to dump loafers off the dole, few ex-
> perts would agree that the nation's general assistance rolls
> include many truly able-bodied adults, or that jobs are avail-
> able to those who lose their benefits. . . . Many are function-
> ally unable to get or hold a job—some because of medical or
> psychological problems; others lack access to transporta-
> tion. A few are drug or alcohol dependents.[57]

Dan Rather intoned on the *CBS Evening News*, "Take an election year, add a budget crunch, and one sure result is an assault on
the welfare system: help for the poor. Still, most of the people who attack welfare have little or no contact with the people who depend
on it."[58]

During the 1992 Republican convention, NBC reporter John
Cochran suggested that "Some of these family values issues have
racial overtones, such as Bush's support for welfare reforms which
penalize single mothers who continue having children."[59]

Mimi Abramovitz, a professor of social policy at Hunter College
in New York City and a frequent commentator on welfare-related
subjects, was unusually comprehensive in hitting all of the hot but-
tons of her liberal readership. She decried both Democrats and Republicans for considering welfare reform in the mid-1990s:

> . . . It's almost certain that some kind of regressive welfare
> "reform" will become law before the 1996 election. Welfare
> reform is bad for women, because they are the direct target of
> a drive to modify women's behavior; bad for children, who
> will see less of their mothers; bad for labor, who will face
> more competition for fewer jobs; bad for the poor, because it
> makes them poorer; and bad for the middle class, because
> their programs are next.

Welfare reform has turned into a mean-spirited campaign to modify women's behavior and dismantle the welfare state. When Aid to Families with Dependent Children (AFDC) was created in 1935, Congress's intention was to cushion poverty and to enable mothers to stay at home with their kids. . . .

But now things have gone from bad to worse. Instead of fixing AFDC to compensate for the falling standard of living, the new welfare reform deflects attention from the sagging economy by maligning the marital, childbearing, and parenting behavior of poor women.[60]

Welfare apologists insisted that women's childbearing decisions were unaffected by the availability of welfare. But encounters such as Mayor John Lindsay's with a vocal constituent cast doubt. At a public hearing, Lindsay was confronted by an angry welfare mother who announced that "I've got six kids. Every one of them has a different daddy. It's my job to have kids, and your job, Mr. Mayor, to take care of them."[61]

Little had changed twenty years later when District of Columbia mayor Marion Barry scolded a welfare mother with fourteen children for having so many kids at the government's expense. Appearing on the *Donahue* program with Mayor Barry, Jacqueline Williams proclaimed that "it is my body and I can have as many children as I want. . . . If I could have fourteen more, I'd have fourteen more."[62] Donahue sided with Williams, urging Barry to apologize and sniping that Barry's comments "would be cheered by the Archie Bunkers of this world" and "would get a standing ovation from the all-white Rotary Club." Barry snapped back, "I'd get a standing ovation from the all-black Rotary Club too."[63]

By making unwed childbearing practicable, the welfare state exacerbated the problem of poverty. And by increasing long-term, generation-to-generation poverty, liberalism created far more misery and social chaos than it relieved. The poverty rate among black children was actually slightly higher in 1995 than it had been in 1971.[64] By the 1980s, the United States did not so much have a poverty problem as an illegitimacy problem. As Isabell Sawhill and others pointed out, family structure was a better predictor of poverty than race. *A child born to an African American married couple was less likely to be poor than a child born to a single white woman.*[65] Nearly all of the increase in poverty since 1970 is attributable, Sawhill argues, to the prevalence of unwed childbearing.[66]

Another fact about poverty in America that liberals had difficulty accommodating in their worldview was the importance of work. Only 2.6 percent of those age sixteen or above who work full time are poor, according to the Bureau of the Census. But 23.6 percent of those who do not work are poor. For African Americans, the number in poverty who do not work is 44.7 percent.[67] It is constantly urged that the reason people don't work is that jobs are unavailable, yet according to a Census Bureau survey, only 4.1 percent of the idle list inability to find work as the reason for their joblessness.[68]

In 1992, Barbara Sabol, New York City's welfare commissioner, disguised herself in a baseball cap, sweatshirt, and jeans, and visited two of New York's welfare offices. She explained to the welfare workers that she desperately needed a job in order to care for her children. But despite her pleas, none of the welfare workers she spoke to would offer to help find her a job.[69]

## Reform and Its Enemies

Throughout the decade of the 1980s, welfare reform percolated on the national agenda. States experimented with work requirements, family caps, and time limits. These met with predictable opposition from the Left. A writer for *The Nation* magazine denounced "workfare" as "indentured servitude."[70] By the early 1990s, it was clear that public pressure for reform was building. Seeing the political opportunity, "new Democrat" Bill Clinton promised to "end welfare as we know it" in his 1992 campaign, and peppered his speeches with terms like "work" and "two years and out."

Upon assuming the presidency, however, Clinton proved that his welfare reform rhetoric had been merely election-year positioning.

Rather than reform welfare, his administration increased funding for all of the major welfare programs without significant change.

It was only in 1994, when Republicans gained a majority in Congress for the first time in forty years, that welfare reform finally got rolling. The outlines of Republican proposals soon ignited one of the fiercest struggles in recent political history. For, unlike abortion, physician-assisted suicide, affirmative action, homosexual marriage, and other contentious domestic matters, welfare reform was not decided in the courts. The people's elected representatives actually settled a serious social and cultural issue themselves.

When word of what the Republican majority was planning leaked out—a five-year lifetime cap on benefits, the requirement that nearly all welfare recipients either work or seek work on a full-time basis—liberal politicians and opinion makers hit the panic button. Columnist Bob Herbert of the *New York Times* was typical:

> There is something creepy about the welfare debate. . . . The politicians have gotten together and decided it's a good idea to throw a million or so children into poverty. But they can't say that. The proponents of this so-called "reform" effort have gone out of their way to avoid being seen for what they are—men and women of extreme privilege who are taking food out of the mouths of infants and children, the poverty-stricken elderly, the disabled . . . old women, small children. . . . A country that would single out such individuals for deliberate harm falls somewhere well short of greatness.[71]

*The Nation* magazine warned:

> The Republican Congress is intent on shredding the safety net for the poor and disabled. The proposed changes are structural and systemic. Republicans would terminate the federal guarantee—passed as part of the Social Security Act in the Great Depression—that every child shall have some minimal level of support, and cut billions from the program. . . .

These structural changes will have shameful effects. Conservative estimates suggest an additional 1.2 million children condemned to poverty. Hundreds of thousands of disabled children will be denied help. Workers displaced from jobs through no fault of their own won't find much of a safety net to break their family's fall. Inequality, already at extreme levels, will grow worse.[72]

Columnist Judy Mann of the *Washington Post* condemned the use of the word "illegitimacy." She called it "a moralistic word used to denounce certain children as bastards." It was all part of a "blueprint for a war against poor women whose misfortune has been to have children they can't support."[73] Misfortune?

The *New York Times* pronounced the legislation "atrocious." "This is not reform," declared the editorial board, "this is punishment."[74]

Writing in the *Progressive*, Frances Fox Piven announced, "For the poor, it's back to the workhouse and the orphanage." Feigning confusion about why a program, AFDC, "that costs only about 1 percent of the federal budget," should have been propelled "to the center of American politics," Piven found the proposed reforms "chilling." Besides, she countered, it is not welfare, but low-paying jobs that constitute a "trap":

> If anything, it is increasingly the low-wage job with no mobility that is the trap. Welfare sometimes provides an opening–to go back to school or enter a good training program that would be impossible without some assured income. Slashing welfare is a way to seal the low-wage trap.[75]

Andrew Hacker was certain he detected the unspoken agenda of the welfare reformers:

> A near consensus is emerging that solicitude and sympathy haven't worked. Hence the calls for tougher measures to curb

dependency and irresponsible reproduction. Of course, those proposing these policies say they are race-neutral. The drive to make single mothers work will apply to everyone on the welfare rolls. . . . Yet despite these assurances, there can be little doubt that the chief targets of the crackdown are members of this country's principal minority race.[76]

The Republican Congress sent President Clinton two welfare reform bills. He vetoed both. In 1996, he was presented with another bill, very like the first two. Many in his cabinet and White House staff urged another veto. But strategist Dick Morris warned the president against it. "I told him flatly that a welfare veto would cost him the election," Morris later wrote. "Mark Penn [a pollster] had designed a polling model that indicated that a welfare veto by itself would transform a fifteen-point win into a three-point loss."[77]

When it became clear that President Clinton was "going wobbly" on welfare reform, liberals sent in reinforcements to buck him up. The National Organization for Women (NOW) organized a vigil outside the White House to urge the president to veto the legislation. "Millions more will swell the ranks of the poor and hungry as a result of this bill," predicted NOW president Patricia Ireland.

"With 4 to 10 million children scheduled to be cut from the nation's welfare rolls in the next seven years through caps on AFDC and Supplemental Security Income, two major assistance programs, [Los Angeles County child welfare official Peter] Digre predicts that Los Angeles will see more than 17,000 new cases of child abuse due to poverty and family stress," reported *Time* magazine.[78]

NBC's Tom Brokaw addressed welfare reform in an interview with President Clinton in the summer of 1996. "Mr. President . . . I wanted to follow up just for a moment on welfare if I can. If in fact you sign the Republican bill that's likely to come down from the Hill, all the projections show that that will push, at least short term, more than a million youngsters in this country below the poverty line. That's a high risk for youngsters in this country who are already in peril."[79]

The view that welfare reform would be a disaster was nearly universal in 1996. Sam Donaldson on *This Week with David Brinkley* analyzed it this way:

> **DONALDSON:** "Congress has suddenly realized there's an election coming up, so all right, they're going to pass a bunch of legislation . . ."
>
> **COKIE ROBERTS:** "Concentrates the mind."
>
> **DONALDSON:** "Like hanging, and in Congress's case, in my view of what they did, perhaps hanging would have been better, because the welfare bill, we're going to regret as a country. It's not just anyone in poverty, it's the children. Throwing women and children off the rolls. Everyone's for workfare, everyone's for changing the welfare system. Bill Clinton promised it. He said, however, it would take $10 billion more to ease people down the ramp off this train. Instead, we just throw them off now and say 'Good luck.' "[80]

Dan Rather, questioning Senator Chris Dodd of Connecticut during the Democratic National Convention in the summer of 1996, challenged him: "You said this a morning that the party's message will focus on the needs and cares of the people. Now, how do you reconcile that with a president who has just signed a, quote, welfare reform bill, unquote, which by general agreement is going to put a lot of poor children on the street?"[81]

In fairness to Rather, he was accurately reflecting what everyone in his circle believed. The Children's Defense Fund predicted that the law "would increase child poverty nationwide by 12 percent . . . make children hungrier . . . [and] reduce the incomes of one-fifth of all families with children in the nation." The law, proclaimed CDF, was "an outrage . . . that will hurt and impoverish millions of American children . . . and leave a moral blot on [Clinton's] presidency and on our nation that will never be forgotten."[82] The Center on

Budget and Policy Priorities predicted that the law "would push 2.6 million people, including 1.1 million children, into poverty, and would cause one-tenth of all American families, including 8 million families with children, to lose income."[83] Senator Daniel Patrick Moynihan, an intellectual giant, believed that welfare reform was going to be catastrophic. "The central provision of this law," he said, "would be the most brutal act of social policy we have known since the Reconstruction. . . . In five years' time, you'll find appearing on your streets abandoned children—helpless, hostile, angry, awful—in numbers we have no idea."[84] At another time, he added, "This disgrace will be taken to the graves of the people who supported it."[85]

"My president will boldly throw 1 million into poverty,"[86] was Rep. Charles Rangel's bitter comment. Jason de Parle, who covered welfare for the *New York Times*, predicted in the summer of 1996, "If he signs the measure as it is, President Clinton will appear to have fulfilled his famous pledge about ending welfare. In truth, he will have abandoned the vision that animated the slogan. Having sought office with the aim of a redefined social contract—health care for every American—he will be seeking reelection with a bill that begrudges poor infants their Pampers."[87] And Robert Greenstein of the Center on Budget and Policy Priorities called the law "a cleverly concocted scam that does not do a single thing."[88]

Senator John Kerry declared that "It [a proposed 1988 revision to the welfare reform bill] contains provisions troublesome to me, such as the 16-hour weekly work requirement for two-parent families receiving benefits."[89] Sixteen hours of work per week is too onerous? Characteristically, Kerry would, in the years that followed, be on all sides of the welfare reform issue. In 1996, debating opponent William Weld, Kerry said, "What we [Democrats] don't do is . . . what's in the Republican plan, which is kick people out without adequate child care and adequate health care and the tools they need to work."[90] On *Face the Nation* in January 2004, Kerry declared, "I have fought hard for responsible welfare reform. I voted for welfare reform." Mickey Kaus, a close Kerry watcher, responded in his blog that:

He did vote for the 1996 reform bill on final passage, but in the Kabuki procedures of the Senate, the final passage vote is often for show, and that was the case with welfare reform. . . . I do know that Kerry voted for both major Democratic substitutes to the GOP-supported bill that finally passed–the Daschle substitute and the nominally bipartisan Biden-Specter substitute–as well as for a defeated Breaux proposal that would have created a non-cash voucher scheme to replace cash welfare when the cash was cut off.[91]

Some demanded that Hillary Clinton, a longtime supporter of the Children's Defense Fund, repudiate her husband's position. CNN's Judy Woodruff put the question to the First Lady as follows:

We were just reminded in that moving film that we saw here of your lifelong work as an advocate for children's causes. And yet, late last week, your husband signed a welfare reform bill that, as you know, Senator Patrick Moynihan and other welfare experts are saying is going to throw a million children into poverty. Does that legislation threaten to undo so much of what you've worked for over the years? . . . Eleanor Roosevelt, whom you admire–you mentioned her again just now–said that much of the time she kept her disagreements with the president to herself in private. But there were times that she felt it was important to disagree publicly. Does there ever come a time [like that] with you, and if not welfare reform, what?[92]

Barbara Walters challenged the president in similar terms, pointing out that the bill was highly controversial within the Clinton administration (two advisers resigned over it): "Even your own aides, many of them, and advisers feel that the bill is too extreme. Two of your advisers recently quit. Under the new bill a sixty-year-old federal guarantee of aid to needy families will end. It's been estimated as many as a million children will go hungry. What are you going to do about that?"[93] NBC's Byrant Gumbel asked Marian Wright Edelman on the *Today* show whether "In light of the new welfare reform bill, do you think the children need more prayers than ever before?"[94] And Gumbel's co-host Katie Couric demanded of President Clinton in April 1997:

> Seventy-four percent of the respondents in a recent poll think young Americans without education or job prospects is the greatest threat facing the country. If that's the case, if that many people think this is such a serious problem, shouldn't government be increasing its role rather than decreasing it? Many people think that your signing the welfare bill only exacerbated the situation of poor kids at risk.[95]

"This bill is anti-family, anti-child, and mean-spirited,"[96] declared Vermont's senator Patrick Leahy. New Jersey senator Frank Lautenberg worried that "I'm afraid that the streets of our nation's cities might someday look like the streets of Brazil."[97] Senator Edward Kennedy issued a press release saying, "[This bill] will leave many welfare recipients unemployable in the real world. It will leave their children ill-fed, ill-clothed, and ill-housed. . . . The gap between rich and poor will be wider, the bonds which tie families together will be weaker, and the dreams of millions of children will be farther from reach."[98] And in a characteristic eruption, Kennedy called the bill "legislative child abuse."[99]

The most concentrated fire came from two former Clinton administration officials. Peter Edelman, husband of Marian Wright Edelman, and Wendell Primus, now with the Center on Budget and Policy Priorities, both resigned when the president announced that he would sign the welfare reform bill. In March 1997, Edelman published a lengthy critique titled "The Worst Thing Bill Clinton Has Done" in the *Atlantic* magazine. "There will be suffering," he wrote:

Some of the damage will be obvious—more homelessness, for example, with more demand on already strapped shelters and soup kitchens. The ensuing problems will also appear as increases in the incidence of other problems, directly but perhaps not provably owing to the impact of the welfare bill. There will be more malnutrition and more crime, increased infant mortality, and increased drug and alcohol abuse. There will be increased family violence and abuse against children and women, and a consequent significant spillover of the problem into the already overloaded child-welfare system and battered-women's shelters.[100]

Primus, too, was very public in his displeasure. Together with Edelman, he gave an interview to *Sojourners*, a liberal Christian magazine, predicting the worst. "Despite all of the rhetoric around the subject of work," Primus said, "there isn't one additional penny in this bill that accomplishes that aim."[101] As everyone knows, he seemed to say, only the government can create jobs.

## The Results Liberals Don't Talk About

Welfare reform did of course become law in 1996. Since that time, every wild prediction the liberals made has been proved false. Poverty did not increase by millions; instead, it has fallen precipitously. Women and children are not sleeping under bridges; instead, millions of women have found jobs that give them a sense of pride and help them reach the first step on the economic ladder. Since 1996, welfare rolls have been reduced by 60 percent. The poverty rate has declined from 13.8 percent in 1995 to 11.7 percent in 2003. Some 3.5 million fewer Americans are poor today than in 1995, including 2.3 million children. Poverty among African American children has reached its lowest point *in history*. Hunger among children has been reduced by half.[102]

Welfare reform has been the greatest domestic policy success of the last thirty years.

A glance at the practices of most state welfare offices today leaves one gaping that things were done differently for so long. Instead of merely handing out checks, most welfare offices have become job centers. Women are offered help writing resumes, practicing interview techniques, making calls, and searching the classified ads. They are offered access to fax machines, copiers, and word processors. Some centers (along with hundreds of churches) even offer clothes to wear to job interviews.[103] In addition to assistance with the mechanics of job seeking, most welfare offices now also attempt to discourage applicants from entering the welfare rolls at all. In a partial return to the welfare policies of the past, when women were asked intrusive questions before being granted eligibility, women today are asked whether they have looked for a job, and whether there is anyone else who can support them. Some states require applicants to make at least twenty job-seeking phone calls from cubicles at the welfare office.[104] Many would-be applicants, faced with this requirement, simply walk out the door.

They walk to a much better future. A Manhattan Institute study found that poverty among single mothers dropped from 41.9 percent in 1996 to 33.6 percent in 2001.[105] Though for decades liberals had argued that welfare recipients would not be able to command a "living wage" in the free market, they have done so in huge numbers. Like other workers, former welfare recipients saw their salaries rise the longer they remained in the workforce. In 2001, only 4 percent of former welfare mothers were earning the minimum wage or less; even among high school dropouts, only 8 percent failed to beat the minimum wage.[106]

Marian Wright Edelman and Donna Shalala, Secretary of the Department of Health and Human Services in the Clinton Administration, among many others, attributed the falling welfare rolls and poverty rates to the booming economy of the late 1990s.[107] But the 1960s and 1980s saw similar economic booms and welfare rolls increased nevertheless. Moreover, the economy did drift into recession in the early part of 2001, yet poverty remained low and the welfare rolls did not explode.[108] Senator Hillary Rodham Clinton grudgingly acknowledged that "we have a lot to celebrate," but added, "I don't think that's the end of the discussion."[109] Even as late as 2001, when the dramatic effects of welfare reform were quite undeniable, Barbara Ehrenreich would say only that there "were some success stories. . . . But overall, it's a sad story."[110] Jason de Parle, the *New York Times* reporter who had covered the welfare debate for five years, admits that he was surprised by the outcome, though, unlike most liberals who averted their eyes from the good news, he did not. "I don't think anyone glimpsed the extent to which enforcing a work requirement would send people off the rolls," he told an interviewer from the Annie E. Casey Foundation. "One big lesson seems to be that if you require people to work for their benefits, great numbers will go off and make other arrangements. . . . They had more survival strategies than I first understood."[111]

Jesse, a former welfare recipient who was fired from one job and got help from welfare workers to find another, told the *City Journal*, "They should've [required work] from the beginning; then a lot more people would have jobs. . . . The program now is: if you get aid, they put you to work. That's a great program because life's not free."[112]

Even seemingly intractable trends like unwed childbearing changed for the better following welfare reform. The number of children born to single women has declined, as has the percentage of children living in single-mother families. Among African Americans, the percentage of children being raised by married parents jumped from 34.8 percent in 1996 to 38.9 percent in 2001, a 10 percent rise in five years.[113]

The reform is not perfect, and much remains to be accomplished. Federal assistance was tied to reductions in welfare rolls. Heather MacDonald explained the formula:

> The bill only required that 50 percent of a state's caseload be engaged in such activities by 2002, and it exempted recipients from working for their first two years on the rolls. But it also gave states a point-for-point reduction of their work-

participation requirement for each percentage-point drop in their welfare rolls. If a state's rolls have dropped 25 percent, say, it will only have to ensure that 25 percent of those remaining on the rolls in 2002 are engaged in some work activity.[114]

Because the rolls shrank so dramatically so quickly, many states no longer have an incentive to encourage those remaining on welfare to work, and half of the two million adults currently on welfare are idle. Additionally, the 1996 reform affected only one program among the sixty-nine major means-tested "entitlements" the federal government administers. Food stamps, housing vouchers, and Medicaid cry out for similar reforms.

That much having been said, the results of welfare reform have been spectacular and gratifying. The success of welfare reform has demonstrated–incontrovertibly–that jobs are available for those willing to work, and that people obliged to fend for themselves will not be "trapped" in "dead end" jobs that fail to afford a decent living. It has also taught a great lesson about the poor. The long-standing liberal attitude toward the poor–the belief that they are childlike, irresponsible, and incompetent–has been revealed for what it was: condescension. The same spirit that shrinks from demanding rigorous academic standards in schools for fear that the poor kids (and, let's face it, the black kids) can't hack it was also at work in sustaining the welfare system for so long.

Liberals claim to be motivated by compassion, but compassion without respect is patronizing. Though it seems paradoxical, it is more respectful to the poor to be a little less generous. To be sure, there are those who truly cannot manage their lives due to mental or physical disabilities, and some of those who have no family, churches, synagogues, or other charities to fall back upon must be cared for by the state. But to treat huge swaths of able-bodied people as a dependent class–and a permanent dependent class at that–is to rob them of their dignity and encourage those qualities that Americans have never admired: sloth and profligacy.

The damage that misguided liberalism did to whole communities will take time to heal. The culture of fatherlessness that has taken root among many Americans and particularly among African Americans is poison. The entitlement mentality so carefully cultivated by liberal academics, politicians, clergymen, and journalists continues to corrode the self-sufficiency that once defined the American character. Welfare reform is succeeding, but it isn't yet clear whether the reversal of some of the most troubling trends–idleness, family breakdown, crime–is either permanent or sufficient.

There is no question, however, that progress toward a healthier and more wholesome society requires undoing so much of the "good" liberals believed they were doing for the past forty years.

# Chapter Four
# REWARDING THE WORST FAMILIES AND DISCOURAGING THE BEST

Just as liberals claim to be pro-worker but urge policies that are antibusiness, they claim to be pro-child while encouraging social mores and government policies that undermine the family. Every liberal initiative, from welfare to antismoking measures, is justified by reference to "the children." Yet the clear result of liberal policies is to harm children even more than adults. Liberals are prepared to erect social welfare scaffolding to support the "families" of single women–those families that are most likely to cause harm to children–and yet they shrink from the most obvious solution to child maltreatment: encouraging and promoting marriage and traditional family structure. The children of divorce and illegitimacy have paid the price for liberalism's attachment to free love and radical individualism. Abused and neglected children have paid the price for liberalism's tendency to sentimentalize the poor.

In fact, liberalism in various guises–feminism, the sexual revolution, gay activism–has been at war with marriage and family for several decades now. And when do-gooders look around at the wreckage of human lives caused by disintegrating families, they call for government to act as father, mother, brother, and sister.

Simone de Beauvoir, one of the mothers of modern feminism, declared that:

Since the oppression of woman has its cause in the will to perpetuate the family and to keep patrimony intact, woman escapes complete dependency to the degree in which she escapes from the family.[1]

"Marriage is the mechanism by which the patriarchy is maintained," advised Gloria Steinem. She also popularized the phrase originated by Irina Dunn, an Australian feminist, that "A woman needs a man like a fish needs a bicycle." Feminists were exuberantly, defiantly antimarriage, ascribing to the institution everything from women's supposedly low self-esteem to war and famine. Betty Friedan had famously declared:

> The feminine mystique has succeeded in burying millions of American women alive. There is no way for these to break out of their comfortable concentration camps except by finally putting forth an effort–that human effort which reaches beyond biology, beyond the narrow walls of home, to help shape the future.[2]

Other feminists argued that marriage itself was abusive. Susan Schechter wrote that "Although men no longer legally own women, many act as if they do. In her marriage vows today, the woman still promises to love, honor, and obey. . . . Battering is one tool that enforces husbands' authority over wives or simply reminds women that this authority exists."[3] Marlene Dixon, a sociology professor at the University of Chicago, wrote:

> The institution of marriage is the chief vehicle for the perpetuation of the oppression of women; it is through the role of wife that the subjugation of women is maintained. In a very real way the role of wife has been the genesis of women's rebellion throughout history.[4]

Jesse Bernard, in her 1972 book *The Future of Marriage*, celebrated the fact that women could no longer automatically expect alimony upon divorce. This "may be one of the best things that could happen to women. It [will] demand that even in their early years they think in terms of life-long work histories; it [will] demand the achievement of autonomy. They will have to learn that marriage is not the be-all and end-all of their existence."[5]

American universities have for decades been blooming with women's studies departments. These worthies teach America's best and brightest young minds that the family is a snare, that husbands routinely mistreat and abuse their wives, that children should be raised in "quality day care" arrangements, and that women must first, last, and always learn to be utterly independent of men. On their reading lists, eighteen- to twenty-two-year-old young women will find not just the works of Freidan and Steinem, but those of writers like Shulamith Firestone, who wrote *The Dialectic of Sex: The Case for Feminist Revolution*. "The institution of marriage consistently proves itself unsatisfactory," she wrote, "even rotten. . . . The family is . . . directly connected to—is even the cause of—the ills of the larger society."[6] Another popular radical feminist from the heady days of the 1960s was Robin Morgan. She (but hardly she alone) called marriage "a slavery-like practice. We can't destroy the inequities between men and women until we destroy marriage."[7] Germaine Greer agreed: "If women are to effect a significant amelioration in their condition, it seems obvious that they must refuse to marry."[8] For those benighted souls who were already married, Greer was unflinching: "Most women . . . would shrink at the notion of leaving husband and children, but this is precisely the case in which brutally clear rethinking must be undertaken."[9] And Kate Millet added the topper: "The complete destruction of traditional marriage and the nuclear family is the 'revolutionary or utopian' goal of feminism."[10]

Though they sometimes deny it today, feminists in the bra-burning radical days of the 1960s and 1970s were positively at war with men and marriage. Helen Sullinger and Nancy Lehmann, two Minnesota feminists, published a manifesto called the "Declaration on Feminism" in 1971. Among its principles was this statement:

Marriage has existed for the benefit of men and has been a legally sanctioned method of control over women. . . . Male society has sold us the idea of marriage. . . . Now we know it is the institution that has failed us and we must work to destroy it. . . . The end of the institution of marriage is the necessary condition for the liberation of women. Therefore it is important for us to encourage women to leave their husbands and not to live individually with men.[11]

It has been a constant irritant to radical feminists that women continue to like men despite the feminists' best efforts to dissuade them. Some are so confused by this attraction that they ascribe it to insanity. Thus, the previously mentioned Jesse Bernard wrote in 1972:

To be happy in a relationship which imposes so many impediments on her, as traditional marriage does, women must be slightly mentally ill. Women accustomed to expressing themselves freely could not be happy in such a relationship. . . . [W]e therefore "deform" the minds of girls, as traditional Chinese used to deform their feet, in order to shape them for happiness in marriage. It may therefore be that married women say they are happy because they are sick.[12]

Other feminists have concluded that women cannot be trusted to make enlightened decisions about their lives. In *Who Stole Feminism*, Christina Hoff Sommers related the following exchange between Betty Friedan and Simone de Beauvoir. Freidan suggested that women should have the choice to stay at home to raise their children if that is what they wish to do. "No," Beauvoir answered:

No, we don't believe that any woman should have this choice. No woman should be authorized to stay at home to raise her children. Society should be totally different. Women should not have that choice, precisely because if there is such a choice, too many women will make that one.[13]

Vivian Gornick agreed:

Being a housewife is an illegitimate profession. . . . The choice to serve and be protected and plan towards being a family-maker is a choice that shouldn't be. The heart of radical feminism is to change that.[14]

Andrea Dworkin has written that all heterosexual intercourse essentially amounts to rape. Thus:

Men use sex to hurt us. An argument can be made that men have to hurt us, diminish us, in order to be able to have sex with us—break down barriers to our bodies, aggress, be invasive, push a little, shove a little, express verbal or physical hostility or condescension. An argument can be made that in order for men to have sexual pleasure with women, we have to be inferior and dehumanized, which means controlled, which means less autonomous, less free, less real.[15]

Not surprisingly then, she declares that, "Like prostitution, marriage is an institution that is extremely oppressive and dangerous for women."[16] Catherine MacKinnon is a professor of law at both the University of Michigan and Chicago Law Schools. Widely considered the guru of sexual harassment law, she is the feminist scholar to whom so many in the major media paid obeisance during the Anita Hill imbroglio. Professor MacKinnon has written that "Feminism stresses the indistinguishability of prostitution, marriage, and sexual harassment."[17]

## "Divorce Is an American Value"

The body blow the feminists delivered to marriage was not the only attack it has endured in the last several decades. The Supreme Court ruled in the 1977 case *Trimble v. Gordon* that states could not prefer legitimate to illegitimate children in matters of intestate inheritance.[18] The Court further ruled that contraceptives had to be sold to unmarried minors despite what states might wish on the subject, and of course that abortion on demand was encompassed within a constitutionally protected right of privacy.

As liberals fought for sexual license they also sought to loosen the bonds of matrimony. *Open Marriage* sold 35 million copies in the 1970s. Norval Glenn, a former editor of the *Journal of Family Issues* recalled that, in the 1970s, "the prevalent scholarly view was that such changes as the increase in divorce, out-of-wedlock births, single-parent families, and stepfamilies were benign and adaptive, if not distinctly beneficial."[19] Barbara DaFoe Whitehead tracked the rapidly changing attitudes toward divorce. After noting that many in the psychotherapeutic world failed to acknowledge that children have a stake in the marriages of their parents, she quoted a psychotherapist, circa 1972, who said

> Many therapists will dismiss as a copout a client's statement that he or she is staying married "for the children's sake," or because I made a commitment for "better or worse." These reasons for staying in a marriage are seen as excuses to avoid making a hard decision based on one's needs.[20]

Whitehead notes that many conservatives who might have been expected to oppose easy divorce on principled grounds nevertheless indulged in it for themselves. But she finds the liberal embrace of divorce even more disquieting:

> Twentieth-century American liberalism, on the other hand, has been vocal in both its concern for the welfare of children and its often skeptical view of the market. Indeed, the notion that there must be a boundary between the domestic domain and the commercial domain, the better to protect children from the corrupting values of the money world, was a defining tenet of liberalism, in general, and turn-of-the-century

progressive feminism in particular. That is why in the 1890s the editors of the progressive magazine *The Nation* saw the commerce in divorce as so threatening to the institution of marriage and the family. But by the late twentieth century many liberals and feminists were embracing a conception of divorce that disenfranchised children and gave the market-place a gilt-edged invitation to burst into the domestic sphere and enter boldly through the front door.[21]

Throw the door open they did. Not only did they deny that di-vorce would harm children, but like Calhoun on slavery, they de-clared it a positive good. A 1974 book, *The Courage to Divorce*, advised that children whose parents divorced would enjoy "greater insight and freedom as adults in deciding whether and when to marry" and would help children "break away from excessive depen-dency on their biological parents."[22] Gloria Steinem, who waited un-til she was past sixty to marry for the first time, declared in 1997 that "The two-parent household is the broken family."[23] The 1970 movie *Airport* caught the spirit of the age. When the character played by Burt Lancaster and his wife decide to break up their twenty-year mar-riage, he reflects soberly on the children, who will now "come from a broken home." She replies tartly, "It's better to come from a broken home than to live in one." A popular advice book for working moth-ers described the benefits of booting the man of the house:

> Given time and space, most women discover that the pleas-ures of being alone are real–and they're not eager to give them up. A single mother can pick her own friends–no more seeing people because of "couple ties." Your children, too, can sometimes pick friends that Dad didn't approve of. And without another adult questioning your values, your child-rearing methods, or your wants, you can come to treasure the sense of being in control that you've worked so hard to achieve.[24]

Judith Stacey, author of *In the Name of the Family: Rethinking Family Values in the Postmodern Age*, has acknowledged that "two compatible, responsible, committed, loving parents generally *can* offer greater economic, emotional, physical, intellectual and social resources to their children than can one from a comparable social milieu." But then she added, "Of course, if two parents are generally better than one, three or four might prove better yet."[25]

Nor does Stacey exactly lose sleep over the decline of two-parent families:

> Perhaps the postmodern "family of woman" will take the lead in burying The Family at long last. The Family is a concept derived from faulty theoretical premises and an imperialistic logic, which even at its height never served the best interests of women, their children, or even many men. . . . The Family is dead. Long live our families![26]

For many years Barbara Ehrenreich wrote a column for *Time* magazine. From that influential perch, she dispensed feminist guidance on many subjects. Regarding divorce, she wrote, "Yes, divorce is bad–but so is the institution that generates it: marriage."[27] Unabashedly hostile to traditional marriage, she insists that

> There is a long and honorable tradition of "anti-family" thought. The French philosopher Charles Fourier taught that the family was a barrier to human progress; early feminists saw a degrading parallel between marriage and prostitution. More recently, the renowned British anthropologist Edmund Leach stated, "Far from being the basis of a good society, the family with its narrow privacy and tawdry secrets is the source of all discontents."[28]

There is a long and dishonorable list of miseries children have been obliged to suffer because intellectuals defamed and undermined traditional marriage. Historians Steven Mintz and Susan

Kellogg argued in their 1988 book *Domestic Revolutions* that "There is no clear-cut empirical evidence to suggest that children from 'broken homes' suffer more health or mental problems, personality disorders, or lower school grades than children from 'intact' homes."[29] Arlene Skolnick rejects the very idea that intact traditional families are superior to other kinds. "We [liberals] should have no part of efforts to hold children hostage to a narrow definition of family that looks only at form and not at love, care, and responsibility."[30] Barbara G. Cashion, writing in the *Journal of Marital and Family Therapy* in 1982, celebrated fatherless families. Girls who grow up without fathers, she argued, are more "open" and "independent" than girls in traditional families. And family dynamics improve without fathers too:

> The two-parent family is hierarchical with mother and father playing powerful roles and children playing subordinate roles. In the female-headed family there is no such division. Women and children forego much of the hierarchy and share more in their relationships. . . . Single mothers report that they enjoy their ability to set norms and make decisions about time schedules and routines that suit their own and their children's needs. There is a general lack of conflict, and decisions are made more easily and quickly, provided resources are adequate.[31]

Americans took the advice of the feminists, Hollywood, the Playboy Philosopher, women's magazines, college professors, and family therapists and began bailing out of marriages in droves in the 1960s. The divorce rate doubled between 1960 and 1997.[32] The number of children who saw their parents divorce rose from 463,000 in 1960 to 1,052,000 in 1995.[33] Eight million children currently live with a divorced parent, and 50 percent of the rest can expect to experience the divorce of their parents sometime before their eighteenth birthdays.

The rate of illegitimate births also exploded. In 1960, only 2.3 percent of white births and 23 percent of black births were to unmarried mothers. By 1997, the white rate had jumped to 25.8 percent, and the black rate had reached 69.2.[34]

Again, this is no bad thing if you ask liberals and feminists. In *The Way We Really Are: Coming to Terms with America's Changing Families*, author Stephanie Coontz is untroubled by the high divorce rate:

> Alongside a continuing commitment to marriage, other arrangements for regulating sexual behavior, channeling relations between men and women, and raising children now exist. Marriage was once the primary way of organizing work along lines of age and sex. It determined the roles that men and women played at home and in public. It was the main vehicle for redistributing resources to old and young, and it served as the most important maker of adulthood and respectable status.
>
> All this is no longer the case. Marriage has become an option rather than a necessity for men and women, even during the child-raising years.[35]

"Divorce is an American value," declared Katha Pollitt of *The Nation* magazine in 1997.[36] More than that, she suspects she knows the real reason conservatives seek to discourage divorce:

> The real aim of conservative divorce reform is to enforce a narrow and moralistic vision of marriage by rendering divorce more painful and more punitive. . . . The antidivorce campaign may be a nonstarter, legally and practically, but it has an ideological function. As more people are spun off into economic instability as the safety net is shredded, family values becomes a way of explaining downward mobility as an individual moral failing: The selfish quest for happiness is what makes women and children poor.[37]

Divorce may be a liberal value–part of the liberal embrace of personal autonomy above all else–but it is far from clear that it is, as

Pollitt claims, an American value. Or at least, not anymore. Americans have witnessed the damage that easy divorce and its companion, unmarried childbearing, have done to children, and are having second thoughts. Indeed, after rising for three decades, both the divorce rate and the rate of out-of-wedlock childbearing have begun to subside.

On the subject of family structure, conservatives look at trends over the past several decades and see breakdown, dissolution, and damage. Liberals look at the same trends but tend to see the birth of new family styles or, as they sometimes label it, "alternatives." Sometimes, liberals refer to all non–husband/wife homes as "single-parent," a technique that they hope drains the stigma from never-married mothers. Stephen D. Sugarman, for example, writing in *All Our Families: New Policies for a New Century; A Report of the Berkeley Family Forum*, asks:

> What do the former First Lady Jackie Kennedy, the chief prosecutor in the O.J. Simpson case, Marcia Clark, the pop star Madonna, and the TV character Murphy Brown have in common? They all are, or at one time were, single mothers–unmarried women caring for their minor children. . . .
> . . . Just mentioning these four prominent women vividly demonstrates the diversity of single mothers. . . . [38]

(Four women? One is a fictional character.) In any case, the point is clear. It is irrelevant to your moral standing whether you are a widowed mother of young children, a divorced wife, or a slutty pop star who chooses to have both of her children out of wedlock with different fathers; all are alike–"single mothers" united in diversity.

Not only did women's magazines, Hollywood, and academia join the chorus for single-parenting, the producers of children's television ensured that the propaganda got started early. Tiny tot viewers of the popular PBS show *Barney*, for example, saw children chorusing:

> *I know a boy named Tim who lives with his mom;*
> *His dad lives far away;*

*Though he sees his parents just one at a time;*
*They both love him every day.*
*Oh, a family is people and a family is love;*
*That's a family.*
*They come in all different sizes and different kinds,*
*But mine's just right for me.*

The producers would probably protest that they are simply re-flecting life as it really is. This is a harder case to make for *Sesame Street*, where one little girl sings, "I've got one daddy," and her friend chimes in, "I've got two!" Another boy explains his family: "There's my mom and me, and baby makes three, and it works per-fectly, don't you see? We're a family."

"Single Mother, and Proud" read the title of a *Washington Post* op-ed piece in 1996. The subhead reinforced the message: "Working Two Jobs and Raising a Daughter: What's to Be Ashamed Of?"[39]

If a father and mother are unnecessary to a child's healthy devel-opment and happiness, then it only follows that the sexual orienta-tion of parents should not matter either. Judith Stacey quoted with approval the declaration of an eighteen-year-old reared by her di-vorced mother and her mother's lesbian lover:

> A happy child has happy parents, and gay people can be as happy as straight ones. It doesn't matter what kids have–fathers, mothers, or both–they just need love and support. It doesn't matter if you are raised by a pack of dogs, just as long as they love you! It's about time lesbians and gays can have children. It's everybody's right as a human being.[40]

Unmarried motherhood became downright chic for a time, dur-ing the 1990s. Actress Michelle Pfeiffer explained her decision to have a baby alone this way:

> I thought about all my options, and certainly one of those op-tions was to just have a baby with somebody, which I guess is

the obvious option. But when it came right down to it, I just couldn't do it. I thought, I don't want some guy in my life forever who's going to be driving me nuts.[41]

When the writers of popular TV situation comedy *Murphy Brown* decided to include the main character bearing an out-of-wedlock baby, Vice President Dan Quayle mentioned it in a speech about family weakness. "Marriage is a moral issue that requires cultural consensus, . . ." he cautioned. "It does not help matters when prime-time TV has Murphy Brown—a character who supposedly epitomizes today's intelligent, highly paid, professional woman—mocking the importance of a father by bearing a child alone and calling it just another 'lifestyle choice.'"

The response from the chattering class was sulphuric. *Newsweek*'s Eleanor Clift saw a Republican smear campaign: "There they go again. Only this time, instead of Willie Horton, the GOP is making Murphy Brown the symbol of what's wrong with liberal elites." Steve Roberts of *U.S. News and World Report* decried the use of a "wedge issue":

> This was not an accident. This was not a casual speech. This was a speech very much a part of the White House game plan, a very deliberate attempt to use these family values, which are an amorphous collection of ideas, but to use them as a wedge issue to drive divisions in this country along cultural lines, along social lines, and to some extent along racial lines.[42]

*USA Today*'s Barbara Reynolds asked "Murphy Brown or Dan Quayle? Which one is the most wretched excuse for a role model in this country?"[43] *Houston Post* Washington Bureau Chief Kathy Kiely detected code words: "I do think values are a code word . . . they are a code word saying I want to exclude certain people. I think they're a code word for saying 'I'm against including homosexuals in government, I'm against maybe including women in certain positions.'"[44] *Tonight Show* host Jay Leno joked, "Maybe the vice president should

stop watching *Murphy Brown* and start watching *Sesame Street*."[45]
Ellen Snortland of the *Los Angeles Times* thought she saw through
Quayle: "Traditional family values is a right-wing euphemism for 'a
white family where Daddy's the boss.' . . . Our country's government is not pro-motherhood or even pro-parenthood. It's antichoice,
pro-married, and in favor of 'traditional motherhood' because the
guys in government want the old fairy-tale days back . . ."[46]

CBS's Bruce Morton delivered a stern lecture to the vice president on national television:

> If you want to see the problem, visit a housing project called
> Clifton Terrace. It's only about a ten-minute drive from your
> house. You could talk to, say, a fifteen-year-old mother of two
> who doesn't want her kids; wants instead to be a child herself,
> and play with a doll. She might have been helped by a good
> sex education course, by readily available condoms, maybe
> even an abortion. Your administration disapproves of
> those.[47]

Morton might have taken a walk just a few blocks from CBS's stu-
dios to discover that the public schools in the District of Columbia *do*
hand out condoms to students and *do* teach sex education.[48] As for
the availability of abortion, there are at least three Planned Parenthood clinics in the Washington area as well as other facilities that
perform abortions. The ready availability of these "solutions" didn't
do much for the fifteen-year-old mother, did they?

Liberal hostility to the traditional family helped to undermine
centuries of accumulated wisdom and experience about what was
best for children and adults. Far from benefiting only men, marriage
confers enormous advantages on women and children as well—a fact
that has been thrown into sharp relief by its breakdown over the past
forty years.

Some children can endure the divorce of their parents without
suffering any short- or long-term effects, but the cheery notion that
children would somehow be happier if their parents were happier has

been shown to be total fantasy. In fact, large numbers of the children of divorce continue to suffer from its effects throughout their lives. Compared with peers from intact families, for example, teens whose parents have divorced are one and a half times more likely to use illicit drugs by age 14, and are more than two-thirds more likely to use illicit drugs sometime in their lives.[49]

Incarceration rates for children of divorced parents are twelve times higher than for children from intact, two-parent homes. Researcher Judith Wallerstein began studying the children of divorce in 1969. Like other experts, she expected to find that the hammer of divorce would fall most painfully on the youngest children, but that within months of the trauma, they would recover fully. Instead, when she examined the children eighteen months after a divorce, she found a high rate of sudden, serious psychological problems. Sixty-five percent of the children who had been functioning well before the divorce began to experience problems: inability to concentrate in school, trouble eating or sleeping, difficulty making friends, and withdrawn or hostile behavior.[50]

While at first it did seem as if older children coped better than younger ones, longitudinal studies show just the opposite. Ten years after a divorce, the older siblings showed signs of distress—inability to trust others, and difficulty forming lasting bonds with members of the opposite sex.

On nearly every measure of childhood well-being, children of divorce score lower than children from intact families. They have more trouble at school, are more likely to repeat a grade, experience more health problems, are much more likely to live in poverty, are more likely to be abused and neglected, are more likely to experience depression, and have higher rates of suicide. Children whose parents divorce spend less time with both parents than they did before the divorce. Forty percent of children in fatherless homes report that they have not seen their dads in at least one year. Of the remaining 60 percent, only one in six sees his father an average of once a week. Even ten years after a divorce, Judith Wallerstein found, children felt "less protected, less cared for, and less comforted," than children in intact families.[51] Children of divorce are much more likely to divorce themselves and are less likely to want children of their own.

Except in the wealthiest families, divorce always means reduced circumstances for the mother and children (if she gets custody). The average decline in income for wives and children postdivorce is 50 percent.[52] In fact, the economic effects of divorce can wipe out the advantages of a college education. A single-parent college graduate, on average, enjoys a lower family income than an intact family of high school graduates.[53] And while the economic condition of the children often improves if and when the mother remarries, the psychological effects of divorce are not erased. Children in stepfamilies were still two to three times more likely as children in intact homes to experience emotional and behavior problems, and almost twice as likely to show developmental or learning problems.[54]

The previously mentioned Barbara DaFoe Whitehead, a nonpartisan academic, wrote an influential article for *Atlantic* magazine in 1993 titled "Dan Quayle Was Right." She expanded the article into a book, *The Divorce Culture*, that demolished many of the comfortable assumptions about "alternative family structures" liberals had been recommending for decades. While 50 percent of divorced men and 80 percent of divorced women claimed to be happier postdivorce, the results were quite different for children:

> To be sure, there are children who say that their parents' marriages were so desperately unhappy or conflictual that they were relieved when their parents parted. Yet not even the most optimistic interpretation of the evidence would permit the conclusion that 80 percent of children are better off because their parents' marriages ended. Particularly for children in stepfamilies, the evidence strongly disputes the "happy ever after" scenario. A 1990 survey of more than nine hundred children ages ten to seventeen found that children in stepfamilies were more likely than children in either intact or single-parent families to wish for more time with their mothers, to report frequently feeling "sad and blue,"

and to lack parental participation in school or homework activities. Indeed, the weight of the evidence suggested that parental divorce, with its chain of disruptive events, is a significant source of disadvantage for children and an important and relatively recent factor contributing to sharp divergence in school, employment, and economic achievement outcomes between children in intact families and those in families disrupted by divorce.[55]

The "wicked stepmother" was a fixture of children's literature for centuries because it was so common for women to die in childbirth and for men to remarry. Today, the wicked stepfather might be the more appropriate bogeyman. According to researchers of family violence, the rate of sexual abuse suffered by girls is at least six and possibly as much as forty times higher for children living with stepfathers than for children living with their biological fathers.[56]

Boys who grow up in intact families are less likely than those in fatherless homes to get into trouble with the law. Robert Sampson, a professor at the University of Chicago, studied 171 cities with populations of 100,000 or more and found that the robbery rate tracked closely with the divorce rate.[57]

Another study followed 6,400 boys over the course of twenty years. Those who grew up without fathers were two to three times more likely to commit crimes that resulted in jail time than were those who grew up in intact families. In Wisconsin, juvenile incarceration rates for children of divorced parents were twelve times higher than for children in intact homes, a Heritage Foundation study found.[58] And a number of studies agree that roughly 70 percent of inmates in juvenile correction facilities are children of single-parent homes.[59] As with all other social ills, divorce and single-parenting are far more common in African American than other families. Today, 68 percent of all black births are to unmarried mothers. Two-thirds of black children (as opposed to 27 percent of all children) do not live with both of their biological parents. And, not surprisingly, only 15 percent of African American children who do

live with their married parents are poor, compared with 57 percent
of those who live with their mothers only.[60]

Women and children both suffer when children are born out of
wedlock. According to the Department of Justice's National Crime
Victimization Survey, never-married mothers experience twice the
rate of domestic abuse that married, divorced, or separated mothers
do. They also suffer much higher rates of violent crime.[61] Children
who grow up with only one of their biological parents are three times
more likely to have a child out of wedlock themselves, 2.5 times more
likely to become teen mothers, twice as likely to drop out of high
school, and 1.4 times as likely to be out of school and unemployed as
children who grow up with both parents.[62] The poverty rate for children of single mothers is 45 percent. For children of intact families,
the poverty rate is 6 percent.[63] Not surprisingly, a child born and
reared outside of marriage is six times more likely to receive welfare
than a child raised in a two-parent home.[64] Illegitimate children are
also far more likely to be depressed and to experience a variety of
mental and developmental problems than children from intact families. Further, 72 percent of America's young murderers, 70 percent
of long-term prison inmates, and 60 percent of rapists come from
single-mother families.[65]

Some liberals have distanced themselves from the antimarriage
crowd. William Galston, President Clinton's domestic policy adviser,
has written that "Marriage is an impressive social good, associated
with an impressively broad array of positive outcomes for children
and adults alike."[66] President Clinton and Vice President Gore (perhaps recognizing which way the wind was blowing) also made rhetor-
ical bows in the direction of marriage. And certainly advocates of gay
marriage *claim* to be pro-marriage as well, though their claim causes
consternation among conservatives and liberals alike–but for different reasons. Writing in *The Nation* magazine, Lisa Duggan expressed her discomfort with the drive for gay marriage:

> How about abolishing state endorsement of the sanctified re-
> ligious wedding or ending the use of the term "marriage" al-

together (as lesbian and gay progressives and queer leftists have advocated for decades)? In a bid for equality, some gay groups are producing rhetoric that insults and marginalizes unmarried people while promoting marriage in much the same terms as the welfare reformers used to stigmatize single-parent households, divorce and "out-of-wedlock" births. If pursued in this way, the drive for gay marriage equality can undermine rather than support the broader movement for social justice and democratic diversity.[67]

Gwendolyn Mink and Anna Marie Smith, professors at Smith College and Cornell University, respectively, were critical of the Massachusetts Supreme Judicial Court's decision in favor of gay marriage on the same grounds.

The Massachusetts court argued that lesbian and gay couples should be able to marry because marriage is good for society. The rationale of this ostensibly liberal decision leaves individuals who choose not to marry–or to exit from an existing marriage–out in the cold. Especially stigmatizing unmarried parents–mostly mothers–the Massachusetts court's decision abetted efforts currently touted by conservatives to cajole, pressure and coerce low-income mothers to marry. . . .

The Massachusetts court went so far as to endorse the idea that children do better when they are raised by a married couple, even though many scholars argue that marital status, in itself, has no bearing on child welfare. Happy, stable families benefit children, but such families need not be marital families. . . . Marriage, after all, is the historical core institution of patriarchy; the wellspring of men's subordination of women; the justification for women's second class citizenship.[68]

The Bush administration responded to the scholarly evidence and commonsense case for marriage by introducing several modest proposals to encourage matrimony among the poor. This was too much for the Left. The NOW Legal Defense and Education Fund decried this attempt, as they put it "to tell poor women it's more important to find a good man than to find a good job."[69] It may well be—just as it is more important to the long-term health and happiness of men to find a good woman rather than a good job. But as a famous study by the Annie E. Casey Foundation discovered, those who do four simple things will not be poor in America. Those four steps are (1) get married, (2) get a job, (3) finish high school, (4) wait until after marriage to have your first child. Though liberals think promoting marriage shoos women back to the kitchen, barefoot, and pregnant, the truth is that marriage tends to make women safer, wealthier, happier, and better mothers.

Feminists are in flight from this reality. Here is the NOW Legal Defense and Education Fund again:

> It is important for Congress to remember that there are currently more non-marital families than married families in America. These include single, separated, divorced, widowed, cohabiting, gay and lesbian, and extended families, among others. Congress should not attempt to coerce low-income individuals into one type of family structure.[70]

Barbara Ehrenreich was similarly dismissive of what she called "prodding the poor to the altar":

> Most of us insist on marrying potential soul mates and, of course, divorcing them when our souls begin to flutter apart. . . . More Americans every year choose not to marry at all rather than settle for a sub-perfect spouse. . . . My suspicion—completely unsupported, of course, but who's talking evidence?—is that conservatives want all women married because, statistically speaking, married women are more likely to vote Republican than single women are.[71]

Forty years of family disintegration have not led to the free and happy world liberal do-gooders envisioned. Through painful experience, we've discovered that family breakdown is devastating for everyone—the couple, the children, and society. In *Fatherless America*, David Blankenhorn sketched the chaos we have created:

> When fatherhood decomposes in a society, this is what happens: Confusion and deception about who a child's father is. Increasingly nuanced distinctions between "biological" and "social" fathers, along with ugly contests pitting one against the other. Lots of new work for lawyers, social workers, and court-appointed psychologists. Titillating new program topics for *Geraldo* and *Donahue*. The fragmenting of adoption as an institution, since adoption can be a coherent idea only if motherhood, fatherhood, and marriage are coherent ideas. Growing numbers of children with either no father or too many "fathers." In short, the paternity of the Sperm Father: male procreation in a kind of postmodern state of nature.[72]

Particularly in inner cities, where majorities of children are born to and raised by single mothers, we have witnessed something far more drastic than simple human unhappiness—we've seen the breakdown of civilization itself.

## Child Welfare or Parent Welfare?

The liberal response to this misery and chaos was to excuse and justify it. They erected a child welfare system that perpetuated the very trends that were most damaging to children. Along the way, they demonized those who questioned their hegemony.

In the heady days after Republicans won control of the House of Representatives in 1994, Newt Gingrich mentioned one idea that had been percolating among conservative think tanks—bringing back orphanages for the children of single, destitute girls. Democrats, still shell-shocked from their stunning reversal at the polls, erupted in manufactured outrage. First Lady Hillary Rodham Clinton denounced the idea as "unbelievable" and "absurd" and declared that Republicans wanted to put children into orphanages "because their mothers couldn't find jobs."[73]

David Liederman, executive director of the Child Welfare League of America, complained that "What they're talking about is unnecessarily separating children from families who have only one problem: They're poor."[74] Columnist Cynthia Tucker jumped on the orphanage remark as proof that the new Speaker of the House had a split personality, and had just revealed the "bomb-throwing Newt . . . reckless, arrogant, mean-dominated."[75] New York governor Mario Cuomo declared that "our strong suit as Democrats has always been our concern for the vast majority of Americans who must work for a living. . . . We'd rather preserve a family than build an orphanage. We believe that we're too good as a people to seek solutions by hurting the weakest among us, especially our children."[76] House Democratic Whip David Bonior vowed to oppose welfare reform and added, "We are not about tearing away babies from their mothers."[77] And Leonard Greene of the *Boston Herald* penned a satirical poem about the new House Speaker containing the lines:

> *Mr. Gingrich, you're a troll.*
> *You are nasty, Mr. Gingrich.*
> *Your heart is as big as a dime.*
> *You'd put children in an orphanage,*
> *just to pass the time.*[78]

The dust-up was typical of liberal/conservative confrontations over the welfare of children, with liberals claiming the moral high ground—and conservatives often retreating. Gingrich later said that "orphanages" might have been the wrong word.

He needn't have backed down. In truth, the child welfare system in the United States was then and continues to be a scandal—one that should offend the consciences of all men of goodwill. In light of the dismal performance of foster care, a number of serious reformers have recommended a return to orphanages, or group living, for some of the hardest-to-place children in the system.

Imagine the view of a young child burned and starved by his drug-addled mother. Assume that he has no one to fight for his best interests. Who would you guess would stand in the way of his welfare, a liberal or a conservative? The answer in 2004 is most often the liberal. The policies that hurt these children have been put into place by liberal advocates, foundations, and politicians (though many rank-and-file Democrats might not support these policies if asked).

Liberals are masters at cloaking themselves in the rhetoric of child welfare. Marian Wright Edelman is the prima donna of the do-gooder libretto. "Why," she asks, in a typical plea, "is there no room for our children in our twenty-first-century inn in the wealthiest nation on earth? Why are our political leaders cutting the heating and shelter and child care and child health assistance children desperately need while squandering hundreds of billions of dollars on tax cuts for millionaires?"[79] Such invocations of children are so common at Democratic National Conventions–"the children" were mentioned ninety times in the 1996 Democratic platform[80]–that they could be permanently imprinted on the teleprompters. But liberal policies often have the effect, sometimes intended and sometimes overlooked, of harming children in fundamental ways. Liberals have won many battles over social policy during the past generation–and the results for children, particularly poor children, have been disastrous.

Not everyone spat out Newt Gingrich's orphanage suggestion untasted. The late Mary McGrory, liberal columnist for the *Washington Post* and an eloquent advocate for children, noted that the response to Gingrich's remark "underscores the sad fact it has been impossible to have a rational discussion of the problem. . . . Nobody is saying that an institution is better than a home. But what Gingrich and others are saying is that an institution is better than a crack house or a life on the street."[81] And Ellen Goodman, while characterizing the orphanage idea as "off the wall," did acknowledge that "some families are irreparably broken down." She hoped to find "what we can agree on here," and included the idea "that the kids should come first."[82]

Though she may not have been aware of it, Goodman was actually voicing heresy by naïvely asserting that "the kids should come first." That is not at all how the child welfare system—devised and run by liberal social workers, psychologists, and judges—is run. In fact, the system treats incompetent or abusive parents as its clients, and only secondarily considers the needs and well-being of the children involved.

## "Orphans of the Living"

There are, according to most estimates, 600,000 children in the United States in the foster care program—that is, those who have been removed from their biological parents and placed with state-approved foster families. They call themselves "system kids." Once removed from their homes, children typically remain in foster care for three years (which means about half stay longer), and children are placed, on average, in three different homes during that time. These foster placements vary enormously in quality. In many states, the requirements to qualify as foster parents are considerably lower than those for adoptive parents. And in all cases, caring for foster children brings with it a monthly check from the government which can and sometimes does attract the worst candidates. Each year, 20,000 to 25,000 children "age out" of the system. They reach their eighteenth birthdays never having had a permanent home or real parents.[83] In many cases, these children go on to become single mothers themselves or get into trouble with the law.

There are also, it should be noted, cases in which perfectly innocent parents are investigated by child welfare authorities, and occasionally even deprived of their children, on the basis of false or malicious accusations. Those cases are infuriating, but they do not lead to the deaths of children. Mistakes made in the other direction often do.

It is outrageous enough when children are shuttled around the foster care system. It is far worse when those kids are sent back to their abusing parents time after time. Some go to their deaths. Sister Josephine Murphy, a social worker who runs the St. Anne's Infant and Maternity Home in Hyattsville, Maryland, described a boy whose back had been shredded from beatings inflicted by his mother. It required months for the lacerations to heal. A judge sent the child back to his mother. "Why," asked Sister Josephine, "do we leave children with mothers who can't or won't protect them? These children are orphans of the living, victims of the child slavery maintained by our legal system and our welfare departments."[84]

A glance at any large newspaper in the country for any one-year period will yield numerous stories of children who have been tortured or killed by their parents, or injured or mistreated in foster care, often after having been evaluated by child welfare authorities. Conna Craig was a foster child herself who lived with a family that had cared for more than one hundred children over the years. Craig was eventually adopted and went on to attend Harvard College and found her own child welfare advocacy group—the Institute for Children. She recalled seeing her foster brothers and sisters returned to abusive parents time after time. One mother tied her daughter to a space heater, causing third-degree burns on the girl's face. Craig recalls another, Catrina:

> Catrina is 12 years old. She has spent most of her life in state-run, government-funded substitute care. When asked "What's it like?" she responds matter-of-factly that by the time she was 2 years old, she had been taken away from and returned to her biological mother 10 times. Catrina explains, "I understand the first nine times, the judge was trying to give my mom a fair chance." On the tenth time, however, then 2-year-old Catrina was found with 48 cigarette burns on her head.[85]

In Collingswood, New Jersey, in 2003 a man notified police when he heard someone rummaging through the trash in the house next door. When police arrived, they discovered that it was Bruce Jackson, searching for food. The story, as it unfolded, was this: Four brothers had been adopted out of foster care by Vanessa and Raymond Jackson. When police arrived, they at first thought Bruce was an extremely thin ten-year-old. He was nineteen–and weighed just forty-five pounds. Then they saw the other boys: the fourteen-year-old weighed forty pounds, and the ten-year-old weighed twenty-eight pounds, and the nine-year-old weighed twenty-three pounds. None stood more than four feet. The Jacksons had starved the boys for their entire lives, locking the doors to the kitchen and giving the boys uncooked pancake batter from time to time. The children had eaten portions of the wall and the insulation behind it. The Jacksons received a stipend from the state of about $28,000 to care for their adopted children.[86]

An investigation revealed that case workers had made thirty-eight visits to the home and somehow failed to notice anything amiss. Nor was this the first horrific case to come to light in New Jersey in 2003. In another case, the decomposing body of a seven-year-old boy was discovered in the basement of a Newark house, while another two starved boys were found in the same home. In Florida, state child welfare officials acknowledged that they had lost track of 500 children. The *South Florida Sun-Sentinel* assigned several reporters to look for the children and they rapidly located nine of them by dialing directory assistance.[87]

The story of six-year-old Elisa Isquierdo made headlines in New York in 1996. A dark-haired, large-eyed little beauty, Elisa was born crack-addicted. Custody was granted to her father at birth, but he died when the child was five. Though his family fought to gain custody of the little girl, the court granted custody instead to the mother–still crack-addicted, unmarried, and the mother of five other children. Social workers, court officials, and teachers all noticed signs of abuse. Yet Elisa remained with her mother, who reportedly believed her daughter was "possessed by the devil." When Elisa was six and a half, she was beaten to death. Her body was found to be covered with wounds from cigarette burns and other injuries, some old, some new. Her hair was almost completely gone.[88]

Joseph Wallace of Chicago was three when his mother stood him on a chair, wrapped an electrical cord around his neck, and kicked out the chair from under him. At Amanda Wallace's trial, prosecutors introduced her statements to police when they arrived at her apartment. She told them that Joseph had "waved at" her before she killed him. The child had been removed from his mentally ill mother's care three times before his death.[89] But what is more devastating is that he was returned. Joshua Wallace was Joseph's younger brother. He was fifteen months old when his mother killed Joseph, yet three years later, Amanda Wallace's parental rights remained intact. Joshua was not free to be adopted. Instead, he was bounced around the foster care system.[90]

Brianna Blackmond had been removed from the care of her mentally retarded mother as an infant. The mother, whose IQ was estimated to be fifty-eight had eight other children, all of whom had been removed from her care. Brianna and a sister were living with loving foster parents who very much wanted to adopt them, yet the child welfare authorities, and a judge who expressed concern about the "destruction of the black family," sent the child back to her mother. Within twelve days of her return, two-year-old Brianna was dead. Her head was smashed against the floor by her mother's housemate.[91]

Some child deaths capture the headlines. Many do not. Monica Wheeler's was one of the silent ones. So was her older brother's. Two-year-old Andre Wheeler had drowned in a bathtub while under the care of his mother's boyfriend, Michael Tubman. Though the boy had bruises on his head, police ruled the death an accident. Three years later, a doctor noticed bruises on Monica's body. A social worker and police officer visited her home once, talked briefly with her mother, and ruled the doctor's suspicions "unsupported." A few weeks later, on September 23, 1997, Tubman beat and strangled Monica to death. The imprint of a fist was found on her back.[92]

In 1996, one of Kendra Anderson's older siblings was the subject

of a teacher's report. She alerted District of Columbia authorities
that the child was very dirty. A social worker assigned to the case did
not check the mother's history. If she had, she would have learned
that Anderson had been accused of child neglect dating back two
years in the state of Maryland. Case workers closed the books on the
family in 1997. In 1998, Kendra was born. A month later, she was
beaten to death. Her death certificate read "blunt impact head injuries" as the cause of death.[93]

In 2002, according to the Department of Health and Human Services, 1,400 children were killed by their parents or guardians in the
United States. Most were under the age of four and the overwhelming majority–81 percent–were killed by their parents.[94] At least half
of the children who died were known to child welfare authorities before they were murdered.

In 2003, the *San Francisco Chronicle* reported that "California's
system of care for abused and neglected children, under fire in two
Bay Area cases and from the state itself, fails to meet national stan-
dards for protecting kids and for training case workers and foster par-
ents. . . ."[95] The *Philadelphia Inquirer* related in that same year that
"New Jersey's Division of Youth and Family Services . . . is considered to be among the worst in the nation."[96] A 2002 headline in the
*Charlotte Observer* reflects the pervasiveness of the problem:
"Deaths of Children in State System Rise; Social Services Officials
Say They Can't Explain Increase in Recent Years."[97] The *Atlanta
Journal-Constitution* editorially scoffed at a new child welfare official's promise to "raise the bar" on investigations of child abuse. "At
this point," said the editorial board, "the bar has been raised so
many times it's a threat to low-lying aircraft . . . [yet] abuse and neglect cases are still on the upswing."[98]

In 1992, the National Commission on Children declared, "If the
nation had deliberately designed a system that would frustrate the
professionals who staff it, anger the public who finance it, and aban-
don the children who depend on it, it could not have done a better job
than the present child welfare system."[99] The U.S. Advisory Board on
Child Abuse and Neglect had sounded the same theme a couple of

years earlier, declaring, "In spite of the nation's avowed aim of protecting children, each year hundreds of thousands of them are being starved and abandoned, burned and severely beaten, raped and sodomized, berated and belittled."[100]

Defenders of the status quo cite a number of excuses for this nationwide failure; lack of funding heads the list. The National Commission on Family Foster Care, convened by the Child Welfare League of America, declared in the 1990s that "family foster care and other child welfare services have never been given the resources necessary."[101] In late 2003, the president of the Child Welfare League reiterated that "Only through significant new resources and strategies for federal, state, and local communities can we effectively promote safety and permanence for children and prevent child abuse and neglect in America."[102] But the nation spends more than $16 billion annually on the child welfare system. Lack of funding is the ready-made excuse for every government failing, but it is a feeble one. In fact, the reason so many do-gooder initiatives fail is not lack of money but bad ideas. The realm of child welfare has been choking on them.

## Family Preservation

The foster care system began in the late 1930s and 1940s when it was discovered that babies raised in orphanages displayed a syndrome called "failure to thrive." Though well-fed and clean, these babies simply wilted without ongoing, loving interaction with one adult. The emotional coldness of an institution, it was discovered, could kill. Adoption became the preferred alternative for orphaned children, and where adoption was not possible, foster care took the place of the orphanage. (Fewer and fewer children were orphaned after the 1940s when medical science made parental death far less common.) Foster care had troubles of its own. Foster parents' circumstances could change through the birth of another child, a move to another state, or a job change. Further, foster parents were discouraged from bonding to their foster kids, since impermanence was a key aspect of the system. And some foster families were child abusers who signed up with the system merely to obtain a steady supply of victims.

Adoption is the one social intervention with an unequivocal history of success. Adopted children score higher than their middle-class counterparts in school, have better social skills, and are more optimistic than the general population. Compared with children raised by single parents, adopted children have lower rates of depression, alcohol abuse, vandalism, and trouble with the police. Adopted children score better on measures of self-esteem, confidence, and feelings of security within their families. They are more likely to grow up with both a mother and father than the average child, and they tend to enjoy better health care and a higher standard of living than the average.[103] Because adoption meets the needs of children so successfully, and because there have long been waiting lists of couples hoping to adopt babies and children, it would seem that the solution for abused or neglected kids was obvious. But not to the do-gooders. To remove a child from an abusive parent, sever the parent's parental rights, and permit the child to be adopted by a couple who would give the child a loving home began to seem too "judgmental" in the sixties.

During the maelstrom that Francis Fukuyama has described as "The Great Disruption"—the flower power era—liberal child welfare experts decided that child abuse was not evidence of a moral or character flaw in the abusing parent. Instead, like poverty, crime, and homelessness, child abuse came to be viewed as evidence of a societal failure. People abused their kids because they were poor, or lived in overcrowded conditions, or suffered from racial discrimination. To take their children away was to "blame the victim." Race, of course, played a role in these opinion shifts, since most foster children were black and most foster and adoptive parents were and are white. In 1972, the National Association of Black Social Workers (NABSW) issued a broadside, branding transracial adoption as "cultural genocide." The group's statement elaborated:

In our society, the developmental needs of black children are significantly different from those of white children. Black children are taught, from an early age, highly sophisticated coping techniques to deal with racist practices perpetrated by individuals and institutions. . . . Only a black family can transmit the emotional and sensitive subtleties of perception and reaction essential for a black child's survival in a racist society.[104]

Many blacks, at the time and since, including a majority of the membership of the National Association for the Advancement of Colored People, disagreed. But as the *New Republic* put it, "the intimidation worked on a pool of largely white, liberal social workers."[105] In 1973, the Child Welfare League of America, the most influential child welfare organization in the nation, changed its guidelines to conform to the wishes of the NABSW. Placements of black children with white parents, which had been on the rise, plummeted.[106] To his credit, liberal senator Howard Metzenbaum made this cause his own in the 1990s and helped to write a law that discouraged the practice. "Keeping a black child in a foster home because some black social worker doesn't believe it's right to cross the race barrier is horrendous," Metzenbaum said. "It means that the child may go from one home to another, without . . . a chance of ever having real parents."[107] But Metzenbaum's reform, while enthusiastically endorsed by the National Council for Adoption, was opposed by some of the most influential so-called children's advocates. The Children's Defense Fund lobbied against the change behind the scenes as did the North American Council on Adoptable Children, and Adoptive Families of America.[108]

In 1980, Congress passed the Adoption Assistance and Child Welfare Act. It was poorly named. Rather than encourage adoption for children whose parents abused or neglected them, the act enshrined a new fad into law: "family preservation." Through concentrated social work, including parenting advice, anger management, housekeeping help and more, social workers would repair the damaged families. What society had broken, well-intentioned liberal social work would fix. The law required that before an adoption plan was prepared for a child, each state would undertake "reasonable efforts" to reunite the child with his or her "family" (in nearly all cases, this meant the unmarried mother).

The legislation did not define "reasonable efforts," and since the child welfare system nationwide was in the grip of enthusiasm for "family preservation," social workers and judges sped down the raceway oblivious to warning flags. Children remained in foster care for years, having only the most cursory contact with their birthparents. Many of these children, particularly those who were very young when they entered foster care, would have been perfect candidates for adoption. Many conscientious and loving foster parents pleaded with child welfare authorities to be able to adopt the children in their care. They watched helplessly as the children they cared for were sent back, time and again, to their abusive, drug-addicted, or mentally unstable single mothers. Even when there was zero chance that the mother (or in rare cases, father) would ever be able to resume custody of a child, limbo in foster care was guaranteed, because the system was in thrall to biological family reunification. Universities taught the practice. The Family Preservation Institute at New Mexico State University was typical:

> Family preservation is a practice philosophy guided by values which uphold the uniqueness, dignity and essential role which a family plays in the health and well-being of its members. In keeping with this philosophy, programs, policies, and organizations are family-focused. As an approach, family preservation provides services ranging from prevention to intensive in-home services based upon the family's strengths and needs.
>
> People of all ages can best develop, with few exceptions, by remaining with their family or relying on them as an important resource.[109]

A social worker with Casey Family Services explained, "We work with the entire family. . . . Sometimes they need recreational activities, academic help, medical services, or something even more basic like clothes to wear, food to eat, and a bed to sleep on. . . ."[110] The concept became fashionable in charity circles as well. Two foundations, the Annie E. Casey Foundation and the Edna McConnell Clarke Foundation, contributed millions to public/private partnerships promoting family preservation. As recently as February 2004, the Junior League of Dallas advertised that its charity ball would raise funds for family preservation among other programs.[111] Richard Wexler, executive director of the National Coalition for Child Protection Reform and a family preservation booster, described the program as follows:

> . . . [F]amily preservation workers combine traditional counseling and parent education with a strong emphasis on providing "hard" services to ameliorate the worst aspects of poverty. Family preservation workers help families find day care and job training, and get whatever special education help the children may require. They teach practical skills and help with financial problems. They even do windows. Faced with a family living in a dirty home, a family preservation worker will not lecture the parents or demand that they spend weeks in therapy to deal with the deep psychological trauma of which the dirty home is "obviously" just a symptom. The family preservation worker will roll up her sleeves and help with the cleaning.[112]

Though the words sound traditional, the family preservation movement was not about traditional families at all. The overwhelming majority of the "families" to whom social workers extended services were single mothers with children. Neither were they the most competent single parents, nor the ones most likely to benefit from extra help. No, what triggered the cascade of government-funded assistance was the imminent prospect of a child being removed from the home. Patrick Murphy is the Cook County, Illinois, Public Guardian. He described family preservation in the following terms:

Take any floor in a typical low-income housing project. In one apartment, there might be a single woman in her mid-20s with two kids, struggling on a meager welfare check to keep the kids dressed, clean and in school. Down the hall is a family of six. Despite months of looking, Mom works as a maid and Dad, unemployed, does a few odd jobs. At the end of the hall, there is a woman with three kids. She is a heavy crack cocaine user. Her present boyfriend is also her drug supplier, and when he gets angry he hits the kids. Sometimes they lock the kids in the apartment and go off for hours of partying.

The state decides to make life easier for one of these families. Which one? Under welfare laws in Illinois and other states, the mother doing drugs and allowing her boyfriend to belt the kids is the only one entitled to a free housekeeper up to five days a week. She can also receive up to $2000 for a security deposit and the first month's rent on a new apartment, as well as furniture and up to $500 in cash. . . .

How does it work in real life? In December 1991, the aunt of a 3-year-old girl [called Senomia B.] told the family services department that her sister and sister's lover had physically abused the child. State investigators confirmed the abuse: the child had bruises and rope burns on her body. Instead of bringing the case to a court, the department provided a housekeeper and a social worker who between them went to the home a total of 37 times over the next 90 days. The housekeeper helped the mother clean up and make dinner. The social worker took her out for meals and shopping.

On March 6, 1992, the aunt telephoned the family services agency again, pleading that the child was still being abused. The agency ignored her. On March 17, the agency closed the case with a glowing report on how well the family was doing. Several hours later, the girl was dead. An autopsy revealed that boiling water had been poured on her genitals and that she had been struck on the head with a blunt instrument. Her body was covered with 43 scars, bruises, and rope burns. . . . She weighed 17 pounds.[113]

In 1993, Murphy proposed a law in Illinois that would have required court approval for family preservation services in cases of physical or sexual abuse. The American Civil Liberties Union lobbied against it, and Governor Jim Edgar, a Republican, vetoed it.[114]

The term "family preservation" is bitterly ironic. In all but the rarest cases, the "families" the social workers are so keen to preserve consist only of one parent and one or more children. In every other context–parental notification laws for abortions, waiting periods for divorce, the debate over gay marriage–liberals tend to disdain the idea that families are in any way sacred. Yet when it comes to mothers who are drug-addicted, irresponsible, and abusive, liberals suddenly decide that, in the words of Robert Little, head of the Child Welfare Administration of New York City under former mayor David Dinkins, "All families have strengths as well as weaknesses."[115] A caseworker interviewed by Bill Moyers on a television special decried the "labeling process" that makes distinctions between a working family unable to afford day care and a crack-addicted single mother. "If we're a country that believes in the integrity of families," he pronounced, "we should keep all families together."[116]

Such is the dogmatism of the do-gooder.

## Biology *Über Alles*

Whereas before 1981, proof of a parent's illegal drug use created a presumption of unfitness as a parent in New York, the law was changed in 1981. To escape the presumption of unfitness, all that a parent had to do was to enroll in a drug treatment program. When Carla Lockwood gave birth to a crack baby, New York authorities asked her to sign up for drug treatment. She complied, and the child welfare office closed the case. Several years later, the baby was found dead. She weighed just fifteen pounds.[117] Another drug abusing mother in Chicago prostituted her eleven-year-old daughter in exchange for money, heroin, and, in one instance, a pair of sneakers. This woman had received "intensive family preservation services" for the better part of a year, including a homemaker who came to the house four times a week.[118]

In many cases, the whole poverty/welfare establishment would weigh in on behalf of parents and against the interests of battered or abused children. New York's Legal Aid Society and the Legal Services Corporation have provided free lawyers to parents whose children are the subject of placement outside the home. They have shown themselves to be absolutists on the subject of family preservation. Sadly, the "law guardians" sometimes appointed by the courts to look after the children's best interests are often under the sway of the same ideas, as are all too many judges. They believe that the best interest of the child is always served by keeping him or her with the biological parent.[119]

When people are intent upon hiding something obvious, they can spout copious amounts of gobbledygook. Glance at the Web site of the Administration for Youth and Families, a division of the federal Department of Health and Human Services. In a section entitled "Risk and Preventive Factors for Child Abuse and Neglect," the department notes that "Important characteristics of the family are linked with child maltreatment. Families in which there is substance abuse are more likely to experience abuse or are at a higher risk of abuse. . . . Domestic violence and lack of parenting or communication skills also increase the risks of maltreatment to children."[120] Similarly, the Doris Duke Charitable Foundation's Web site announces that "Child abuse and neglect occur in all segments of our society, but the risk factors are greater in families where parents: seem to be having economic, housing, or personal problems; are isolated from their family or community; have difficulty controlling anger or stress; are dealing with physical or mental health issues; abuse alcohol or drugs; appear uninterested in the care, nourishment or safety of their children."[121]

Well, yes. But that's a little like saying people who swerve down the highway at high speeds are more likely to die in car crashes than others. It tells us nothing that is not obvious.

## Unmentionable

In truth, what all of these liberal groups avoid mentioning–and what is hardly measured at all in the United States–is that the safest place for a child is with his married mother and father. Data from Britain and Australia make crystal clear that the biggest risk factor for child abuse is having a never-married mother. Children of divorced or never-married mothers are six to thirty times more likely to suffer from serious abuse than are children raised by their two biological or adoptive parents. In Britain, a child whose mother lives with a man other than the father of her children places her children at thirty-three times the risk for abuse as a woman who gets married to the father. When researchers examine the backgrounds of children who have been murdered by parents or caregivers, they find that the lowest rate of fatalities is among married parents. The rate is three times higher for stepfamilies, nine times higher for a single mother raising her children alone, eighteen times higher for cohabiting biological parents, and seventy-three times higher for a mother living with a boyfriend who is not the biological father of her children.[122]

Researcher Barry Maley, writing in the *Courier Mail* of Australia, discussed a reality that is often slighted in the United States:

Child abuse in the United States has increased 134 percent since 1980, in tandem with an accelerating rate of children affected by divorce and sole parenthood. . . . We must be wary, of course, of assuming that all sole parent families, stepfamilies, or cohabiting couples are inevitably risky for children, or that married natural parents are an absolute guarantee of safety and happiness, for this is clearly not so. What does seem to be the case is that, *on average*, the risk to children increases as we move away from an environment in which the biological parents of the child are married. . . .

Although low income is associated with more child abuse, and although it is easy to imagine that poverty brings stresses that may spill over into child abuse or neglect, we cannot jump to the conclusion that poverty causes abuse or neglect. It is plausible that prior family dysfunction leads to both poverty and child abuse or neglect. This would explain why *abuse is relatively uncommon in intact but poor families where a parent is working, even though such families might be forced to live in neighborhoods made disorderly by dysfunctional families and the prevalence of crime* [emphasis added].[123]

It would be false and unjust to suggest that anyone associated with the child welfare system condones child abuse or neglect. On the other hand, it is fair to note that some ideological mind-sets can be blinding. Advocates of family preservation do not wish to "judge" a mother who beats or starves her children–particularly if she is a member of a minority group. Though liberals love the idea of children's rights when it comes to a suburban teenager who wants an abortion, they shrink from recognizing the rights of poor and minority children to be free from abuse. They sentimentalize poor adults–sympathizing with them even when they commit crimes against the weakest members of society, their own children.

For a number of years, family preservation policies were declared successes due to a tautology. Instead of removing a child from an abusive home, social workers would shower the family with services. They would then triumphantly announce that fewer children were being sent to foster care. As Heather MacDonald pointed out, "The fact that a child is not placed during family preservation is part of the treatment, not a result of the treatment."[124] When careful experimental and control group studies were finally undertaken, no advantage accrued to children who had participated in family preservation programs.[125] And, as we have seen, a great deal of harm came to some. Faced with the daunting prospect of thousands upon thousands of dysfunctional single-mother households hardly able to manage the basics of life, Columbia University professor of social work Brenda McGowan was unruffled: "These families can maintain loving homes and meet their children's basic developmental needs only if they are provided a range of supports on a sustained basis, perhaps until their children are grown."[126] *Until their children are grown!*

In 1997, in response to burgeoning foster care caseloads, Congress passed the Adoption and Safe Families Act. The law eliminated language requiring states to exert "reasonable efforts" to reunite children with their birth families and instead stressed permanency planning. Richard Gelles, head of the Family Violence Research Program at the University of Rhode Island and a severe critic of family preservation, discussed the old law on the PBS program *Frontline*:

> It's almost immoral to hold a child's development hostage while you wait for parents to turn their lives around. What if it takes a parent five or six or eight years to turn their life around, with three or four relapses? Is it fair to ask the child to . . . stay in foster care for eight years with multiple moves? Or for the child to be some sort of guinea pig to test whether the change has been effective and thereby restore the child to the home and have the child re-injured, taken out of the home? You keep running this revolving door and the only way you know you've failed is the child is injured or harmed.[127]

The ASFA requires that states begin the process of terminating parental rights and seeking to place children for adoption if they have been in foster care for fifteen of the most recent twenty-two months. The act, responding to the failures of the Adoption Assistance and Child Welfare Act of 1980, specifies that termination of parental rights can be undertaken if the parent has abandoned the

child, killed a sibling, or when a court determines that reasonable efforts to reunify the family are not appropriate.[128]

Within four years of the bill's passage, adoptions out of foster
care doubled. This result pleased Gelles.

> I've been in the system for 35 years. The system was set up as
> a residual system to make sure that . . . children wouldn't
> suffer at the hands of inadequate parents. And that was al-
> ways the purpose of the system. The system was never de-
> signed to be a default welfare system, a default parental
> training system, a default drug abuse and alcohol treatment
> system. That's not what it was set up for. It was set up to
> watch out for vulnerable children. That should be its prime
> objective. . . . [129]

Some conservatives loathe the idea of the state terminating anyone's parental rights, and in the ideal world, family relationships
would be sacred. But if you believe that each life is precious–an end
in itself, not a means to an end–then there is no alternative to state
intervention to save children in perilous situations.

This country is in the midst of a responsibility deficit the likes of
which we have not seen before. While most adults continue to marry
and raise children in man/woman households (73 percent of households with children under the age of eighteen in 2000 were headed by
married couples),[130] a significant and rising number of Americans
seem to regard childbearing as a gratification to the adult rather than
as a duty to the child (far less to society). Personal fulfillment, not the
best interests of the child, determines many adults' decisions. Sixty-
two percent of young, unmarried singles cheerfully tell pollsters
that, while not ideal, it is okay for a woman to have a child on her own
if she has not found the right man to marry.[131] Among the poor in the
inner cities, the illegitimacy rate hovers around 80 percent. It is this
reality that social welfare types so assiduously seek to downplay.
With their "all families have strengths" happy talk, they avoid the
simple truth that children raised outside of marriage tend to be at

higher risk for every social pathology from crime to drugs to teen pregnancy.

Liberalism has created this world in which parents freely divorce their children, many children never know their fathers, and toddlers are cruelly abused with the acquiescence of the state. What children need is the opposite of what liberalism encourages: children require adults to behave like adults. They require adults to keep their commitments, to control their appetites, and even to put their own needs second or third to those of their spouses and children. When adults fail to do their duty—when they neglect and mistreat their children—it is they, and not the children, who should pay the price.

# Chapter Five
# THE "GRATE" SOCIETY— HOW LIBERALISM CREATED HOMELESSNESS

It's a peculiar thing about liberals. When it comes to middle-class people who are fully capable of caring for themselves, liberals seek to undermine their independence in every way possible. With seductive "entitlements" like guaranteed retirement, health care, nutrition, education, and jobs, liberals attempt to lure the middle class into dependence on the state. But when it comes to those who are truly incompetent, those whose mental afflictions render them unable to manage their lives at all, liberals are suddenly transformed into absolutists for personal autonomy. In some cases, the results are downright cruel.

The story of the homeless is an ironic one. Though liberals have portrayed themselves throughout the past several decades as champions of the homeless, they are actually guilty of having created and perpetuated their condition.

As is often the case, the Supreme Court played a starring role. In 1971, in the case of *Papachristou et al. v. City of Jacksonville*, the court swept away all but the most narrowly tailored of America's vagrancy statutes. The Jacksonville ordinance, written in a pre-politically correct era, read as follows:

Rogues and vagabonds, or dissolute persons who go about begging, common gamblers, persons who use juggling or unlawful games or plays, common drunkards, common night walkers, thieves, pilferers or pickpockets, traders in stolen property, lewd, wanton and lascivious persons, keepers of gambling places, common railers and brawlers, persons wandering or strolling around from place to place without any lawful purpose or object, habitual loafers, disorderly persons neglecting all lawful business and habitually spending their time by frequenting houses of ill fame, gaming houses, or places where alcoholic beverages are sold or served, persons able to work but habitually living upon the earnings of their wives or minor children shall be deemed vagrants and, upon conviction in the Municipal Court, shall be punished as provided for Class D offenses.[1]

Justice William O. Douglas, a Roosevelt appointee, writing for a unanimous court (Justices Rehnquist and Powell did not participate in this case) was dismissive:

The Jacksonville ordinance makes criminal activities which by modern standards are normally innocent . . . "the habitual wanderer" or, as the ordinance describes it, "common night walkers." We know, however, from experience that sleepless people often walk at night, perhaps hopeful that sleep-inducing relaxation will result.

And he was arch:

Luis Muñoz-Marín, former governor of Puerto Rico, commented once that "loafing" was a national virtue in his Commonwealth, and that it should be encouraged. It is, however, a crime in Jacksonville. . . .

Persons "wandering or strolling" from place to place have been extolled by Walt Whitman and Vachel Lindsay. The qualification "without any lawful purpose or object" may be a trap for innocent acts. Persons "neglecting all lawful business and habitually spending their time by frequenting . . . places where alcoholic beverages are sold or served" would literally embrace many members of golf clubs and city clubs.[2]

Very amusing. The justices, of course, being the very types of people who belong to country clubs, are most unlikely to be troubled by vagrants in their buffered neighborhoods. With one decision, the Court invalidated centuries of commonsense law and practice that kept the public sphere reasonably orderly and civilized for people at all levels of income. Police lost the power to tell derelicts, petty criminals, and bums to move along. Living on the street became a right.

The lower courts piled on. In 1987, St. Petersburg, Florida, passed an ordinance narrowly aimed at purse-snatchers, prostitutes, and drug dealers who congregated at a busy intersection. The law required police to have "probable cause" before arresting a suspect. Nevertheless, the Florida Supreme Court struck down the law, objecting that it was too vague and might implicate those simply hailing cabs.[3]

In 1994, a homeless man in Morristown, New Jersey, was expelled from the public library. Though a number of homeless men had spent time in the library, Richard Kreimer was particularly disgusting. Patrons complained of his foul smell and his tendency to lean close and stare directly at people. In response to complaints, the library issued two regulations. One specified that the library would not permit "staring at another with the intent to annoy" and the other permitted "patrons whose bodily hygiene is so offensive as to constitute a nuisance to other persons" to be ejected. In due course, police escorted Mr. Kreimer from the library.

Kreimer contacted the American Civil Liberties Union and took the library to federal court. Judge Lee Sarokin (whom President Clinton would later appoint to the Court of Appeals) intoned: "If we wish to shield our eyes and noses from the homeless, we should revoke their condition, not their library cards." As to Kreimer's antisocial behavior, Sarokin offered that "our revulsion may be of our own making." The library could not condition access on "behavior, appearance, or hygiene" because to do so would be to impose an "unreasonable wealth classification." While he was at it, Sarokin added that the library could no longer "shhh" people. Kreimer was awarded $230,000 in damages.[4]

It was a liberal impulse that would be expressed again and again in many different contexts—a tendency to exalt personal liberty at the expense of communal order. No behavior, no matter how offensive, if it stopped short of criminality (and sometimes even when it did not), would be discouraged.

At the same time, liberal civil libertarians were agitating in another direction that would help to create the homeless.

## Who Are We to Apply Labels?

In the early 1960s, Americans became aware of abuses in mental hospitals. Both the mentally retarded and the mentally ill were often cruelly neglected in state-run institutions. At any other time, such revelations would have led to scandal and then to reform. But coming as they did in the roiling 1960s, the mistreatment at mental hospitals was hijacked for the counterculture agenda then gaining steam. Perhaps, said the intellectuals, the mentally ill were treated poorly because they refused to conform to the soul-stifling strictures of American life. Perhaps they possessed a higher consciousness that most pedestrian dullards could barely guess at.

The ideas of Thomas Szacz, Erving Goffman, and others gained currency. Szacz, author of *The Myth of Mental Illness*, popularized the idea that mental illness did not exist but was merely a label that a rigid and intolerant society placed upon those who were nonconformists of any stripe. Mental illness, said Szacz to the applause of the academic world, was a social construct, a prejudice, not a diagnosis. Goffman, in his influential book *Asylums*, insisted that most of the symptoms of mental illness displayed by residents of mental hospitals—raving, hearing voices, paranoia—were responses to being locked up, not evidence of illness per se.[5] All institutions, Goffman argued, were more alike than dissimilar. Psychiatrist Willard Gaylin recalls a meeting at which Goffman argued that Groton and Andover (posh private schools) were more similar to Attica prison and Creedmoor State Hospital than they were different.[6] And Ken Kesey, author of *One Flew Over the Cuckoo's Nest*, a best-selling book and movie, popularized the notion that mental institutions were run by Gestapo-type nurses and inhabited by slightly eccentric free spirits who needed nothing more than the keys to their wards.

R. D. Laing, a British psychoanalyst, provided the capstone to the evolving liberationist dogma of the day with his influential *The Politics of Experience*. Laing argued that modern society itself was twisted and unnatural, deformed by materialism and regimentation. Echoing Rousseau's paean to the "noble savage," Laing taught that society's coercion alienated human beings from their instinctive, natural, and intuitive selves. The people society called mentally ill were merely attempting to recapture the ecstatic and intuitive parts of their souls. Who were we, he asked, to label them insane when society itself was so sick?

It would be difficult to overstate Laing's influence among intellectuals, and from there to the larger society. It was but a short jump from Laing's "inner liberation" to the sixties' slogans "Do your own thing" and "Let it all hang out." The mentally ill, intellectuals insisted, already had hold of an "altered consciousness" that the larger society would soon attempt to experience through drugs. Harvard professor Timothy Leary, the guru of LSD, quickly seized upon Laingian ideas to promote a quick route to inner liberation. "Tune in, turn on, drop out" became a catechism for thousands. College dorm rooms were festooned with posters reading "Reality is for people who can't take drugs."

The mentally ill thus became a cultural and political symbol–an example of the repression society imposes on its most creative citizens, its nonconformists. The ground was prepared for the wholesale abandonment of the mentally ill to the tender mercies of the streets. Deinstitutionalization was born. In obedience to the ideas that had captured the medical schools and the universities, states simply unlocked the doors of mental hospitals and wished their patients a cheery goodbye. Legislatures across the country were delighted to shut down mental institutions, since it saved money. Vague promises were offered all around for "community mental health clinics" that would pick up the slack and care for those few mental patients who really were psychotic. But under the sway of Laing and his acolytes, such community mental centers as were built tended to see their mission as curing society of its pathologies rather than caring for the mentally ill. Myron Magnet, in *The Dream and the Nightmare*, described the results:

> . . . Community mental health centers began to busy themselves hectoring landlords of slum housing, setting up remedial education courses, registering the poor to vote so they could cast their ballots for social hygiene, and counseling the worried but mentally sound on how to preserve their mental health.[7]

In other words, the community mental health clinics went about "curing" society, not the mentally ill. Only 6 percent of the clinics had day hospitals. More than 50 percent had no inpatient beds at all, and 33 percent did not have facilities to handle emergencies.[8]

In 1955, state psychiatric hospitals housed some 558,000 patients. By the late 1990s, that number had dropped to 70,000.[9] Bearing in mind that the baby boom population bulge was maturing during those years, the expected number of patients today would have been greater than 900,000.

Thousands of schizophrenics and manic-depressives descended upon the nation's cities. Though antipsychotic drugs were available, many patients, now unsupervised, simply did not take them. One of the hallmarks of mental illness is an inability to understand that one is sick. Confused, insane, and alone, the mentally ill slept in cardboard boxes and curled up in doorways. They pushed their meager belongings through the streets in stolen shopping carts. Their bodies became wracked with parasites, skin lesions, and other diseases. Many became victims of violence and sadism by street criminals. "Youths Set Homeless Man on Fire" reads a not untypical headline from the *New York Times* in 2002.[10] Some starved. Most became addicted to street drugs.

A series of liberal initiatives made treating the homeless mentally ill difficult to impossible. Involuntary commitment laws in many states were diluted to the point that a psychotic person would have to be caught in a violent act in order to be hospitalized without his or her consent. New York's law was particularly narrow, making it nearly impossible to hospitalize the mentally ill unless they requested it. The catch-22, of course, was that the nature of the illness made many schizophrenics deny that they were ill. Consider the case of Mr. B, a psychotic homeless man who lived on the streets of Manhattan in the mid-1990s. He was emaciated and dehydrated but refused to eat because he believed that the CIA was poisoning his food. Dr. Sally Satel, then a psychiatrist at Yale, tells the story:

> The owner of a local package store allowed Mr. B to sleep in the basement for $5 a night, but Mr. B couldn't afford to pay after he began to use all his panhandled change to phone the White House operator and complain about the CIA. He started sleeping on the freezing pavement outside the store; instead of eating, he began stuffing newspaper in his mouth, declaring: "The words will feed my soul."
>
> Concerned, the store owner offered to take Mr. B to the emergency room. When Mr. B refused, the owner called the police as well as the psychiatrist on duty at the local hospital, asking them to take Mr. B to the hospital. "Was Mr. B planning to kill himself or others?" they asked. If not, they were powerless to do anything.
>
> Mr. B became suspicious of his benefactor and fled the neighborhood. His toes became frostbitten, and he wanted to see a doctor. He began limping to a local emergency room but became frightened and turned back when he decided that the doctors must be under CIA control.
>
> Soon, Mr. B collapsed in the street and was brought to a hospital, where doctors removed his gangrenous toes. Finally, in order to be closer to his son, he was transferred to a Connecticut hospital where I worked. . . . That Mr. B's deterioration had to reach such an extreme–and that he had to

leave New York State before he could receive the treatment he so desperately needed—is a tragic indictment of the state's mental health system.[11]

Unlike New York at the time, Connecticut permitted mentally ill people to be treated without their consent if mental illness had seriously impaired their ability to tend to basic needs like food, clothing, shelter, health, and safety. But New York clung to a "danger to self or others" standard for involuntary commitment (until 1999, when a series of murders committed by the homeless insane finally spurred the New York legislature to act). Unless the mentally ill person was caught in an attempted suicide or homicide, he could not be hospitalized and treated without his consent.

As Dr. Satel observed, "Admitting a resistant patient to the hospital is usually an uphill battle for psychiatrists."[12] Liberal civil libertarians, still under the sway of Thomas Szasz and Ken Kesey, and perhaps "The King of Hearts"—a popular sixties' movie in which inmates from a French asylum are actually far saner than their caretakers—thought of the mentally ill as free spirits who should be permitted to express their eccentricities. They ensured that every commitment hearing was run like a criminal trial. Each patient was provided with a lawyer at public expense, a jury trial if requested, and the right to confront witnesses.

## The Right to Sleep Under Bridges

In 1995, Tanya P, a pregnant, homeless, mentally ill woman, was arrested after attempting to set fire to the shelter in which she lived while high on crack. Delivered to Bellevue Hospital, she agreed to undergo treatment with antipsychotic medications. A month before her baby was due, she decided that she was finished with treatment and asked to leave. The hospital refused, citing a law that permitted involuntary drug treatment for pregnant patients. Thanks to legal assistance from the New York Civil Liberties Union (NYCLU), Tanya P sued the hospital and won. The decision, declared NYCLU lawyer

Donna Lieberman, "affirms the principles of equality for women in our society when it comes to medical care. A woman does not lose her constitutional rights when she becomes pregnant."[13] Note that the "principle of equality" at issue here is the "right" to decline medical treatment and to harm one's unborn child.

In 1991, the Giuliani administration in New York City attempted to move a clot of homeless men who were living outside the Fifth Avenue Presbyterian Church into shelters. The church and "homeless advocates" sued, and a liberal judge agreed that they had a "right" to sleep on the street. On another such occasion, TV personality Rosie O'Donnell used her show to send the following message to the mayor: "News flash, Rudy–it's not good to arrest the homeless people."[14] Warming to her subject, O'Donnell declared, "He's out of control, this guy. Sure, just, you know, arrest all the homeless people."[15] During her run for the U.S. Senate, Hillary Clinton chimed in as well on Giuliani's homeless policy. Christmas, she admonished, was about "the birth of a homeless child. . . . Criminalizing the homeless with mass arrests for those whose only offense is that they have no home is wrong."[16]

In the 1980s, Joyce Brown, aka Billie Boggs (she liked to be called by the name of the TV character she admired), became a national celebrity. She was a raving thirty-nine-year-old woman who took up residence above a steam grate on New York's Second Avenue. She screamed obscenities at people who passed by, urinated against the wall of the local bank, and defecated on the street. When black men passed her she would shout, "Kiss my black ass, you m—f—nigger." She would then lift her skirt and shake her naked rear end at them. "Kiss my black ass. Come s—my big black d—!"[17] When pedestrians offered her less than she was hoping for in handouts, she would upbraid them volubly and often set fire to the bills she was handed. But when Mayor Ed Koch attempted to have her committed involuntarily to a treatment facility, she phoned the New York Civil Liberties Union. As Myron Magnet detailed in his excellent book on the underclass, *The Dream and the Nightmare,* her commitment hearing and all that followed became a form of political theater:

. . . the city, backed by expert testimony that Brown was severely insane, argued that she was a danger to herself, slowly
dying from self-neglect. The NYCLU saw her predicament
with different eyes. In its view, she was the victim of a city
drive to hide evidence of its failed housing policy. Her only
lapse: affronting the aesthetic sensibilities of New York's
Haves, to whom the mayor was obsequiously pandering.

Abnormal? the NYCLU's expert witness demanded. Not
Joyce Brown. Do not cabdrivers also pee on the street? Does
not every modern movie use bad language? Hadn't protesters burned draft cards, just as Brown—presumably in a similar protest against imperialist America's oppressiveness—
symbolically burned dollar bills?

. . . A month later, having made the rounds of the TV
talk shows, she was the guest speaker at a Harvard Law
School forum on "The Homeless Crisis: A Street View." "We
need housing, housing, and more housing," she declared.
"My only problem was that I didn't have a place to live and
that's the city's fault." Scarcely two weeks later, she was back
on the street, screaming and panhandling again.[18]

Though Americans from Miami to San Francisco to Washington
sought to help the homeless, they were stymied by liberals who
rushed into court to defend their "right" to reject treatment.
"Lawyers are doing what they think is right in terms of civil rights,
whether it is good for the person or not," acknowledged Bruce Ennis,
a NYCLU attorney.[19]

In 1989, the city's Metropolitan Transportation Authority, in a
bid to clean up the subway system and get the homeless into more
suitable situations, issued a series of regulations. These prohibited:
vandalizing cars with graffiti, jumping or evading turnstiles or other
fare-beating tactics, solicitation, panhandling, drinking alcoholic
beverages in the subway system, littering, urinating in public areas,
lying down on the floor, and blocking stairs or exits. It was, in retro-

spect, a rather feeble attempt to enforce the bare minimum of civilized public conduct and it reveals the pathetic decline in civil order New York had inflicted upon itself.

Advocates for the homeless rushed to object. They responded by demanding "nooks and crannies" for the homeless–places within subway stations where they would be free to sleep, eat, and presumably eliminate–and protested that panhandling had to be permitted. The Transit Authority declined. The homeless advocates filed a class action lawsuit in federal court, and the district court agreed with them. Panhandling, the court ruled, was protected speech under the First Amendment.[20]

## Reagan's Legacy

It's enough to make one cynical. Could it be that liberals were reluctant to see the homeless mentally ill cared for because their presence on the streets of America's largest cities provided such a convenient stick with which to beat the Reagan and Bush I administrations, and then society generally? For more than a decade, the homeless became liberals' favorite moral crusade. But, for the political barb to sting, they first had to becloud the distinction between those who were temporarily down on their luck (a small percentage of the so-called homeless) and the drug addicts, alcoholics, and former mental patients who comprised the vast majority.

Thus, *Time* magazine noted in 1987:

> The stereotype of the homeless as vagrants or mentally ill is increasingly out of date. Families with children constitute one-third of the homeless population in 26 major cities, according to a study released last week by the U.S. Conference of Mayors. Moreover, 22 percent of the homeless hold full- or part-time jobs, but the lack of affordable housing means some low-wage workers cannot find shelter. . . .
> The task force blames the homeless crisis on the Reagan

administration's cuts in federal housing aid, food stamps, and programs to care for the mentally ill. . . . [21]

*U.S. News* had a similar take, estimating that "500,000 youngsters" were growing up "uneducated, unhealthy and angry at society."[22] ABC's John Martin condensed the liberal lesson nicely: "In the 1980s, the Reagan years, the amount of government money spent to build low-income housing was cut drastically. Then the homeless began to appear on streets and on doorsteps and housing became a visible human problem."[23]

The numbers, of course, were from outer space. Mitch Snyder, leader of the homeless advocacy group Coalition for Creative Non-Violence, became the media darling of the 1980s. S. Robert Lichter surveyed television news on the subject of homelessness for the period 1986 through 1989 and found that homeless people were quoted far more often than any government official or academic expert, and Snyder was quoted more frequently than either Ronald Reagan or George Bush.[24] It was Snyder who originated the figure of three million homeless. He was frank about how he came up with it:

> Everybody demanded it. Everybody said we want a number. . . . We got on the phone, we made a lot of calls, we talked to a lot of people, and we said, "Okay, here are some numbers." They have no meaning, no value.[25]

Still, the number was repeated until it was taken as true. A typical network news report, explained former CBS news correspondent Bernard Goldberg in his book *Bias*, would focus on a picturesque family, usually white and consisting of a married mother and father and their children. Such families, viewers were invited to conclude, were typical of the homeless in America. While there were occasional acknowledgments that most of the homeless did not fit this image, the viewer was left with the indelible impression of "people just like us" facing ruin. In a 1987 report for ABC News, Jackie Judd put it this way:

It's a problem growing larger. The National Coalition for the Homeless surveyed 20 cities. It found a 25 percent increase in the number of homeless in the last 12 months and estimates there are three million Americans nationwide without a permanent roof over their heads.

. . . Who are they? Certainly there are the derelicts, the mentally ill, the underclass who fall through society's safety nets. But the fastest-growing group is down-on-their-luck poor families. It's a problem critics blame on the administration's housing cuts.[26]

On CBS's *Evening News*, reporter Lee Cowan told viewers:

On any given day, the nation's economic downturn can be measured by those down on their luck, and that population is on the rise. There are now more homeless families on the street than ever before, up an estimated 19 percent. . . . There are now more homeless families in Manhattan than since the Great Depression.[27]

Over at NBC's *Dateline* program, they must have consulted the same expert, because the following night, reporter John Hockenberry said:

Tonight we're going to show you a new true face of homelessness in America. Today's homeless are families, and the families you will meet have done everything right and yet there's no place for them. Still, they struggle to find a home. . . . There are more families homeless in New York City now than at any time in the last 20 years . . . in numbers, it's estimated, not seen since the Great Depression.[28]

*New York Times* columnist Anna Quindlen was also certain that the homeless proved something about American society: "If empty shelves became a symbol for the failure of communism in the Soviet Union, people living in cardboard boxes are the most visible sign that

America is on the skids. They are living, breathing symbols of an economy that, no matter what the astigmatism president says, is a mess."[29]

Speaking at the Massachusetts Institute of Technology, Susan Marsh of the National Coalition for the Homeless explained that homelessness was caused by lack of housing. Homelessness, she said, is "an economic issue, not a personal one." The image of the "single man with a substance abuse problem" was not representative. Rather, Marsh asserted, most of the homeless were families headed by females. "Housing is a right that should be accessible to all people."[30]

Even when the mental disabilities of the homeless population had to be acknowledged, a way was found to blame that too on the conservatives. When a deranged man shot several people at the U.S. Capitol, Kelly O'Donnell had this to say on NBC's *Today* show:

> Could it have been prevented? Did the mental health system do enough? . . . During the Reagan era federal spending for mental health dropped about 25 percent. Funding has continued to go down ever since. Today as many as half of the homeless are believed to be the untreated mentally ill.[31]

Liberal educators have propagandized children and adolescents about the homeless from their perches in classrooms. A teacher handbook prepared by the Graduate College of Education at the University of Massachusetts in Boston offered teachers a number of lessons about the homeless to share with their students. Among them:

> How the underlying economic structure and attitudes of our society have prevented us from solving the problem of homelessness. . . . One of the philosophical issues raised by this unit is the contrast between American ideals and the reality of the American, capitalist system.[32]

The handbook suggests classroom activities, such as dividing the children into groups and forcing one or two students at a time, through no fault of their own, to become "deskless." Another invites teachers to share with students the "fact" that "the top 1 percent have 73 percent of the wealth."[33]

Children's books offering highly romanticized and sentimental views of homeless people have proliferated. Large public libraries have at least a dozen titles. There is Maurice Sendak's *We Are All in the Dumps with Jack and Guy,* Frank Asch's *Goodbye House,* David McPhail's *The Teddy Bear,* and DyAnne DiSalvo-Ryan's *Uncle Willie and the Soup Kitchen,* to name just four.

Robert Hayes, another celebrity "homeless advocate," drove home the political message: "The homeless are indeed the most egregious symbol of a cruel economy, an unresponsive government, a festering value system."[34] Kay Young McChesney, a sociologist, declared in 1987 that "What we are dealing with is a collapse of moral leadership in this country . . . it's hard to remember that this is America and not Calcutta."[35]

*Time* magazine used a familiar technique to dramatize the issue:

> On the morning that Ronald Reagan stood under the Capitol dome and delivered his Inaugural paean to boundless opportunity, Leander V. Gilmore, 61, of "no fixed address," was found frozen to death in an abandoned house a few miles away. . . . Outside a Washington shelter for the homeless, ragged street people gaped as a purple van from Ridgewell's ("caterers to the elite") pulled up and tuxedoed waiters hopped out to unload leftover canapés, whole hams, mounds of crab claws, shrimp and quiche. That night at the shelter, 1,000 homeless dined like lobbyists.[36]

Years later, the Department of Housing and Urban Development performed a comprehensive survey and reported that there were between 250,000 and 300,000 homeless in the country. Even that figure may have been too high. HUD estimated that Chicago alone had 25,000, but when an independent academic group counted, it found only 2,700.[37]

As for the composition of the homeless population, most surveys have agreed that some 84 percent are male, 97 percent are single (or at least without a spouse at the time of their homelessness), 33 percent have been diagnosed with a mental illness, 27 percent are alcoholics, and 38 percent are in poor health.[38]

## The Mythical Housing Shortage

Many of the homeless mentally ill have wound up in institutions, but not in the ones where they belong. They now populate our prisons in pathetic numbers. According to the Justice Department, 16 percent of American inmates have serious psychiatric illnesses. In New York, a survey of 137 individuals referred for forensic evaluation after arrest found that 50 percent were homeless.[39] Mixed in with the general population of prisoners, they are subject to abuse. Their often bizarre behavior ensures that they will be victimized both by fellow prisoners and by guards who have no special training in understanding mental illness or caring for the psychotic.

But "homeless advocates" haven't noticed. They are focused on solving a nonexistent problem—the mythical "lack of affordable housing." They pointed to the decline in appropriations for HUD's subsidized housing program between 1978 and 1991. But as Christopher Jencks explains in *The Homeless,* his eminently fair and measured analysis of the problem, this figure was highly misleading:

> This assertion is correct, but unless you are a housing junkie, it is also misleading. Contrary to what a lay reader might imagine, "appropriations" are not a measure of how much HUD spends in a given year on housing subsidies. Instead, appropriations measure the increase in HUD's future commitments. A cut in appropriations is not, therefore, a cut in the size of HUD's programs; it is a cut in the rate at which these programs will grow.[40]

When HUD undertakes to subsidize a housing unit or a family, Jencks explained, the commitment stretches over decades. Due to the large number of commitments begun between 1977 and 1981, HUD would have continued to add subsidized housing to the market well into Reagan's first term even if Congress did not make any further authorizations for new spending. But Congress did authorize new spending—another 1 million subsidized housing units between 1982 and 1989. Further, when the authorizations undertaken during the Carter years expired, Congress renewed them all. So the total number of subsidized housing units grew from 2.9 million in 1977 to 4.7 million in 1992.[41] The number of shelter beds increased from 98,000 at the start of the decade to 275,000 at the end without appreciably reducing the numbers of people sleeping on sidewalks.[42]

## The Federal Cure?

The combination of media distortion and activist lobbying was successful in opening the government spigot. The federal government made former mental patients eligible for Medicaid, Medicare, Supplemental Security Income (SSI), the Disability Insurance Trust Fund, food stamps, and housing assistance—but only if recipients were no longer in state treatment facilities. This added to the incentives already in place for states to empty their institutions. As E. Fuller Torrey pointed out in the *City Journal,* it changed the way state officials framed the issue of care: "No longer did mental health officials ask, 'What is in the best interests of patients?' The question now became 'What will the federal government pay for?' "[43] The newly independent mentally ill were thus receiving between $500 and $700 a month with no strings attached and no questions asked. A great deal of that money went to finance drug and alcohol habits, and, in effect, to subsidize vagrancy.

The federal government also initiated fifty different programs administered by eight different agencies to aid the homeless. Most of these were authorized in the McKinney Bill signed by President

Reagan in 1987. Under McKinney, the Department of Housing and Urban Development administers four big programs designed to end homelessness in America: the "Emergency Shelter Grants," "Supportive Housing Programs," "Shelter Plus Care," and "Section 8 Single-Room Occupancy Moderate Rehabilitation." Sixteen programs—costing $1.7 billion in 2001—were targeted only for the homeless. The homeless were also eligible for another thirty-four federal programs, including housing, health care, job training, and transportation. Twenty-six programs administered by six agencies offer food and nutrition services.[44]

Big cities like New York and San Francisco have lavished services on the homeless only to be shocked, shocked by their increasing numbers. New York spends $1 billion a year on the homeless.[45] San Francisco has made itself the Mecca of the homeless. Starting in the 1980s, under Mayor Art Agnos, a devout believer that the homeless were victims of Reaganism, the city began offering a $345-a-month general assistance allotment for single adults, thousands of freshly made beds in shelters across the city, free health and dental care, and a hammock of other services and "supports."[46] Agnos instructed the police not to arrest the homeless who slept in public parks. Within a very short time, San Francisco was overrun. Civic Center Plaza, in front of City Hall, became a camping ground that was quickly dubbed "Camp Agnos."[47]

In fact, it was a source of confusion and frustration for many liberal mayors during the 1990s to discover that no matter how many shelters they built to provide for the homeless, it never seemed to be enough; they were always full. As CNN put it, "People are beginning to wonder whether building shelters only exaggerates the numbers: they argue that poor people who wouldn't otherwise be homeless are attracted to shelters as a way of quickly tapping into government assistance."

There's a thought. The CNN report might have added that shelters also provided an easy means of escaping from under the roof of your dyspeptic sister or annoying mother. "It didn't take long for people to figure out that this was a way to scam the system," acknowledged Andrew Cuomo, secretary of housing and urban development in the Clinton administration.[48]

All the while, of course, network television continued its drumbeat (supplied by liberal advocacy groups). On CBS's *This Morning* program, for example, Charles Osgood intoned, "It is estimated that by the year 2000, 19 million Americans will be homeless unless something is done and done now."

Similarly, CNN's Lou Waters warned:

> A new research report is warning that homelessness in this country could easily double or triple if there is a mild recession. Current estimates on the number of homeless people in the United States range from about 655,000 to four million, and the study by researchers at Rutgers University says the total is growing 20 to 40 percent each year. It says there are now up to 40 million Americans living on the knife edge of homelessness, many of them just one paycheck or one domestic argument from the streets.[49]

This was the third leg of the liberal contribution to homelessness— the first being judicial invalidation of vagrancy and related laws, the second being paying the homeless to remain in their condition. Having carefully obfuscated the true nature of the homeless population— 85 percent of whom were alcoholics, drug addicts, mentally ill, or a combination of all three—liberal policy makers found themselves offering "services" and "housing" that served only to perpetuate the problem.

What most of the homeless truly needed was recommitment to mental institutions (involuntarily where required) or mandated care as outpatients (with the proviso that failure to take medicine and comply with a treatment plan would result in involuntary hospitalization). The liberal position came to resemble that which was satirized by Anatole France: "The law, in its majestic equality, forbids the rich as well as the poor to sleep under bridges, to beg in the streets, and to steal bread." But its modern form would substitute

"The law, in its majestic equality, permits the sane as well as the insane to sleep in urine-soaked alleys, to rant at strangers, and to pick
amid the trash for food." Or, as Heather MacDonald has put it: "Give
the 'advocates' credit for this: they may not have done a thing for the
'homeless,' but they have accomplished a tour de force–turning
cruel neglect into self-righteous virtue."[50]

For those homeless who are not mentally ill, the warm shower of
entitlements and no-strings-attached goodies that has descended
upon them since the mid-1980s is an irresistible enticement to remain irresponsible and dissolute. There are, of course, always unfortunate individuals who find themselves in trouble through no fault of
their own, but the current system of public and private shelters is
more than adequate to help one cope with life's unavoidable miseries. The existence of a large, intractable homeless population,
however, is a creation of liberal soft-headedness.

## The "Wild Man of 96th Street"

The homeless mentally ill have undoubtedly suffered the most from
liberal concern, but society as a whole has been punished as well. Because liberals insisted upon romanticizing the homeless, they were
unable to deal with the dramatic and painful consequences of having
thousands of mentally ill, alcoholic, and drug-addicted people wandering the streets unsupervised.

Paris Drake would certainly be called homeless, but he hardly fit
the sentimental imagery the "advocates" prefer. He was arrested for
the first time at age fourteen. He served time for drug-dealing,
weapons possession, burglary, larceny, and assault, serving sentences ranging from one day to four years.[51] One day in November
1999 he was in a particularly foul temper and picked up a paving
stone and smashed the skull of Nicole Barrett, a young woman who
happened to be walking by. She survived, but barely.

In the mid-1990s, Larry Hogue became known as the "wild man
of 96th Street." A large man, Hogue was certainly insane. He was
also addicted to crack. Hogue announced his presence in the neigh-

borhood by strewing trash over the sidewalks and inserting gasoline soaked rags into the gas tanks of cars parked along 96th Street. He would also break off the cars' side-view mirrors. When he had smashed one New Yorker's car windows for the second time, she pressed charges. In response, he threatened her with a lead pipe and leapt out at her at night. He chased another woman into the vestibule of her building, screaming and pounding on the glass when he could get no further. Hogue hurled cinder blocks through the windows of the Christian Science Church, causing $10,000 damage. And he shoved a sixteen-year-old girl into the path of an oncoming truck, which had to swerve wildly to avoid her.

Though Hogue was arrested at least nine times, he failed to serve longer than one year for any offense. And his tour of the mental health system was like something out of Alice in Wonderland. As Heather MacDonald described it:

> Hogue has been in and out of mental hospitals since 1972, but he has never been hospitalized for longer than six months. Usually the hospital releases him within 24 hours after the police bring him in. The city's psychiatric emergency rooms are intimately familiar with him. On one occasion the police were turned away from six emergency rooms with Hogue restrained in the back seat.[52]

When a group of neighbors asked for a meeting with Hogue's medical team, they were astonished at what they were told:

> The hospital staff told the victims, "Hogue is more violent than you think, but we can't tell you what's in his record." Many of the community representatives were crying, "Why are you telling us this without protecting us?" . . . Hogue's medical team answered that they were "unable to hold him because of his rights." When the effect of the crack wears off, the hospital team claimed, "he becomes a model patient, and we have to release him."[53]

This charade continued for years. Hogue haunted the neighborhood, threatening people's lives, scratching cars with screwdrivers, brandishing a machete, screaming, charging, and on one occasion, painting himself green. *Sixty Minutes* did a segment about him, filming him cashing his VA check, getting high at a crack house, and rampaging through the streets. He was arrested countless times and treated in psychiatric emergency rooms only to be released again—"because of his rights." The rights of the community to live free from fear, vandalism, and filth went unrecognized. A breezy Robert Levy of the New York chapter of the ACLU offered, regarding the Hogue case, "Society can't eliminate risk."[54]

That includes risk posed by Julio Perez, a mentally ill homeless man who had been convicted of a felony, who shoved Edgar Rivera onto the subway tracks in April 1999, causing both of Rivera's legs to be severed.

In another case, Buford Furrow Jr. had tried to commit suicide several times, drank so heavily that he passed out, committed several assaults, and voiced extreme hatred toward all nonwhites. He told police of his fantasy about going to a mall and randomly shooting people, and when he attempted to have himself admitted to a psychiatric facility, he threatened to stab two women there. In October 1998 he opened fire on children at a Jewish Community Center in Los Angeles.[55]

In Salt Lake City, social workers were familiar with Brian David Mitchell and his wife, Wanda Ilene Barzee. He was, they believed, a schizophrenic who needed treatment, but there was nothing they could do. The homeless Mitchells are now accused of kidnapping fourteen-year-old Elizabeth Smart, having originally gained entry into the Smart home by doing odd jobs.

In a similar case, a woman in Akron, Ohio, who was doubtless influenced by the media's misrepresentation of the homeless as people "just like us but down on their luck," told the *Washington Times* she had a "save the world policy." In 2002, she offered a spare bedroom to Mike Dennison, because "he had no place to live." She did not know that he had a criminal record that included forgery, car theft, and sexual assault. He was arrested after raping the woman's eight-year-old daughter.[56]

Reuben Harris pushed Song Sin to her death under a New York subway train in 1995. He was an untreated paranoid schizophrenic.

Colin Ferguson, a schizophrenic, opened fire on a Long Island train in 1993, killing six people and wounding nineteen as he methodically walked up and down the train's aisle blasting people in the face. Ferguson was a black racist originally represented by left-wing attorney William Kunstler, who wanted to mount a "black rage" defense, but Ferguson rejected this strategy, preferring to represent himself.

Juan Carlos Aguilar, a homeless thirty-five-year-old, was arrested in Glendale, Arizona, on charges that he molested no fewer than nine little girls, ages four to ten, at a public library.[57]

Jackson Roman had fired a shotgun onto the tracks of a subway station in 1987. He was treated and released. He groped a passenger on a subway car. Doctors said he was schizophrenic. He even spent an entire year in a psychiatric facility, but was released to a "supervised mental health program" from which he walked away. Officials began searching for him and contacting shelters. They were about to phone the police when they heard that he had been arrested for attempted murder. He shoved Latchmie Ramsamy, a nurse and mother of two, onto the subway tracks. She lost a foot, suffered several skull fractures, and sustained neck and spinal cord injuries.[58]

Andrew Goldstein signed himself into mental hospitals thirteen times over a two-year period. Each time, he was medicated and then released within a few days or weeks, despite a history of violent attacks on strangers. In January 1999, he shoved thirty-two-year-old Kendra Webdale to her death in front of a subway train.[59]

The Justice Department estimates that there are about one thousand killings by untreated psychotic people in the United States every year.[60]

Following Webdale's death, New York joined forty other states adopting "Kendra's Law," a mandatory treatment statute. But the habits of several decades seem to die hard. In 2004, a psychotic man caused pandemonium in a subway station by tossing metal objects and other trash onto the third rail, causing a series of explosions and fires. Hundreds of passengers fled the scene in terror. It turns out that Bonergy Quelal, who had a long rap sheet, had recently been released from Cornell Medical Center's psychiatric ward despite the pleas of his family to keep him locked up.[61]

Intractable homelessness has also degraded life in America's cities for reasons going beyond crime. The presence of multitudes of aggressive, bizarre, and filthy homeless people is destroying what was arguably America's most beautiful city, San Francisco. Across the nation, cities are losing residents and businesses due to the atmosphere of threat and disorder the homeless help to create. When the Commonwealth Fund and the Manhattan Institute conducted a survey of former New York City residents, 59 percent said they had moved out of the city to improve their "quality of life." Sixty percent responded that graffiti, homeless people, noise, and panhandlers contributed to their decision to leave.[62]

Homelessness came into being because liberal policy makers embraced a series of foolish ideas. They themselves were alienated from society, and so they romanticized the mentally ill and transformed them into social critics. This was unjust both to American society and to the mentally ill themselves, who paid a terrible price for the liberals' social experiment.

Having blundered badly by dumping hundreds of thousands of mentally ill people onto the streets, the libertarian impulse in liberalism–most often represented by the ACLU–insisted that living on the street was a right. Judges rushed in to agree that people could not be forced into shelters–not even when the thermometer dropped below freezing. Nor could they be involuntarily committed to mental hospitals–not unless they were setting fires or assaulting strangers.

Liberals then offered an engraved invitation to anyone on the fringes of society who might want to escape a less than ideal living arrangement by funding homelessness as an alternative lifestyle. Hundreds of government programs and government-funded shelters swelled the population of vagrants.

When the homeless then dotted many street corners around the nation, liberals added the coup de grace: This terrible epidemic of homelessness, they cried, was all the fault of heartless conservatism! Liberals made great use of those pictures of ragged men and confused women. It confirmed their belief (and helped to persuade the undecided) that America is a fundamentally cruel and inhumane country whose economic system rewards the wealthy and oppresses the poor.

In fact, of course, there has never been a more humane country in the whole history of humanity. But liberals have shown that terribly inhumane policies can issue from ideologically blinkered people who congratulate themselves on their own virtue.

# Chapter Six
# THE LIBERAL WAR ON RIGOR AND PATRIOTISM IN AMERICA'S CLASSROOMS

If you care, really care, about the well-being of young people and particularly of the poor, then you must really, truly care about what happens to American children when they step into their classrooms 180 days per year. Liberals certainly loudly proclaim their concern about education, but their interest has proved toxic for the basic competence of suburban schools while proving disastrous for the inner-city schools containing the most vulnerable populations.

Liberals own education in America. They have been at the forefront of every major education reform (until vouchers—a conservative reform aimed at giving parents a choice about where to educate their children) of the past century. They have promoted progressive methods, whole language, new math, open classrooms, whole math, noncompetitive grading, teachers as "facilitators," bilingual education, child-centered education, cooperative learning, outcome-based education, and more. Education in America has been a liberal enterprise for more than a century. Progressive reformers have brought us one innovation after another, even as lay people have struggled, usually unsuccessfully, to keep schools focused on the basics. Schools of education are dominated by liberalism, as are teachers' unions, textbook writers, and administrators.

Liberals are romantics. They believe that children come into the world possessed of deep and inspiring knowledge and that we would do well to simply unlock this treasure. Education should accordingly be fun—a process of discovery more than instruction.

Though children, liberals tell us, are "natural" learners and wiser than adults in many ways, it requires gobs and gobs of money to release all of that knowledge from their little heads. All liberals insist that we are failing to "invest" properly in our children. Pick a year, any year among the past forty, and you will find liberal politicians (including some Republicans) claiming that we are parsimonious with education dollars. In 1965, inaugurating one of the first federal education spending programs, President Lyndon Johnson declared, "The answer for all our national problems comes down to a single word and that word is education."[1] In 1984, Democratic presidential candidate Walter Mondale expounded the same boilerplate:

> Getting this nation's schools back on track will be one of the top priorities of the Mondale administration. Everything depends on strong schools and strong colleges: a healthy economy, a strong defense, social justice, opportunity for all. There is no reason whatsoever why the next generation of Americans cannot be the best educated and trained in this nation's history.[2]

It was a long way from it. But instead of probing the reasons behind our failures, liberals continued to sing the same song. Nearly twenty years later, Nancy Pelosi (D-CA) could say pretty much the same thing as if the subject were still fresh. "Investing in our children is the best investment we can make. And Head Start is an extraordinarily effective investment."[3] Actually, Head Start has never been shown to be effective–a subject to which we will turn soon. But in any case, to read liberal statements on education is to encounter a stuck needle. In 2000, Al Gore said virtually the same things without even a thought as to how the old money had been spent. He proposed an additional $176 billion over ten years on universal preschool, special education, after-school programs, and more. "We've got to recruit 100,000 new teachers," Gore declared, "and I have budgeted for that. We've got to reduce the class size. . . . And we ought to make college tuition deductible up to $10,000 a year. I want the federal government . . . to make improvement in our schools the number one priority."[4] Or was it Kerry? His 2004 proposal reads exactly the same way.

The truth, of course, is that we've been doing it the liberal way for forty years. We've sat by as liberals have drained education of rigor, of content, and of the most essential ingredients to good citizenship. We've catered to every minority, often to the detriment of those minorities; genuflected before the power of the teachers' unions; indulged in every mindless fad concocted by schools of education; and turned out citizens who can scarcely read a newspaper or balance their checkbooks. Perhaps worst of all, we've permitted the liberals who control education to teach American history with a jaundiced, cynical, and left-wing bias. When the World War II memorial was dedicated in Washington, D.C., on Memorial Day 2004, the *Washington Post* ran a story about what high school students in the area know about the war. Tiffany Charles, a B student, was typical. She could not name the president who served during World War II, nor could she name a single battle or any general. But she is quite aware the United States interned Japanese-Americans during the war. Of seventy-six students surveyed by the *Post*, 66 percent knew about the Japanese-American internment but only 33 percent could name even one American general.[5]

## All the Money They Need

How long will the charade go on? Each and every time a Democrat demands more money for education, he or she should be asked how we spent all of the previous money and how well students performed. Full stop.

In 1965, the average per-pupil expenditure for primary and secondary schools students was $3,000 per year. By 1995, it had more than doubled to $6,500 (in constant dollars).[6] Performance (i.e., test scores) did not improve. Indeed, in many areas, performance has declined. Spending rose in every category—salaries, equipment, special programs, transportation, and administration. Spending also rose at every governmental level—local, state, and federal. By 2003–2004, local, state, and federal governments spent *half a trillion* dollars on elementary and secondary education.[7] It tends to put into perspective that 1980s slogan, emblazoned on thousands of hippie T-shirts, that read: "Wouldn't it be great if the schools had all the money they needed and the Pentagon had to hold a bake sale to buy a bomber?" In 2003–2004, the United States spent $375 billion on defense, so education spending *far* outstrips defense spending. We've already reached the nirvana liberals have been preaching for decades–but don't hold your breath waiting for them to admit it. They simply pocket the gains and persist in bleating for more and more.

The national average per-pupil expenditure in 2001 was $8,745. In some states, spending was much higher. The District of Columbia, for example, is near the top, spending $15,122 per pupil.[8] And how does this munificence affect student performance? The District of Columbia's students are at the very bottom of national rankings.

For more than three centuries, Americans educated their children in private, religious, and local public schools. Children thus educated managed to build the United States into the world's largest economy and preeminent military power. Yet in 1979, the Democrats discovered that the United States could not go forward without a federal Department of Education. Democrats and the new department's chief beneficiary, the National Education Association, quieted fears about its cost and intrusiveness by assuring critics that the department would be modest. And so it was, at first. At its birth, the department's budget was $14 billion and it employed 450 people. But the new Department of Education followed the iron law of federal spending, which reads: Federal programs always spend at least triple what they are projected to spend. By 2001 the department's budget had soared to $43 billion and its workforce increased to 4,800 without, as Martin Gross has tartly noted, educating a single child.[9]

It's actually worse than that. Not only has the federal Department of Education failed to educate a single child, it has foisted upon local schools throughout the nation the fads and enthusiasms of its Washington-based bureaucracy. These include circulating curriculum guides to children as young as kindergarten age instructing them on how to recognize and deal with sexual harassment. Five-year-olds are taught to say, "Stop it! That's sexual harassment and sexual harassment is against the law."[10] In the wake of the Columbine massacre, educrats circulated antibullying curricula. In 1996, when the Clinton administration's feminists were in charge at the Department of Education, the department's Office of Civil Rights issued so many regulations about sexual harassment that school boards were worried sick. As Christina Hoff Sommers reported, "The National School Board Association has complained that the Education Department's guidelines 'appear to be more involved with trying to help plaintiff's attorneys win cases against school districts.' "[11]

## "Buckets of Money"

Perhaps the most emotionally charged accusation liberals have lodged against America's public education system is that of unequal funding. This, they feel sure, is the explanation for everything that is wrong with public schools–particularly inner-city schools populated by black and Hispanic youngsters.

*New York Times* columnist Bob Herbert voiced the conventional wisdom in 2002 when he condemned: "the chronic lack of resources that has condemned one generation of youngsters after another to a public school experience that is all too frequently inadequate, and in some instances little more than a joke."[12] Andrew Hacker, in *Two Nations: Black and White, Separate, Hostile, Unequal*, declared:

> That black children have not been well served by the schools
> hardly needs recounting. In the view of growing numbers of
> black educators, the reasons are inherently racial. In all parts
> of the country, as they see it, school systems are organized
> and administered by white officials who have little under-
> standing of the needs of black children. Even in schools that
> have black principals and are staffed largely by black teach-
> ers, state rules shape most of the curriculum, often limiting

the choice of books and imposing uniform testing. To a casual
visitor, such a school may seem "all black." Yet further obser-
vation reveals the influence of white power and authority.[13]

The notion that inner-city schools are in the deplorable shape
they're in because of lack of funding is an article of faith in liberal circles. Speaking at a New York school in 2002, Jonathan Kozol, author
of *Death at an Early Age* and *Savage Inequalities*, was asked whether
throwing more money at schools would make any difference. "Yes!
Yes!" he exclaimed, "Buckets of money! Just throw it down from the
skies!"[14] Even the two most recent Republican presidents have
thrown money at education. During George W. Bush's first three
years in office, spending on education increased by $56 billion. Nev-
ertheless, Senator Blanche Lincoln (D-AK) protested in 2002 that
"President Bush and his allies in Congress have placed education reform on a starvation diet."[15]

Jonathan Kozol has argued passionately that disparities in funding account for the poor performance of America's urban schools.
The theme is echoed in courtrooms across the United States as the
American Civil Liberties Union brings suits against school districts,
arguing that funding disparities violate the equal protection clause of
the Constitution. In 1991, *Time* magazine reported the story this way:

> The notion of equal opportunity is central to the American
> ideal. For that goal to have any meaning, it must be rooted in
> an education system that gives every child a chance to suc-
> ceed. But for decades, a gulf has been widening between the
> quality of public schooling for children of privilege and that
> for those born in poverty. By relying on local property taxes as
> a crucial source of funds, the U.S. has created a caste system of
> public education that is increasingly separate and unequal.[16]

Rep. Maxine Waters (D-CA) asserted that "Our children are failing because, in many cases, there's just plain lack of resources in districts that are poor. . . ."[17]

But as Abigail and Stephen Thernstrom proved in *No Excuses: Closing the Racial Gap in Learning*, actual disparities in spending between inner cities and suburbs are actually quite negligible.

> Minority children are more likely to live in big cities, where everything is more expensive: transportation, janitorial and food services, housing and other living costs for teachers. Big-city students also cost more to educate because a higher proportion are classified as Limited English Proficient or as in need of "special education." . . . When adjustments are made for these differences, it turns out that districts with more minority students did have a little less money. But the differences were surprisingly small . . . a discrepancy of just 6.5 percent.[18]

## Good Money After Bad

How much of education spending goes into the classroom? In the 1950s, before the federal fire hose of cash was trained on our schools, 80 percent of all employees in public schools were teachers. Today, in nearly every major urban school district in the nation, teachers are a *minority* of school district employees. From 1960 to 1984, student enrollment increased by 9 percent while the number of teachers employed increased by 57 percent. But the number of principals and other supervisors ballooned by 79 percent during the same period. The number of other staff, including specialists, counselors, psychologists, and aides, increased by 500 percent.[19] The Los Angeles superintendent of schools rode to work in a chauffeur-driven car.[20]

In 1990, Wayne Johnson, then head of the United Teachers of Los Angeles, went public when he discovered the level of waste in the Los Angeles Unified School District budget. In an article for the union magazine *United Teacher*, Johnson wrote:

> This is going to infuriate you. It will also shock and disgust you. . . . In a district with 600,000 students and a budget of

$3.5 billion, the people in charge spent only 2% on books and supplies for kids and 6% for certified administrators' salaries. The district spends 36% of its budget on teachers' salaries plus textbooks and supplies. The question should then be asked: What is the remaining 64% of the budget spent on that is more important than teachers and books and supplies for kids?

$1,027,500,000 was spent on running the offices at 450 North Grand and the Region Administrative Offices. This figure does not include any administration costs actually on school campuses. That $1,027,500,000 to run non-school-based administrative offices comes to 31% of the total budget.

Almost one-third of the District's $3.5 billion budget was spent on people who never see a kid—and they spend only $83 million on textbooks and supplies for kids![21]

In New York City, the situation is similar. When two education authors, Terry Moe and John Chubb, contacted the New York City public schools attempting to discover how many administrative employees worked at central headquarters, they were met with delays, transfers of calls, and promises to get the information at some later date. As Sol Stern recounts in his excellent book *Breaking Free*, they never did get an accurate count, though the number was suspected to hover around 7,000 (for a student population of about 1 million).[22] But when Moe and Chubb contacted the Catholic Archdiocese of New York and asked the same question, he was asked to hold for a minute. ". . . the aide said that if he stayed on the line he would have an answer shortly. As he waited, Chubb could hear someone counting heads—'one, two, three, four.' The aide then got back on the phone and told him that a total of twelve people worked at central headquarters."[23] The Catholic Schools educate 150,000 students.[24] This works out to one administrator for every 12,500 students in the Catholic system, versus one administrator for every 142 students in the public system.

As recently as 2003, House Minority Leader Nancy Pelosi was

calling proposed education spending "appalling" and proclaiming that without even more funding it would be "impossible for the schools to meet the mandates [of the No Child Left Behind Act]."[25]

Liberals are like the characters in the musical *Cabaret* who sing "Money, Money, Money" with such relish. It's for the children, they insist, with knitted brows. Taxpayers fork it over. And what do they get?

Compare academic performance in states that spend lavishly with those who spend only somewhat lavishly (there are no American states that stint on education). Montana is twenty-fifth in terms of expenditures but second highest in achievement. Delaware is eighth highest in spending but twenty-sixth in achievement.[26]

Money, money, money. Seven percent of our gross domestic product is spent on education, and yet the siren call for more spending continues year after year. In 2001, for example, the Senate New Democrat Coalition issued a press release endorsing "significantly increased funding and flexibility, increasing federal investment in education by $35 billion over the next five years. . . ."[27]

## Losing Ground

And students are becoming dumber with every passing decade. The Organization for Economic Cooperation and Development (OECD) is a group of industrialized nations that includes all of Europe and North America as well as Japan, South Korea, and a few others. The United States—surprise, surprise—is at the very top for K–12 spending. Yet our fifteen-year-olds perform only in the middle of the pack academically.[28] And our trajectory is not encouraging. Despite ever-increasing spending and liberal innovations across the board, our rates of high school completion have dropped compared with other nations, plunging from first place twenty-five years ago to ninth place in 2003.[29]

Even America's best students now lag behind those of other nations. On international tests comparing mastery of advanced algebra, twelfth graders in Japan and Hong Kong scored twice as high as American high school seniors.[30] In tests among twenty nations measuring math performance, eighth graders in the United States scored tenth in arithmetic, twelfth in algebra, and sixteenth in geometry.[31] Among elite students who take the toughest courses, Americans performed very poorly. Of sixteen nations competing on the advanced math portion of the Trends in International Math and Science Study test (TIMSS), America was second to last. And among those taking the advanced physics portion, American twelfth graders were dead last.[32]

The longer a student remains in the U.S. school system, the worse he performs as compared with other nations. At age nine, American kids are slightly above the international average (though well below South Korea and Holland). By age thirteen, they've fallen below the international average and have dropped well below the high-scoring nations like Singapore and Holland. By age seventeen, Americans outrank only Lithuania, Cyprus, and South Africa.[33]

## Class Size, Buildings, Equipment

Despite our enormous investment in education, our students do not perform as well as those in other nations who make do with much larger class sizes and much less luxurious buildings. The average class size in America has dropped from thirty in 1961 to twenty-three today. In Japan, the norm is thirty-six. In Taiwan, forty-four students per class is the average, and in South Korea, the average class size is forty-nine.[34] Defenders of the status quo argue that it isn't fair to compare the United States with other nations because we attempt to educate everyone while they cream off the best students. But this pleasing excuse is quite wrong. Most of the countries in the TIMSS sample have secondary school enrollment rates similar to our own. The United States also falls below the OECD average in high school completion rates.[35] Japan, the Slovak Republic, Hungary, Germany, the Netherlands, South Korea, Denmark, Finland, Israel, France, Switzerland, Belgium, and Iceland all graduate more of their high school students than does the United States.

Imagine a liberal fairyland in which a benevolent liberal master were able to dictate spending on education. It's been done. In 1985, a federal judge in Missouri assumed control of the entire Kansas City school district. He did so as the result of a desegregation case that had been wending its way through the courts for years. In what would become the model of sky's-the-limit funding, Judge Russell Clark took it upon himself to reorganize the Kansas City schools and to mandate spending. He mandated with a backhoe.

Clark ordered the district to build fifteen new schools in order to "remedy the vestiges of segregation." Among the amenities he demanded were an Olympic-sized swimming pool; a robotics lab; a twenty-five-acre wildlife sanctuary; a model United Nations complete with simultaneous translation facilities; a Soviet Olympic fencing coach; a temperature-controlled art gallery; greenhouses; and more. The bill came to more than $2 billion.

How did all of this largesse affect student performance? It didn't. Kansas City students still score well below the national average on the Iowa Basic Skills Test. And when the city's eleventh graders took Missouri's statewide test in 2000, only 5 percent of black students scored a "proficient" in reading.[36] As for the "vestiges" of segregation in Kansas City, nothing has changed.

## Sacred Cows

Designed during Lyndon Johnson's Great Society as a way to boost the school performance of poor children, Head Start has managed to become the most sacred of sacred cows on Capitol Hill. Yet it has never worked. Since 1965, 15 million preschoolers have participated in Head Start's program combining lessons, nutrition, and play at a cost of $35 billion. But when the Department of Health and Human Services examined the results of multiple surveys on the program's effectiveness, they concluded that any benefits were short-term. By the second or third grade it was impossible to distinguish children who had attended Head Start from those who had not.[37]

Similarly, Chapter I, the federally funded program to boost the achievement of poor and minority children in grade school has nothing to show after nearly forty years and more than $130 billion. The program began in 1965 with the hope that extra funding for economically disadvantaged students might close the achievement gap. But the gap remains as large as ever.[38]

All of this forced-march spending on programs that demonstrably do not work does more than merely pick the pockets of taxpayers. It starves funds from other ideas that might just work and permits the terrible dumbing down to accelerate.

## Illiterate in Two Languages

Bilingual education, by contrast, was not just ineffective, it was downright harmful. Sold by liberals as a benefit to non-English-speaking children, bilingual education became a jobs program for teachers instead and did actual harm to children by keeping them from learning English rapidly. In fact, many children consigned to the bilingual track never mastered English at all. In California, for many years teachers from foreign countries who spoke one of the languages used in a bilingual program did not have to pass the competency tests required of other teachers and did not have to demonstrate fluency in English.[39] This led to a situation in which many students were being taught to be illiterate in two languages. The existence of bilingual education not only required hiring lots and lots of Spanish-speaking teachers, it also meant, in large cities, holding jobs fairs for Spanish-speaking psychologists, speech therapists, social workers, nurses, and other specialists.

Senator Patty Murray, a Washington Democrat, demonstrates the indifference to results characteristic of liberals: "Many children are learning English as a second language. They need bilingual teachers who can help them learn to read. Unfortunately, we don't have all the bilingual teachers that we need today. We should be investing more in bilingual education."[40]

Bilingual programs also became ghettos of ethnic separatism. Assimilation into American society was slighted in favor of Mexican festivals, holidays, political memories, and traditions. Bilingual apologists insisted that such programs were necessary to boost the "self-esteem" of Spanish-speaking students. But self-esteem arises from mastery, not spoon-feeding. Like other immigrants who had come before them, Hispanic families were fully capable of transmitting their language and ethnic heritage to their children at home. The gift of bilingual education was a Trojan Horse, locking Hispanic kids into permanent inferiority to their native classmates.

Sugary words from Democrats disguised the reality. Senator Harry Reid, a Nevada Democrat, flaunted his sensitivity:

> The increasing diversity of our nation enriches our communities. It also challenges our public schools to meet both the English language and literacy needs of our expanding limited English proficient student populations. . . . Think about it. You go to school and they are speaking one language there, and you go home and they are speaking a different language. How do you improve upon what you don't know? It is hard to do.[41]

Yes, it's hard to do. But millions upon millions of immigrant children have managed to accomplish just that. They came from homes where the native language was Italian, Greek, Portuguese, Spanish, Polish, Yiddish, Russian, German, and hundreds of others. And because children are little sponges, they learned English quickly—often helping their parents navigate the new country.

Immigrants haven't changed—but American education has. Parents of Spanish-speaking children hated these programs. In poll after poll, parents stated their preference for learning English as quickly as possible. A former bilingual teacher, Rosalie Pedalino Porter, switched sides on the bilingual debate after years in the trenches. Writing for the *Atlantic*, she noted:

> In the past ten years several national surveys of the parents of limited-English schoolchildren have shown that a large majority consider learning English and having other subjects taught in English to be of much greater importance than receiving instruction in the native language or about the native culture.[42]

Yet the education establishment persisted with bilingualism. In New York, Hispanic parents actually sued the city in an attempt to free their children from the program.[43] Some children with Spanish surnames found themselves relegated to bilingual classes even if they were completely fluent in English and over the strenuous objections of their disbelieving parents. In Los Angeles, hundreds of Hispanic parents boycotted their local school for two weeks in 1996 to protest the bilingual program.[44]

In 1998, California voters approved Proposition 227, a bill to end bilingual education. It passed by a huge majority of 61 percent. Throughout the campaign season, the initiative enjoyed strong Hispanic support. As many as 80 percent said they approved of ending bilingual education. But in the final two weeks, the California Teachers Association carpetbombed the state with deceptive ads suggesting that 227 would vitiate local control and deny parents options. Typical was a warning by Josephina Villamil Tinajero, president of the National Association of Bilingual Education: "It will be an evil day if this initiative succeeds. Everyone will be hurt if this initiative passes. Everyone."[45]

Well, everyone in her organization, anyway. It was, on the other hand, wonderful news for the children when the initiative passed. Test scores for former bilingual students rose dramatically in the years after 227 passed. Because the law permitted districts to implement the new regulations in different ways, a laboratory of sorts was provided. In the Oceanside Unified School District, Spanish-language instruction was simply eliminated. Reading scores on the Stanford 9 test jumped from the twelfth percentile in 1998 to the thirty-second percentile in 2000. In the neighboring district, where bilingual programs were continued through a parental waiver provision, scores improved only modestly. "Originally, I thought 227 was too extreme," admitted Oceanside superintendent Kenneth Noonan, "but the results speak for themselves." He later added, "This is not news the bilingual industry is interested in hearing."[46] True enough. A Stanford University bilingual advocate told the Associated Press that the scores "don't tell us anything, nor will they ever."[47]

That's a familiar do-gooder trope. If the facts don't support your point of view, dismiss the facts as irrelevant.

## A Nation Still at Risk

The data could not be clearer. Our students are not performing as well as they did thirty or forty years ago when we spent far less. Though the number of students taking the SAT has risen consistently over the past several decades, the number of high scorers has declined. In 1972, 116,630 Americans scored 600 or above on the verbal section of the test.[48] In 1992, though many more students took the test, only 75,243 scored 600 or above. Math scores, after plunging in the early 80s, have rebounded, but the designer of the test, Educational Testing Service, "recentered" the test scores in 1994, making comparisons over time far more difficult (as was intended). Though the College Board reports the average verbal SAT score as 505, it would actually be 428 on the old scale.

Another window into America's educational decline can be found in the International Adult Literacy Survey. During the mid 1990s, sixteen- to sixty-five-year-olds from fourteen countries in Europe and North America participated in a literacy test. Our older age groups, those whose schooling did not include sex education, child-centered learning, cooperative learning, and creative spelling, did very well. Americans aged fifty-six to sixty-five ranked second highest among those nations participating. But the youngest group, those aged sixteen-to twenty-five, ranked fourteenth–dead last.[49]

The education establishment–what Bill Bennett calls "the Blob"–has been devilishly clever about avoiding the pedagogy that works and selling "reforms" that don't. As Charles Sykes has said:

> It's the education disease; they're addicted to it. We're always having these waves of reform, and the only thing they have in common is that there's never any empirical evidence of whether they in fact work. And the worst part is when these things [whole language, new math, outcome based

education] fail, they are repackaged with a different title, presented as innovations and then go on to fail again.[50]

Employers are noticing the education deficit. A 1991 survey of Fortune 500 executives found that 58 percent had difficulty finding workers with basic skills.[51] Eighty percent of major employers in Pennsylvania, a 1998 survey found, said students were not graduating from public schools with adequate skills to enter the workforce.[52] Americans have spent fortunes—and if liberals prevail, will spend further treasure—on community colleges. Yet community colleges are often doing the work that is not done in elementary and high schools. The Education Commission of the States, a subdivision of the National Conference of State Legislatures, found in 2000 that 41 percent of all first-time community college freshmen and 29 percent of university freshmen require some kind of remediation before attempting college-level work.[53] At California State University, 54 percent of freshmen in 1994 required remedial math courses and 49 percent required remedial reading.[54] Yet Cal State admits only the top third of the state's graduating high school seniors. Nationwide, 30 percent of first-time college freshmen require remedial courses—and 80 percent of four-year colleges provide such courses.[55]

Nor is it just advanced skills that American graduates lack. U.S. manufacturers report that 40 percent of all seventeen-year-olds lack the math skills to hold a manufacturing job and 60 percent lack the reading skills.[56] Seventy-six percent of college professors and 63 percent of employers believe that "a high school diploma is no guarantee that the typical student has learned the basics." The Nevada Policy Research Institute followed 10,000 high school graduates who were receiving remedial courses in 2003. They found that "in too many cases, they needed help with knowledge and skills that should have been learned in the third or fourth grade."[57]

The federal government currently spends more than $15 billion annually on worker retraining. In other words, the U.S. government spends billions to teach adults what they should have learned in primary and secondary school. Call it failure cubed.

In 1983, the Department of Education issued a report from an independent commission titled "A Nation at Risk." Authored by a number of prominent educators, including David P. Gardner and Glenn T. Seaborg of the University of California, Gerald Holton of Harvard, and A. Bartlett Giamatti of Yale, the report rang with alarm about the decline of standards and performance in American education.

In its most quoted passage, the commission's report declared that America's education system was threatened by "a rising tide of mediocrity that threatens our very future as a nation and a people. If an unfriendly foreign power had attempted to impose on America the mediocre educational performance that exists today, we might well have viewed it as an act of war. As it stands, we have allowed this to happen to ourselves."[58]

One way we disguise our weakness is through importation of top talent. At every level of higher education–bachelor's, master's, and Ph.Ds–the percentage of math and science degrees awarded to American citizens has declined over the past few decades. In 1980, for example, 76 percent of doctoral degrees in the physical sciences went to Americans. By 1999, that number had dropped to 54 percent.[59] And while some of these well-trained graduates remain and make contributions to the United States, many do not.

## The Tests Are the Problem

There is little doubt that American education at the primary and secondary levels has been infantilized and drained of rigor for the past forty years. The two big teachers' unions, in concert with schools of education, have foisted a huge number of nonacademic functions on the schools while slighting instruction. Indeed, educationists do not bother to deny this. They scorn traditional methods as "drill and kill." Teachers, they insist, should no longer attempt to be "the sage on the stage" but should adopt the pose of the "guide on the side." (Perhaps they take sloganeering lessons from Jesse Jackson.)

At most public schools around the nation, students spend an

inordinate amount of time on sex education, safety rules, drug and alcohol education, and brainwashing about the environment. Classroom hours are devoted to "cooperative learning." Teachers pride
themselves on teaching "the child, not the subject." Great stress is
laid upon encouraging the child's creativity and building self-esteem.

Every antiintellectual excuse that can be imagined has been trot-
ted out by the education establishment to justify the retreat from
content. They spurn mere facts and claim instead to be teaching the
"tools of learning." They claim to be imparting "critical thinking
skills" instead of dull information. The "whole language" reading
method–founded on the dubious notion that reading is as natural as
speaking–focused on making reading fun and letting children teach
themselves, through context, what the words meant and how they
were pronounced. Ken Goodman, a whole language advocate, described the joyful atmosphere this method would induce: "Whole
language classrooms liberate pupils to try new things, to invent
spellings, to experiment with a new genre, to guess at meanings in
their spellings, or to read and write imperfectly. In whole language
classrooms risk-taking is not simply tolerated, it is celebrated."[60]
And the children can neither spell nor punctuate.

Rita Kramer's experience is recounted in J. Martin Rochester's
book *Class Warfare*. She visited dozens of education colleges around
the nation and came away with these impressions:

> Everywhere, I found idealistic people eager to do good. And
> everywhere, I found them being told that the way to do good
> was to prepare themselves to cure a sick society; to become
> therapists, as it were, specializing in the pathology of educa-
> tion. Almost nowhere did I find teachers whose emphasis was
> on the measurable learning of real knowledge. . . . The
> school is to be remade into a republic of feelings–as distinct
> from a republic of learning–where everyone can feel he de-
> serves an A. In order to create a more just society, future
> teachers are being told they must focus on the handicapped
> of all kinds–those who have the greatest difficulty learning,

whether because of physical problems or emotional ones, congenital conditions or those caused by lack of stimulation in the family . . . in order to have everyone come out equal in the end.[61]

In that spirit, during the past four decades curricula have been watered down and requirements eliminated. A U.S. Department of Education study in 1983 examined high school transcripts from 1964 to 1981. As Diane Ravitch recounts in *Left Back*, researcher Clifford Adelman found a "systematic devaluation of academic (and some vocational courses)":

> High schools students were spending less time in academic courses and more time in credit-bearing nonacademic courses. The curriculum had become "diffused and fragmented." Enrollments in the "general track" had jumped "from 12 percent in the late 1960s to 42.5 percent in the late 1970s," said Adelman, and the general track had become "the dominant student track in high school." Neither academic nor vocational, the general track consisted of courses such as driver education, general shop, remedial studies, consumer education, training for marriage and adulthood, health education, typing, and home economics.[62]

In the last few years, as part of a backlash against the liberal destruction of education, a standards movement has spread throughout the country. Many states have instituted—gasp—tests for high school graduation. The late senator Paul Wellstone (D-MN) expressed his disdain for the idea:

> Today in education there is a threat afoot to which I do not need to call your attention; the threat of high stakes testing being grossly abused in the name of greater accountability, and almost always to the serious detriment of our children.
>
> Allowing the continued misuse of high stakes tests is, in

itself, a gross failure of moral imagination, a failure both of educators and policymakers, who persistently refuse to provide the educational resources necessary. . . .

First and foremost, I firmly believe that it is grossly unfair to not graduate, or to hold back a student based on a standardized test if that student has not had an opportunity to learn the material covered on the test. When we impose high stakes tests on an educational system where there are, as Jonathan Kozol says, savage inequalities, and then we do nothing to address the underlying causes of those inequalities, we set up children to fail.[63]

Senator Russ Feingold (D-WI) presented a liberal's greatest hits on education in a 2003 Senate floor speech:

I am extremely concerned that the new federal testing mandate will not achieve the desired result of better schools with qualified teachers and successful students. I fear that this new mandate will curtail actual teaching time and real learning in favor of an environment where teaching to the test becomes the norm. The unfortunate result of this would be to show our children that education is not about preparing for their futures, but rather about preparing for tests—that education is really about sharp No. 2 pencils and test sheets, about making sure that the little round bubbles are filled in completely, and if their school districts and states have enough money, maybe about exam booklets for short answer and essay questions. I am also deeply concerned that this focus on testing will rob teachers of valuable teaching time and will squelch efforts to be innovative and creative, both with lesson plans and with ways of measuring student performance. If we fail to provide adequate resources to these schools and these students, we run the risk of setting disadvantaged children up for failure on these tests—failure which could damage the self-esteem of our most vulnerable students.[64]

In fact, by resisting rigor and standards, it is liberals who set up children to fail. The American economy does not coddle adults with easy outs and soft expectations. It does not accept excuses. Performance counts. Children who emerge from the warm cocoon of American public schools are simply unprepared for what awaits them. This hurts poor and minority children the most. They are the most in need of solid educational achievement to boost them up the economic ladder.

Liberals are equally sour on imposing teacher standards. A suburban New York school district advertised jobs available for thirty-five teachers. They received 800 applications and decided to thin the ranks by administering an eleventh-grade state examination in English. Only 25 percent of the would-be teachers answered forty of the fifty questions correctly.[65] In Massachusetts, 59 percent of prospective teachers flunked a state licensing exam.[66]

Debby Feldman, a geometry teacher at Brockton High School, scorned the idea of teacher testing. "For years we've known that kids' achievement is affected by loads more things than just what the teacher is saying in the classroom," she told the *Boston Globe*. "I think that instead of putting money into testing, it would be nice if they would put that money into being more supportive in the schools."[67] Just ignore the test results and keep pouring good money after bad.

## The Shame of the Nation

But the shame of the nation is unquestionably the nature of what goes on in urban public schools. Mediocre suburban schools are a disservice to youngsters who arrive ready to learn and full of promise and represent a rebuke to those who claimed that massive spending would improve things. But poor inner-city schools are a disaster for children who arrive already burdened with serious social problems and leave unready for much. These are the students that liberals claim to be most concerned about and these are the ones to whom liberal policies do the most damage.

*Education Week* estimates that "most fourth-graders who live in U.S. cities can't read and understand a simple children's book, and most eighth-graders can't use arithmetic to solve a practical problem."[68] And as Abigail and Stephen Thernstrom heartbreakingly document in *No Excuses*, the situation is much worse for blacks and Hispanics than for other Americans.

According to the National Assessment of Educational Progress (NAEP) tests, black twelfth graders are, on average, four years behind white and Asian students. As the Thernstroms note:

> To function well in our postindustrial, information-based economy, students at the end of high school should be able to read complex material, write reasonably well, and demonstrate a mastery of precalculus math. Imagine that you are an employer considering two job applicants, one with a high school diploma, the other a dropout at the end of eighth grade. Unless the job requires only pure brawn, an employer will seldom find the choice between the two candidates difficult.[69]

In fact, blacks in their final year of high school score only about as well as white seventh-graders on tests of math and geography. Hispanics do slightly better but only about as well as white eighth graders.[70]

The NAEP test reveals that about 20 percent of white students have not mastered basic skills by the time they graduate from high school. The NAEP establishes four categories:

1. Below basic, which means that the student has not shown even "partial mastery of prerequisite knowledge and skills that are fundamental for proficient work" at that grade level,
2. Basic, or partial mastery,
3. Proficient, which requires a "solid academic performance," and
4. Advanced, which represents "superior" performance.

For blacks and Hispanics the numbers are truly astounding. In five subjects–mathematics, science, U.S. history, civics, and geography–more than half of black high school seniors scored below basic. In science, the number was close to 80 percent. Among Hispanics, the numbers were only slightly better.[71] This appalling gap is rarely discussed. Conservatives are afraid of being labeled racist for mentioning it, and liberals–the authors of a thousand education "reforms" that have failed to ameliorate it–would like to change the subject.

But how is it possible that our well-funded public schools are failing black and Hispanic kids so thoroughly? Liberal educrats point to problems within the families and communities. And those handicaps certainly make a difference. But the education system cannot excuse itself so easily.

The atmosphere at many public schools in urban areas is chaotic and unsafe. In 2001, the Pennsylvania House of Representatives prepared a report on Philadelphia's public schools detailing the level of violence that had become common. Offenses were committed against children as young as age eight and on teachers and principals, too. The crimes cited in the report included: gropings, beatings, arson, stompings, and knifings. And as *City Journal* reports, the obstacles to discipline are Byzantine:

> Thanks to a bewildering accumulation of federal, state, and district regulations, a suspended student usually returns to class after just three to five days. Even worse, expelling a student to one of the district's "alternative" schools for miscreants takes 20 separate steps, including filling out 26 documents and sending them to 13 people. Miss a deadline, fail to fill out a form just right, and the whole process begins all over again–while the attacker remains in class. Expelling a student permanently is next to impossible. Some principals just try to transfer the worst cases to other schools, without alerting the new school to the transfer's bad habits–a poor solution but arguably better than the more common Philly alternative of transferring the victim and letting the punk stay.[72]

A mother who visited a Cleveland middle school in the late 1990s reported in horror: "I didn't want to go in. . . . The school was a madhouse; it was filthy. Who's in control here? The kids?" In Washington, D.C., within waving distance of the Capitol dome, a young football star was shot dead by a classmate in 2004.

In 1999, students ages twelve to eighteen were victims of 2.5 million crimes at school; 186,000 were serious, violent crimes.[73] The National Center for Education Statistics reports that in the academic year 1996–97, 57 percent of American schools reported at least one crime to the police. A 1996 survey found that 41 percent of black high school students felt that disruptive students were "a very serious problem" in their schools.[74] Almost the exact same number of teachers, 40 percent, said disruptive students "interfere with my teaching."[75] Eighty-eight percent think that academic achievement would improve "substantially" if unruly students were removed from the classroom.[76] And while extreme violence is not the norm at American schools, disorder and mayhem are not uncommon, particularly in urban public schools.

When a *Newsday* reporter decided to teach at a public school in Brooklyn for a year, she discovered that many kids had never been required to sit still, to pay attention, to police their language, or to behave in a minimally civilized fashion. Some of her students called her "c— face," told her to "f— off," spat in her face, played radios during class time, and threw furniture around the room.[77] In a 1991 survey, 58 percent of teachers said they had been verbally abused at least once in their teaching career, and 23 percent said they had experienced such abuse within the previous four weeks.[78]

## "Uncontrolled and Uncontrollable Liberty"

How did schools get to be so squalid? In part, changes in society, particularly in family structure, have reverberated within the classroom. But the work of liberal activist lawyers must also be taken into account.

Schools have been intimidated and cowed from enforcing discipline by generations of liberal lawyers and judges who have undermined adult authority. It began, as so many awful things did, in 1969 with the Supreme Court case of *Tinker v. Des Moines School District*. Three high school students (one was thirteen) had been suspended for wearing black armbands to school to protest the Vietnam War. They sued on the grounds that their free speech rights had been violated, and the liberal majority on the Supreme Court agreed with them. Protests against the Vietnam War had high status in the eyes of liberal judges. The judges used the opportunity to create a new era in school discipline. "It can hardly be argued," wrote Justice Abe Fortas, "that students or teachers shed their constitutional rights to free speech or expression at the schoolhouse gate."[79]

The message was clear, adults had lost a large measure of their authority. Children had free speech rights within the school building that trumped the need for teachers and principals to maintain a quiet and respectful learning environment.

Justice Hugo Black, often considered a First Amendment absolutist, dissented in *Tinker*. His reasoning is one of the best distillations of conservative sentiment in American letters—and he was not a conservative in the traditional sense:

> Change has been said to be truly the law of life, *but sometimes the old and the tried and true are worth holding* [emphasis added]. The schools of this nation have undoubtedly contributed to giving us tranquility and to making us a more law-abiding people. Uncontrolled and uncontrollable liberty is an enemy to domestic peace. . . . school discipline, like parental discipline, is an integral and important part of training our children to be good citizens. Here a very small number of students have crisply and summarily refused to obey a school order designed to give pupils who want to learn the opportunity to do so. One need not be a prophet or the son of a prophet to know that, after the Court's holding today, some students in Iowa schools—and, indeed, in all schools—will be ready, able, and willing to defy their teachers on practically all orders.[80]

Kay Hymowitz, writing in the *City Journal*, describes some of *Tinker*'s cascading effects:

"At each elementary and middle school door, you have some guy making a constitutional decision every day," observes Jeff Krausman, legal counsel to several Iowa school districts. Suppose, says Krausman by way of example, that a student shows up at school wearing a T-shirt emblazoned "white power." The principal wants to send the kid home to change, but he's not sure it's within his authority to do so, so he calls the superintendent. The superintendent is also unsure, so he calls the district's lawyer. The lawyer's concern, though, isn't that the child has breached the boundaries of respect and tolerance, and needs an adult to tell him so, but whether disciplining the student would violate the First Amendment.[81]

Having constrained the authority of teachers and principals in the realm of speech, the Supreme Court further undermined discipline with a 1975 decision on school suspensions. A principal in an Ohio high school had suspended a number of students after a riot broke out in the school lunchroom. The students appealed their ten-day suspensions as violations of their due process rights, and in *Goss v. Lopez*, the liberal majority of the Supreme Court agreed. "Since misconduct charges, if sustained and recorded," the Court ruled, "could seriously damage the students' reputations, as well as interfere with later educational and employment opportunities, the States claimed right to determine unilaterally and without due process whether that misconduct has occurred immediately collides with the Due Process Clause's prohibition against arbitrary deprivation of liberty."[82]

Remaining in school, the Court ruled, was a "property interest" in the student's possession that could not be removed without "oral or written notice of the charges," an explanation of the evidence against the student, and an opportunity for the accused to present his version.[83] In other words, ordinary day-to-day discipline in the nation's schools was to become a legal battleground, with courts looking over educators' shoulders at every pass, ready to decide whether a particular punishment violated the student's constitutional rights.

Justice Powell, writing in dissent, was disgusted:

> . . . the Court ignores the experience of mankind, as well as the long history of our law, recognizing that there *are* differences which must be accommodated in determining the rights and duties of children as compared with those of adults. Examples of this distinction abound in our law: in contracts, in tort, in criminal law and procedure, in criminal sanctions and rehabilitation, and in the right to vote and hold office. Until today, and except in the special context of the First Amendment issue in *Tinker*, the educational rights of children and teenagers in the elementary and secondary schools have not been analogized to the rights of adults or to those accorded college students. Even with respect to the First Amendment, the rights of children have not been regarded as "coextensive with those of adults."[84]

Even more than *Tinker*, the *Goss* decision swung open the door to chaos in the public schools. "Everyone has lawyers today," the president of the Cambridge Teachers Association told the *Boston Globe*.[85] Accordingly, teachers and administrators are very careful and wary about meting out discipline. Virtually no aspect of school conduct has gone unlitigated in the years since. In Montclair, New Jersey, a teacher who grabbed the arm of a student who had been throwing grapes in the cafeteria was sued by the girl's parents and lost his job.[86] Children and their parents, often with legal assistance from the American Civil Liberties Union, have sued school systems over hair length, school newspaper articles, locker searches, grades, class assignments, dances, and much, much more. In 2002, a New York fourteen-year-old went to school wearing a "Barbie Is a Lesbian" T-shirt. When the principal suspended the girl for a day and instructed her not to wear the T-shirt again, she sued in federal court.

"Schools cannot legally engage in this type of selective, content-based suppression of speech," her lawyer explained.[87]

During the 1990s, courts also began to apply civil rights laws to school discipline cases. If schools were found to be disciplining a "disproportionate" number of minority students, the NAACP might bring suit. The Cincinnati public school system, after being sued by the NAACP, was monitored by federal courts to ensure that suspensions were proportional to the number of black students in the schools.[88] The chilling effect this would have on discipline is obvious. The devastating consequences for the majority of kids who are not disruptive is also obvious.

While the courts were doing their corrosive work, the Democrat-controlled Congress too was interfering in classrooms in ways that ensured greater disorder. The 1966 Education of the Handicapped Act, which later became known as the Individuals with Disabilities Education Act (IDEA), required that all schools provide a free, public education to all students without regard to disability.

It was, it should be acknowledged, a generous move. But like so many well-intentioned liberal initiatives, this one was a bit deficient in common sense and workable boundaries. Included in the definition of the "handicapped" were children with "serious emotional disturbances." So while members of Congress could feel virtuous for having provided more educational opportunities for the blind and those in wheelchairs, they also permitted knife-wielding 17-year-olds to be educated in regular classrooms, and restricted the latitude of school officials in dealing with students who were highly disruptive and even dangerous.

Among the rights Congress conferred on children with behavioral and emotional problems were:

=  Due process hearings whenever a change of classroom was contemplated by school authorities,
=  Education in the "least restrictive environment" possible,
=  Supplemental tutoring, and
=  Tailored curricula.

What led America's schools further down the path to chaos was the law's requirement that special education students be exempt from the regular disciplinary rules applicable to general education students. An emotionally disturbed student could not be suspended for longer than ten days unless it could be shown that the misconduct in question was completely unrelated to his disability.

In practice, that is nearly impossible. If a child who suffers from depression or anxiety disorder sets fire to his classmate's hair, can it ever be firmly established that the behavior was completely unrelated to his disability? The consequences on the ground can be absurd, as in Connecticut, when school officials caught one student passing a gun to another. The regular education student received a one-year suspension. The other student, who was classified as special ed due to a stutter, received only a forty-five-day suspension (after a hearing) and received special, individualized services. In New York, special ed teacher Jeffrey Gerstel was confronted one day by a violent adolescent student who rushed the teacher's aide screaming that he was going to kill her. Gerstel restrained the student, but in the course of the scuffle, the student scratched his back on a bookcase. Gerstel was dragged before a hearing where he was forced to justify himself in front of the boy and his mother as well as school officials. The case was settled and the boy was returned to class.[89] In the Bronx, an emotionally disturbed student was discovered in possession of a four-inch knife. The boy was neither suspended nor reported to the police because he was a special ed student.[90]

The IDEA law suffered from a disability of its own, and it is the same disability that affects most liberal thinking. It looks at the world from the perspective of a person with troubles—whether self-imposed or not is irrelevant—and attempts to compensate him without regard for the way this special consideration will affect the majority and without recognizing that special favors are not always good even for their intended beneficiaries.

It is not clear that "mainstreaming" is actually good for children with severe handicaps. They may not get the kind of intensive help they require in a general education classroom, and if their misbehavior goes uncorrected, they may get the message that unacceptable behavior does not entail consequences. At the same time, it is certain that the presence of difficult, demanding, unruly, and sometimes even violent special education students in mainstream classrooms inhibits the ability of all students to learn. As the late Albert Shanker of the American Federation of Teachers put it, "You don't help the bad kid, and you've effectively destroyed the environment for the other kids."

A cri de coeur from a mother who was herself a special education teacher for twelve years made the rounds of the Internet and met with strong agreement in many quarters. It was titled "Isn't My Kid Special Too?"

> My son started kindergarten this year and I'm considering homeschooling him because I believe that the school now caters to the special needs children more than they care about the regular kid. . . .
>
> Since school started I have been hearing about a child named Mikie. I have heard my son have nightmares about Mikie . . . Mikie is the largest boy in the class. He does not speak English and is also obviously developmentally delayed. Mikie does not play on the playground; he runs, he hits, he chokes other kids. He grabs them by the jacket and throws them to the ground. The teachers cannot control Mikie. . . . My son has come home with a ripped jacket, a bruised leg and a bloody lip from Mikie. . . .
>
> If you ask about the regular child, you will be told how good it is for them to be in classes with special needs children. . . . Mainstreaming has gotten out of hand.[91]

Everyone agrees that inner-city schools have major problems. And there is even some agreement about its causes. No one denies, for example, that family chaos–which is particularly acute in black and Hispanic neighborhoods–affects children's ability to learn. Many children in inner-city schools come from homes without fathers, but that is only the beginning.

Think about what a child needs in his home environment in order to succeed in school. He needs to get to bed at a reasonable hour every night in the same bed. He needs to wake up, eat breakfast, and get to school on time. In the afternoons, he needs supervision so that he doesn't wind up planted in front of the television or wandering the streets. He needs parents, preferably two, who are aware of what he is doing in school, check his homework, stay in touch with the teacher, and offer enrichment in the form of family activities, outings, rules, and traditions. He needs to know that his parents take school seriously. For some black and Hispanic youngsters, few or none of those prerequisites to school success is in place.

## Catholic Schools Teach

And yet . . . that isn't the whole story. What happens between 8:30 and 3:00 makes a huge difference in the life prospects of these children too. Coming from disorganized and even miserable families does not prevent many children from succeeding in school and in life.

Compare the work of the Catholic schools in New York City with the public school system. In 1990, the Rand Corporation performed a study and found that while public schools in New York graduated only 25 percent of their pupils, Catholic schools were graduating 95 percent; and while only 16 percent of students in the public system took the SAT, 75 percent of those in the Catholic schools took the test.[92] For those kids who did take the SAT, the Catholic school children significantly outscored the public school kids with an average 815 on the test compared with 642.[93] Research by others, including the U.S. Department of Education, has confirmed these findings. Students in Catholic schools, even when they come from exactly the same sort of homes as children in the public schools, significantly outperform them. Most of the children attending inner-city Catholic schools are not even Catholic. In the boroughs of Manhattan and the Bronx, 85 percent of the children in Catholic schools are non-Catholics.[94]

Sol Stern began his parenting life as a strong believer in the public schools, to which he dutifully sent his two sons. Like many other parents, he was appalled by what he found—incompetent teachers who could not be fired; chaotic classrooms wasting time on "hands-on" projects instead of substantive learning; and generous servings of political correctness. In the course of investigating what had gone wrong, he discovered the Catholic schools. To his shock, he learned that the Catholic schools in New York City were everything that advocates of strong *public* education could have wished. They took all comers without regard to race, ethnicity, or religion. They offered an orderly, safe environment. Catholic schools with the same percentage of minority children as public schools, and often just blocks away, consistently showed better test scores on standardized tests—often by as much as a whole grade level. And they did it with larger class sizes and about half the money the public system enjoyed.[95]

When financier Eugene Lang offered to pay college tuition for minority children who finished high school, he was stunned by how few students at P.S. 44, a public school in the South Bronx, could get to the graduation step. The following year, Lang offered to pay the high school tuition for any eighth grader who wanted to switch to Catholic school. The results were equally dramatic. Of the thirty-eight students who remained in the public system, only two went on to college, but of the twenty-two who went to Catholic high school, all but two attended college.[96]

Where did this fantastic disparity get noticed? Not among advocates for the poor. Not at the *New York Times*. Not by the NAACP. Not on the major television networks. No—only in conservative journals and among certain right-leaning think tanks did the outstanding job of the Catholic schools in minority neighborhoods get noticed. When the subject was raised, liberals tended to dismiss the Catholic schools' success as the result of "creaming"—i.e., being able to skim the best students off the top and leave the rest behind. That said, they closed their minds.

Not even a very newsworthy confrontation on the subject could get much traction in liberal New York. Albert Shanker restated this argument at a public forum at the City University of New York in 1991. "I challenge the Catholic schools to accept the lowest-scoring

5 percent of our public school students," he declared. "Let's see how they do then." The audience applauded. Sol Stern explains what happened next:

> After a moment of silence, a soft-spoken, middle-aged lady stood up to respond. She introduced herself as Catherine Hickey, superintendent of schools of the Archdiocese of New York. "Mr. Shanker," she said, "on behalf of the Catholic schools, we accept your challenge."
>
> . . . Having been challenged to put up or shut up, Shanker's union and the New York City Board of Education had little choice but to engage in exploratory discussions with the archdiocese about the possibility of transferring some students to the Catholic schools and then monitoring their progress. The discussions continued for about eighteen months. Then the perennially revolving doors to the schools chancellor's office revolved again: the incumbent chancellor was out and the new chancellor let the project die.[97]

There was never any real chance that the city would take up the archdiocese on its offer. Yet the reluctance of any political or journalistic figure on the Left to acknowledge this dramatic offer to the poor was itself notable. Only one New York politician seems to have understood and appreciated the irony, and that was Republican mayor Rudolph Giuliani, who repeatedly mentioned the Catholic school system's success and urged that the public schools might have much to learn from them.

Not only have liberals failed to show curiosity about the schools that have succeeded where the public schools have failed, they've become wedded to the status quo at the expense of the students. "My job," declared Clinton secretary of education Richard Riley, "is to protect the public schools."[98] Note that he did not say to improve the public schools, nor did he see his role as protecting students.

The flaws and failures of the American education system cannot be laid entirely at the feet of liberals. The long erosion of standards could not have unfolded without at least tacit acceptance by the majority. And yet, liberal Democrats, by allying themselves so totally with the teachers' unions and with public schools, have become a major obstacle to reform for those they claim most loudly to represent—minorities and the poor.

## "You Have to Work to Stay in School"

In 1955, a then relatively obscure economist named Milton Friedman suggested that the system of public education the United States employed might not be the most efficient nor the best we could do. We had empowered the states to build schools, hire teachers, and dictate curriculum. The result was a bureaucratic, inflexible, nonresponsive, and antiintellectual behemoth. He recommended giving a voucher to each parent for the amount the public schools spend each year educating children and then permitting parents to choose schools for their own children (subject to certain minimum standards set by the state). The G.I. Bill was essentially a voucher system for higher education and it worked beautifully.

The idea percolated in conservative journals and conferences for decades before really hitting stride in the 1990s, when the failure of the public schools to provide a minimally decent chance to poor kids became starkly apparent. A number of philanthropists like Ted Forstmann and John Kirtley began privately funding voucher programs in cities across America. When venture capitalist Kirtley offered vouchers worth $1,500 to 750 students in the Tampa Bay area in 1998, he received 12,500 applications. When financier Forstmann offered vouchers to 40,000 children around the country, he was swamped with 1.2 million applications.[99]

The *City Journal* has published moving stories of the schools "vouchers built" in cities like Milwaukee. At Messmer High School, for example, no security guards or teachers monitor the cafeteria. The kids have part-time jobs working the cash registers. A young teacher whose starting salary at the school was $13,000 explained that he was inspired by "the sense of mission here, of working with

poor students yet holding them accountable and helping them strive
for excellence. We are not in the business of making excuses or allowing the kids to make excuses for themselves." Children in these classrooms are energetic and well-behaved. Unlike in the public schools,
Messmer inculcates a culture of civility. A teenaged girl explained to
the *City Journal* what was different: "They are very tough here," Jennifer explained. "You can't break any rule without being punished.
And you have to work hard to stay in school. In the public schools,
there's a lot of violence and you don't have to work hard." In 1999,
Messmer was spending $4,600 to educate one student compared
with Milwaukee's public schools' $7,200, but no child pays more
than $2,800.[100]

Among the most avid voucher supporters are black parents living
in big cities. The Rev. Floyd Flake, for example, a black minister who
served six terms in Congress and now works for the Edison Project,
has explained:

> When children cannot read or do even elementary math,
> they are doomed in a twenty-first-century economy. . . . We
> only hurt ourselves when we produce a bumper crop of work-
> ers cursed to compete in international markets with unac-
> ceptable skills. Conspiring politicians remain wedded to a
> system of waste and mediocrity because of the fundraising
> prowess of teachers unions and other interest groups.
>
>      . . . I am not against public schools. I am against . . .
> public schools where educational mediocrity goes unchal-
> lenged. I am against public schools that only expect the least
> from our children. I am against public schools where im-
> provement is stifled by strict union rules and regulations. . . .
> Poor children can learn. Set the standards high, and children
> will meet those standards.[101]

Flake is unusually courageous, but he is hardly alone in the black
community. Polly Williams was an early heroine of the choice movement. A member of the Wisconsin legislature, Williams was also a

Jesse Jackson for President organizer. But on the subject of choice in education, she joined forces with conservatives and helped to launch the nation's first publicly-funded voucher program in Milwaukee. "The arrogance of white liberals is amazing," she told the *Chicago Tribune*. "They think they have a monopoly on the world's supply of brains."[102] Nationwide, 57 percent of black Americans support school vouchers (as compared with 49 percent of the general public). But among black parents, support rises to 75 percent.[103]

Research confirms that vouchers significantly improve academic performance among black children. Critics have charged that the superior performance of black children in inner-city Catholic schools was the result of self-selection—that is, parents who have the initiative and resources to send their children to parochial school may be different from parents who lack that commitment. It's possible. But a study by professors from the University of Wisconsin, Georgetown, and Harvard evaluated the voucher programs in New York, Dayton, and the District of Columbia with an eye toward just this potential bias, among others. The survey was carefully designed. For example, to avoid the problem of "self-selection," researchers first assembled a pool of applicants for vouchers. They then randomly divided the applicants into an experimental group, who received vouchers, and a control group, who did not. Family income, education of the mother, and other variables were factored in. The researchers found that receiving a voucher made a big difference in the reading and math scores of African American kids—a rise of 6.3 percent. For children of other backgrounds, no statistically significant difference was noted.[104] Measures of parental satisfaction with private as opposed to public schools are through the roof.

Why then has there not been a tsunami of support for voucher programs nationwide? Because liberal groups like the NAACP, People for the American Way, Americans United for Separation of Church and State, the American Civil Liberties Union, and, most significantly, the two huge teachers' unions, the NEA and the AFT, have formed up a phalanx of opposition that is as rigid and impermeable as any ancient fortress. They stand like modern versions of

George Wallace in the schoolhouse door declaring "Segregation forever."

Jesse Jackson, an ardent voucher foe, sent his children to the very best private schools money could buy. Rep. Jesse Jackson Jr., who attended St. Albans in D.C., declared that the "political foundation" of the voucher movement was "avoidance of racial integration."[105] Meanwhile, a white conservative senator from Indiana, Dan Coats, described vouchers as "quite simply an issue of survival for our nation's poorest students."[106] Harold Levy, former chancellor of New York's public schools, sent his kids to the exclusive Dalton School in Manhattan.[107] Senators Albert Gore (D-TN), Mary Landrieu (D-LA), Arlen Specter (R-PA), and Hillary Clinton are among the many voucher opponents who have exercised "checkbook choice" for their own children.[108] Senator Teddy Kennedy (D-MA), who was prepared to filibuster a bill that would give D.C. parents a choice in education, sent his children to private schools. Of the 273 House members who opposed the school choice provision of the No Child Left Behind Act in 2001, 69 had sent or were sending a child to private school.[109]

Nationally, about one in ten American children attend private schools. Among members of the United States Senate, it is 51 percent. Among House members, 47 percent send their kids to private schools. These numbers would doubtless be even higher if all members of Congress lived in the District of Columbia, whose public schools are a disgrace of major proportions, but many members live in the Virginia and Maryland suburbs, where the public schools are better.

Among the members of the D.C. City Council who oppose vouchers (Mayor Anthony Williams supports them), four—Kevin Chavous, Harold Brazil, Vincent Orange, and Kathleen Patterson—send their children to private schools.[110]

Around the country, teachers in public schools send their own children to private schools in numbers far exceeding those of the general public. In Chicago, for example, 22 percent of the population attends private schools, whereas 46 percent of public school teachers send their children to private schools. In Milwaukee, 50 percent of public school teachers send their children to private schools.[111]

Keith Geiger, past president of the NEA, once questioned why certain students should be able to "escape" the public schools when others could not.[112] His word choice was significant. D.C. mayor Anthony Williams provided an answer, albeit thirteen years later: "If I am a doctor, am I supposed to say to victims who walk through the door that I won't treat you unless I can treat everyone? I think not. I think we have to help those we can."[113] D.C. delegate Eleanor Holmes Norton was disgusted by Mayor Williams's embrace of vouchers, calling him "a sellout."[114] Senator John Kerry (D-MA) once showed some willingness to consider vouchers. "Shame on us," he admonished in 1998, "for not realizing that there are parents in this country who . . . support vouchers not because they are enamored with private schools but because they want a choice for their children. They want alternatives, and seeing none in our rigid system, they are willing and some even desperate to look elsewhere."[115] But in 2004, he told the Associated Press, "I have never supported vouchers."[116]

Liberal groups have lined up behind the teachers' unions to oppose vouchers with everything they've got. In 1997, People for the American Way and the NAACP joined forces to create Partners for Public Education (PPE). A docile Ford Foundation kicked in $100,000.[117] Other foundations have also provided support for PPE to fight school vouchers in court and in electoral contests across the country. The American Civil Liberties Union has filed numerous suits to halt implementation of voucher plans.

But that is small potatoes compared with the immense firepower of the National Education Association. The NEA sees the struggle over vouchers as a matter of life and death. Widespread vouchers, they fear, would spell the end of teachers' unions. In the 1999–2000 election cycle, the NEA Political Action Committee spent $6,108,973. Peter Brimelow of *Forbes* magazine explains the context:

Because of the NEA's hydra-headed nature, the national organization's PAC is only part of its hard-money political spending story. State affiliates and even some NEA locals have PACs too. The NEA has claimed that it does not know how much they spend altogether. Extrapolating from four representative states, however, Leslie Spencer and I estimated in *Forbes* that total state and local spending amounted to a remarkable $16 million in 1992–when it was about seven times what the NEA's PAC spent. If that relationship holds true, PAC spending by NEA state and local affiliates in the 1999-2000 cycle would have been an additional, even more remarkable, $42.5 million. So, the NEA overall may have given roughly $50 million to candidates. By comparison, the Federal Election Commission reports that the total of *all* PAC contributions to *all* federal candidates in the 1999-2000 cycle was a mere $579.4 million. In other words, the Teacher Trust (including the AFT) provided one out of every ten dollars spent in elections.[118]

Naturally, the NEA gives about 98 percent of its contributions to Democrats.[119] And Democratic candidates, like Vice President Al Gore in 2000, have been vociferous opponents of vouchers while supporting every "reform" that pleases the union. Among the acceptable education reforms Democrats recommend are (1) more spending, (2) smaller classes (which means more teachers), and (3) less testing (which means less accountability for teachers).

In March 2004, the union acknowledged that both the IRS and the Labor Department are investigating it for failure to disclose political contributions.[120]

The NEA and the AFT descend to yellow journalism where vouchers are concerned. "Who supports vouchers?" asked one NEA affiliate's Web site. "How about the former military dictator of Chile, alleged torturer Augusto Pinochet?"[121] When D.C. delegate Eleanor Holmes Norton appeared on the *NewsHour with Jim Lehrer* to debate vouchers with then Majority Leader Dick Armey in 1998, she relied on all of the usual liberal arguments: vouchers were unconstitutional because public money might go to religious schools (an argument the Supreme Court later rejected), vouchers would drain money from the public schools, and supporters of vouchers were engaged in a "charade" for political purposes since Bill Clinton (whose daughter attended Sidwell Friends) had promised to veto the bill. Rep. Armey then noted that he had personally donated money to nine D.C. children so that they could attend private schools.[122] Some charade.

Liberals have focused a great deal of intellectual energy on the notion that vouchers will cream off the best students. Kwesi Mfume, president of the NAACP, for example, has said that voucher proposals are intended to disguise the reality that "the best students will be skimmed off–those whom private schools find desirable for their own reasons."[123] What they have not quite grappled with is the idea of competition. As Milton Friedman predicted, those public schools who have been forced to compete with voucher schools have improved. A study by Harvard's Program on Education Policy and Governance found that in Florida "schools receiving a failing grade from the state in 1999, and whose students have been offered tuition vouchers if they failed a second time, achieved test score gains more than twice as large as those achieved by other schools. . . . Schools with failing grades that faced the prospect of vouchers exhibited especially large gains."[124]

Liberal opposition to vouchers can be explained as excessive delicacy about church/state relations. It can be seen as reflecting concern about spending. But consider the following exchange between Matthew Miller, a writer for the *Atlantic Monthly*, and Bob Chase, president of the National Education Association. Miller was attempting to broker a compromise of sorts between opponents and backers of vouchers. He had already approached a number of conservatives, including Milton Friedman, and inquired whether they might accept a compromise in which spending for the public schools was increased while vouchers were offered. Some said yes.

When Miller approached Chase, here's how the exchange unfolded:

"Is there any circumstance under which that would be something that . . ."

"No."

". . . you guys could live with? Why?"

"No."

". . . in inner cities?"

"No."

"Triple it [spending]?"

"No."

". . . but give them a voucher?"

" 'Cause, one, that's not going to happen. I'm not going to answer a hypothetical when nothing like that is ever possible."

"But teachers use hypotheticals every day."

"Not in arguments like this we don't. . . . It's pure and simply not going to happen. . . ."[125]

Sandra Feldman, president of the American Federation of Teachers, was equally adamant. The encounters left Miller, a writer for the (mostly) liberal *New Republic*, wondering if the Democratic Party was supporting its "funders at the expense of its constituents."[126]

## Vanishing Historical Memory

Americans are attached to the idea of public school, but they may be supporting something that has long since ceased to be. The idea of schools that can take children from very different backgrounds, races, and religions, and turn them into Americans maintains its appeal. There is a genuine fear that voucher schools might tend to Balkanize the nation. Yet, in reality, our public schools no longer inculcate patriotism nor even an understanding of America's place in the world. They are doing something else entirely.

A survey commissioned by the American Council of Trustees and Alumni conducted by the Roper organization in 1999 tested college seniors at fifty of our most elite colleges on the basics of American history. Among the universities included in the survey were Harvard, Princeton, Swarthmore, Dartmouth, the University of California at Berkeley, MIT, Rice, Columbia, and Duke.[127]

If the test had been graded, 81 percent of college seniors would have received a grade of D or F. Thirty-five percent thought that the Marxist slogan "From each according to his ability, to each according to his need" could be found in the Constitution. More than half thought Germany, Italy, or Japan was a U.S. ally during World War II. Only 29 percent knew (or correctly guessed) that Reconstruction referred to post–Civil War political arrangements. Fifty-nine percent thought it had to do with repairing the physical damage caused by the war. Only 26 percent knew that the Emancipation Proclamation freed only slaves held in the Confederate states. Sixty-three percent thought it freed all of the slaves. Only 60 percent knew which document established the division of powers among the three branches of government. Twenty-six percent thought the Articles of Confederation deserved the credit, and 8 percent of these elite college students thought it might be the Marshall Plan.

Only 45 percent could correctly choose the date range of Jefferson's presidency from a multiple choice list (these questions were all multiple choice). Thirty-three percent chose 1780–1800, and 2 percent chose 1860–1880!

Only 34 percent could identify the American general at Yorktown. Thirty-seven percent thought it was Ulysses S. Grant. Twenty-eight percent of our best students thought John Marshall was the author of the *Brown v. Board of Education* decision, and 43 percent thought the phrase "government of the people, by the people, and for the people" could be found in the Declaration of Independence. Only 22 percent correctly cited the Gettysburg Address.

When it came to naming government programs from different eras, our students were all over the map. One question read "Social legislation passed under President Lyndon B. Johnson's Great Society Program included" and here are the choices and the percent who chose them:

a.  The Sherman Antitrust Act–16 percent
b.  The Voting Rights Act–30 percent
c.  The Tennessee Valley Authority–19 percent
d.  The Civilian Conservation Corps–22 percent

The rest left it blank.

There were a couple of questions that the kids absolutely aced. Ninety-nine percent correctly identified Beavis and Butthead as television cartoon characters, and 99 percent knew that Snoop Doggy Dog was a rap singer.

Not surprisingly, surveys of elementary and secondary school students provide similarly depressing results. According to the National Assessment of Educational Progress, often called "the nation's report card," 75 percent of fourth graders could not name the branch of government that passes laws. Thirty-six percent of eleventh graders thought the Magna Carta was "the charter signed by the Pilgrims on the Mayflower." Only 39 percent of eleventh graders could correctly place D-Day between 1943–1947. Fewer than 32 percent knew that Jim Crow laws enforced segregation. And only 36 percent could find on a map the territories taken from Mexico in war.[128]

If we lose our history–our collective memory of the struggles, triumphs, and tragedies of our nation–then what are we? A random collection of sports fans, McDonald's customers, SUV drivers, and television watchers? Without a shared sense of history and widely understood cultural terms of reference, our very national identity is in question. A few decades ago, most Americans recognized and understood the meaning of the words: "Give me liberty or give me death," "First in war, first in peace, and first in the hearts of his countrymen," Yorktown, bleeding Kansas, Reconstruction, Ellis Island, *Marbury v. Madison*, "Remember the Maine," the Spirit of St. Louis, Midway, "I shall return," the Battle of the Bulge, the Hiss/Chambers case, and "Ich Bin ein Berliner."

Not so many years ago, this nation was self-confident enough to demand that those who immigrated here adopt our language and customs. Today, we don't even teach our history to our native-born population. Among the fifty-five elite colleges who participated in the Roper survey, not one requires a course in U.S. history for graduation. At 78 percent of these institutions, no history of any kind is required. This ignorance, of course, trickles down to the secondary and primary schools, where the study of history has been almost completely supplanted in favor of a thin gruel called "social studies." The old way worked better.

In 1947, 77 percent of high school graduates knew which party controlled the House of Representatives. In 1996, only 54 percent could answer that question.

But as Mark Twain once said, "It ain't what you don't know that gets you into trouble. It's what you know for sure that just ain't so." And so much of what Americans–particularly college-educated Americans–think they know about our history is just plain wrong. It is wrong because for several decades higher education in this country has been dominated by liberals and Leftists. Left-leaning professors serve up a vision of our history that is a caricature of reality.

Many American schoolchildren are offered a view of our history that is tendentious at best and anti-American propaganda at worst. Some of the social studies textbooks, with their denunciations of Columbus and overemphasis on Joseph McCarthy, are reminiscent of the Gilbert and Sullivan line about "the idiot who praises with enthusiastic tone every century but this and every country but his own."

In *The Language Police*, Diane Ravitch offers this assessment of the widely used middle-school textbook *To See a World*, published by Houghton Mifflin:

... *To See a World* implies that every world culture is wonderful except for the United States. It lauds every world culture as advanced, complex, and rich with artistic achievement, except for the United States. Readers learn that people in the United States confront such problems as discrimination, poverty, and pollution. Those who came to this country looking for freedom, the book says, found hardship and prejudice; the immigrants did all the hard work, but the settled population hated and feared them. Despite these many injustices, people kept trying to immigrate to the United States, but many were excluded because of their race or ethnicity. Compared to other cultures in the world, the United States sounds like a frightening place. Why people keep trying to immigrate to this unwelcoming, mean-spirited culture is a puzzle.[129]

No serious person would suggest that American history should be taught in a cheerleading way or that this nation's many sins and flaws should be glossed over. That would be an offense against the truth. At the same time, taken for all in all, and compared with other nations, we have less to fear from the truth than any other society.

Left-wing professors, on the other hand, present American history as a cartoon featuring big bad capitalists and white males against virtuous, environment-preserving, peace-loving Indians, women, and minorities. The American Revolution is taught as the triumph of one group of property-owning white men over another. In their telling, slavery is not the blot on an otherwise brilliant beginning, but the soul of the enterprise. This is a libel.

C. Sheldon Thorne, professor of history at Golden West University, wrote to the *L.A. Times* in 2002 about his colleagues in the academy:

What is truly unfortunate, however, is that these purveyors of "blame America first, last, and always" at the university level are preaching to the choir. By the time students emerge from 12 years of public education they are exquisitely sensitive to every nuance of racism, sexism, and imperialism in American history, albeit unable to write a coherent paragraph about any of them. Most of my U.S. history students have it all figured out long before they step into the classroom: America is rotten to the core. Ask about the Constitution and they can virtually respond in unison, "A racist document written by rich white men." The Westward movement? A genocidal march driven by capitalist greed. They are utterly convinced that in all of human history the U.S. is the only country to have practiced slavery.[130]

And here is Professor Elizabeth Cobbs Hoffman of San Diego State, making a related point:

There are numerous examples of the castigating tendency of American scholars but my personal favorite is an anthology I reviewed a few years back. This textbook gave undergraduates three articles on World War II. The first was on Japanese internment, the second on the segregation of black troops in the South, and the third on harassment of Italian Americans. Every article discussed an aspect of the war that was absolutely true; yet, collectively, they made for a portrait of the war that was fundamentally false. No Adolf Hitler, no Emperor Hirohito, no Holocaust—only an imperfect America battling its demons.[131]

This is America through the eyes of liberals. It is the horror of slavery without the uplift of the Abolitionist movement. It is the greed of the "robber barons" without the ingenuity of the Edisons and the Wright Brothers. It is the shame of the Japanese internment without the glory of Iwo Jima. America's children are fully versed on the stain of slavery in American history but not on the great benevolence and sacrifice that that evil brought forth. Youngsters know about Sojourner Truth, but not about William Lloyd Garrison, the Underground Railroad, *Uncle Tom's Cabin*, and Frederick Douglass. Few would recognize the powerful words of Lincoln's second Inaugural address, in which he said:

> If we shall suppose that American slavery is one of those offenses which, in the providence of God, must needs come, but which having continued through His appointed time, He now wills to remove, and that He gives to both North and South this terrible war as the woe due to those by whom the offense came, shall we discern therein any departure from those divine attributes which the believers in a living God always ascribed to Him? Fondly do we wish, fervently do we pray, that this mighty scourge of war may speedily pass away. Yet if God wills that it continue until all the wealth piled by the bondsman's two hundred and fifty years of unrequited toil shall be sunk, and until every drop of blood drawn with the lash shall be paid by another drawn with the sword, as was said three thousand years ago, so still it must be said "the judgments of the Lord are true and righteous altogether."[132]

Lincoln's evocation of the terrible price America paid in blood for the "bondman's . . . unrequited toil" demonstrates a largeness of spirit that is exceedingly rare in men and even scarcer in leaders. Every nation has moral stains in its history, but American children should know that their ancestors struggled to–and largely succeeded in–overcoming theirs.

Most nations offer their children an excessively air-brushed version of their own history–massacres are omitted while triumphs are memorized. Under liberal guidance, many American schools have been doing the reverse.

Historian David McCullough has warned that:

> Something's eating away at the national memory, and a nation or a community or a society can suffer as much from the

adverse effects of amnesia as can an individual. . . . If you're
going to teach just segments of history—women's issues—
youngsters have almost no sense of cause and effect. So many
of the blessings and advantages we have; so many of the reasons why our culture has flourished aren't understood,
they're not appreciated. If you don't have any appreciation of
what people went through to get to achieve to build what you
are benefiting from, then these things don't mean very much
to you.[133]

American education is serving not to pass along the great heritage of the most idealistic nation on earth but rather to embitter
children and young people against this country. Following September 11, 2001, American professors let loose with invective—not
against the enemy that had attacked us, but against America herself.
A professor of physics at the University of Massachusetts at Amherst
said, "The American flag is a symbol of terrorism and death and fear
and destruction and oppression." A professor at the University of
Washington said, "Many people consider the United States to be a
terrorist state." A professor at the University of New Mexico said,
"Anyone who can blow up the Pentagon gets my vote." A professor of
English at Brown University said, "What happened on September 11
was terrorism, but what happened during the Gulf War was also terrorism." And a professor of anthropology at MIT said, "Imagine the
real suffering and grief of people in other countries. The best way to
begin a war on terrorism might be to look in the mirror."

Reform of American education, then, is not just about math and
English and global competitiveness. And it isn't just about closing
the vast gap between rich and poor. It is about preserving the very
soul of our country. The liberal-dominated system that exists today
has leeched billions from our pockets and produced many children
who cannot read and write competently and many more who despise
their ancestors. Liberals have hurt the poor, to be sure. But they are
also engaged in a long-term guerrilla war on America's soul.

# Notes

## Chapter One

1. Andrew Peyton Thomas, *Crime and the Sacking of America*, p. 37.
2. *Crime and Punishment in America*, 1999, www.ncpa.org/studies/s229/2ss9.html.
3. Michael Barone, "The Good News Is the Good News Is Right," *Weekly Standard*, September 8, 1997.
4. Robert James Bindinotto, "The Root Causes of Crime," www.libertyhaven.com.
5. *Mapp v. Ohio*, www.supct.com.
6. Ibid.
7. John T. Fennell, "Lock Them Up and Other Thuggery Stoppers," *Policy Review*, Winter 1984.
8. Ernest van den Haag, "The Growth of the Imperial Judiciary," *Policy Review*, Spring 1978.
9. Ibid.
10. William Tucker, "True Confessions: Time to Revisit Miranda," *Weekly Standard*, May 19, 2003.
11. David Tell, "Let's Have a Fight About Judges," *Weekly Standard*, April 15, 1996.
12. www.cnn.com/ALLPOLITICS/1996/news/9604/02/judge.reverses/index.shtml.
13. Tell, "Let's Have a Fight About Judges."
14. John Derbyshire, *National Review* Online, February 5, 2002.
15. Personal interview with author, September 1993.
16. Abigail and Stephen Thernstrom, *America in Black and White*, p. 46.
17. Ibid., p. 48.
18. Ibid., p. 261.
19. William J. Bennett, *List of Leading Cultural Indicators*, p. 12.
20. Charles Murray, *Losing Ground*, p. 115.
21. Ibid., p. 115.
22. National Center for Policy Analysis, "Crime Is Down Because Punishment Is Up," www.ncpa.org/ba/ba247.html.
23. William E. Leuchtenberg, *A Troubled Feast*, p. 154.
24. Ibid., p. 169.

25. "The American Dream Does Not Yet Exist for All Our Citizens: Kerner Commission Members Discuss Civil Unrest," www.historymatters.gmu.edu/d/6465.html.
26. Thernstrom, *America in Black and White*, p. 160.
27. Leuchtenberg, *A Troubled Feast*, p. 170.
28. Thernstrom, *America in Black and White*, p. 161.
29. Ibid., p. 166.
30. Ibid.
31. Jonathan J. Bean, " 'Burn, Baby, Burn': Small Business in the Urban Riots of the 1960s," *Independent Review*, September 22, 2000.
32. Ibid.
33. Edward Banfield, *The Unheavenly City Revisited*, p. 221.
34. Ibid.
35. www.usc.edu/isd/archives/la/watts.html.
36. Banfield, *Unheavenly City*, p. 228.
37. Ibid.
38. Thernstrom, *America in Black and White*, p. 163.
39. Thernstrom, p. 162.
40. Banfield, *Unheavenly City*, p. 224.
41. Ibid.
42. Thernstrom, *America in Black and White*, p. 279.
43. Wendy Kaminer, "Federal Offense: The Politics of Crime Control," *Atlantic Monthly*, June 1994.
44. Vincent J. Cannato, *The Ungovernable City*, p. 488.
45. Cannato, *Ungovernable City*, p. 532.
46. Bindinotto, *Root Causes of Crime*, www.libertyhaven.com.
47. Myron Magnet, *The Dream and the Nightmare*, p. 163.
48. Cannato, *Ungovernable City*, p. 533.
49. Ibid., p. 532.
50. Quoted in William Tucker, "Unbroken Windows: The Good News on Crime," *American Spectator*, March 1998.
51. Cannato, *Ungovernable City*, p. 534.
52. Ibid., pp. 535–36.
53. Ibid.
54. James Q. Wilson, "Crime and the Liberal Audience," *Commentary*, January 1971.
55. Ibid., p. 77.
56. Thernstrom, *America in Black and White*, p. 173.
57. Bean, "Burn, Baby, Burn."
58. Ibid.
59. Thernstrom, *America in Black and White*, p. 521.
60. Ibid., p. 526.
61. Michael Moore, *Stupid White Men*, p. 61.
62. John J. DiIulio, "My Black Crime Problem and Ours," *City Journal*, Spring 1996.
63. Ibid., p. 25.
64. Thernstrom, *America in Black and White*, p. 602, note 94.

65. Ibid., pp. 263–64.
66. Ibid., p. 265.
67. Dinesh D'Souza, *The End of Racism*, p. 261.
68. Bureau of the Census, 2000.
69. Thernstrom, *America in Black and White*, p. 263.
70. Lynne Duke, " 'Hailing While Black' Sparks a Cab Crackdown," *Washington Post*, November 16, 1999.
71. Heather MacDonald, "The Racial Profiling Myth Debunked," *City Journal*, Spring 2002.
72. Ibid.
73. Richard Cohen, "Closing the Door on Crime," *Washington Post*, September 7, 1986.
74. Thernstrom, *America in Black and White*, p. 263.
75. "Violent Victimization and Race, 1993–98," Bureau of Justice Statistics, US-DOJ, www.ojp.usdoj.gov.
76. "Young Black Male Victims," National Crime Victimization Survey, www.ojp.usdoj.gov.
77. www.ojp.usdoj.gov/bjs/cvict_v.htm.
78. "Violent Victimization and Race," www.usdoj.gov.
79. "Bureau of Justice Statistics Victim Characteristics," www.ojp.usdoj.gov/bjs/cvict_v.htm.
80. John J. DiIulio, "The Question of Black Crime," *Public Interest*, September 22, 1994.
81. Ibid.
82. John J. DiIulio, "White Lies about Black Crime," *Public Interest*, Winter 1995.
83. Ibid.
84. Tamar Jacoby, "From Protest to Politics," *Hoover Digest*, 2001, no. 1, www.hooverdigest.org/011/jacoby.html.
85. William J. Bennett, "An Exchange on Crime and Punishment," *First Things*, January 1994.
86. George Kelling and William Bratton, "Taking Back the Streets," *City Journal*, Summer 1994.
87. Ibid.
88. DiIulio, "White Lies About Black Crime."
89. Barbara Kantrowitz, "Growing Up Under Fire," *Newsweek*, June 10, 1991.
90. Personal interview with author, January 1996.
91. George Kelling and Catherine Coles, *Fixing Broken Windows*, p. 167.
92. Sol Stern, "The Legal Aid Follies," *City Journal*, Autumn 1995.
93. Scott Ladd, "Court Bars Drug-Suspect Evictions," *Newsday*, March 4, 1992.
94. Eugene Methvin, "Mugged by Reality," *Journal of American Citizenship Policy Review*, July/August 1987.
95. Jan M. Chaiken, "Crunching Numbers: Crime and Incarceration at the End of the Millennium," *National Institute of Justice Journal*, January 2000.
96. Kaminer, "Federal Offense."
97. Methvin, "Mugged by Reality."
98. Ibid.

 99. Peter Reinhartz, "The Crime War's Next Battles," *City Journal*, Winter 1998.
100. Ibid.
101. Methvin, "Mugged by Reality."
102. William Andrews and William J. Bratton, "What We've Learned About Policing," *City Journal*, Spring 1999.
103. Quoted in Heather MacDonald, "America's Best Police Force," *City Journal*, Summer 2000.
104. Sol Stern, "Turnaround: How America's Top Cop Reversed the Crime Epidemic," *Commentary*, March 1998.
105. Reinhartz, "The Crime War's Next Battles."
106. Fox Butterfield, "Defying Gravity, Inmate Population Climbs," *New York Times*, January 19, 1998.
107. "Two Million Inmates, and Counting," editorial, *New York Times*, April 9, 2003.
108. "Incarceration Brings Down Crime," editorial, *Washington Times*, September 2, 2003.
109. Ibid.
110. Kevin Flynn, "Rights Panel Scolds Police on Race Issues," *New York Times*, April 27, 2000.
111. Heather MacDonald, "Diallo Truth, Diallo Falsehood," *City Journal*, Summer 1999.
112. William K. Rashbaum, "More Police Officers Being Punished, But Not More Severely," *New York Times*, July 28, 2000.
113. Michael Powell and Christine Haughney, "Immigrant Tortured by Police Settles Suit for $8.7 million," *Washington Post*, July 13, 2001.
114. Ibid.
115. Blaine Harden, "Turning Back the Clock on 'Giuliani Time,' " *Washington Post*, January 15, 1998.
116. Matt Bai and Gregory Beals, "A Mayor Under Siege," *Newsweek*, April 5, 1999.
117. MacDonald, "Diallo Truth."
118. Arch Puddington, "The War on the War on Crime," *Commentary*, May 1999.
119. Ibid.
120. "The Diallo Case Unfolds," editorial, *New York Times*, April 2, 1999.
121. Puddington, "The War on the War on Crime."
122. Ibid.
123. Ibid.
124. MacDonald, "Diallo Truth."
125. Tamar Jacoby, "Race and Truth," *City Journal*, Spring 1999.
126. Eli Lehrer, "Crime-Fighting and Urban Renewal," *Public Interest*, Fall 2000.

**Chapter Two**

  1. John Leo, "The Selma Mind-Set," *U.S. News & World Report*, December 18, 2000.
  2. Tamar Jacoby, "Voters and Victims: How Blacks Lost No Matter What," *National Review*, December 4, 2000.

3. Stuart Taylor Jr., "Legal Affairs: Finding Racial Bias Where There Was None," *National Journal*, June 9, 2001.

4. John Leo, "Was the Black Vote in Florida Really Suppressed?" *U.S. News & World Report*, December 18, 2000.

5. Taylor, "Legal Affairs."

6. Kevin Sack, "Seven Blacks Challenge Georgia's Voting System," *New York Times*, January 6, 2001.

7. www.sharpton2004.org.

8. www.rmc.org/realitycheck/pdf/qt1214.pdf.

9. Moore, Michael, *Stupid White Men*, p. 4.

10. Katherine Q. Seelye, "The 2002 Campaign: The Governors, Cast Reassembled, Florida Revives a Drama from 2000," *New York Times*, November 2, 2002.

11. John J. Miller, "Black Mark: The NAACP Discredits Itself in Florida," *Weekly Standard*, December 31, 2000.

12. www.aclu.org/VotingRights/VotingRightsMain.cfm.

13. www.usccr.gov/pubs/vote2000/report/exesum.htm.

14. Thernstrom/Redenbaugh Dissent to U.S. Civil Rights Commission Report.

15. Jennifer Braceras, "Uncivil Commission: In Florida, the Civil Rights Commission Achieves a New Low," *Weekly Standard,* February 26, 2001.

16. Thernstrom/Redenbaugh Dissent.

17. Ibid.

18. Ibid.

19. "A Civil Wrong," editorial, *Wall Street Journal*, June 6, 2001.

20. www.manhattan-institute.org/html/_natljournal-legal_affairs.htm.

21. jointcenter.org/sepaper/pdffiles/blackvot/2000/BlackVote2000.pdf.

22. progressive.org/mplusane1098.htm.

23. www.cbsnews.com/campaign2000results/state/poll_noys-.html.

24. Richard Pearson, "Former Alabama Governor George C. Wallace Dies," *Washington Post*, September 14, 1998.

25. Walter Williams, "Jackson, Sharpton, and Gore Play Racial Rope-A-Dope," *Capitalism*, December 20, 2000.

26. Leo, "Was the Black Vote in Florida Really Suppressed?"

27. Williams, "Jackson, Sharpton."

28. http//archive.salon.com/politics2000/feature/2000/01/18/gore/print.html.

29. Leo, "Was the Black Vote in Florida Really Suppressed?"

30. Roger Clegg, "Racial Divide," *Legal Times*, November 20, 2000.

31. www.gwu.edu/~action/ads2/adnaacp.html.

32. James A. Cooley, "(Some) Victims' Rights," *National Review*, May 8, 2001.

33. www.gwu.edu/~action/ads2/adnaacp.html.

34. Stephen F. Hayes, "The Democrats' Race Conspiracy Theory: Are Republicans Really Trying to Keep African-Americans from Voting?" *Weekly Standard*, November 6, 2002.

35. Ibid.

36. www.townhall.com/columnists/johnleo/printjl20001211.shtml.

37. Quoted in Mackubin T. Owens, "Al Gore's Assault on the Constitution," www.ashbrook.org/publicat/oped/owens/00/gore.html.

38. "GOP Accused of Planning to Harass Minorities at Polls," Associated Press, November 3, 1998.
39. Hayes, "The Democrats' Race Conspiracy Theory."
40. Ibid.
41. Miller, "Black Mark."
42. Jacoby, "Voters and Victims."
43. Ibid.
44. Terry Eastland, "Bork Revisited," *Commentary*, February 1990.
45. Ibid.
46. Suzanne Garment, "The War Against Robert H. Bork," *Commentary*, January 1988.
47. http://faculty.ncwc.edu/toconnor/410/410lect03.htm.
48. Patrick McGuigan and Dawn Weyrich, *Ninth Justice*, p. 102.
49. Mona Charen, "This Nomination Is Not a Quota Filler," *Newsday*, July 10, 1991.
50. Arch Puddington, "Clarence Thomas and the Blacks," *Commentary*, February 1992.
51. Ibid.
52. Ibid.
53. Ibid.
54. Daniel Troy, "Law Review, Bar Brawl: The ABA Prepares to Fight Dirty," *National Review*, November 23, 1998.
55. Jesse Lee Peterson, *Scam: How Black Leadership Exploits Black America*. p. 21.
56. Ibid.
57. Puddington, "Clarence Thomas."
58. Maureen Dowd, "Could Thomas Be Right?" *New York Times,* June 25, 2003.
59. www.rightwingnews.com/quotes/leftwingracists.php.
60. Barbara Reynolds, Media Research Center, *Notable Quotables*, September 16, 1991.
61. Kurt Eichenwald, "Texaco Executives, On Tape, Discussed Impeding a Bias Suit," *New York Times*, November 4, 1996.
62. Kurt Eichenwald, "Civil Rights Groups Asking U.S. to Join Texaco Bias Suit," *New York Times*, November 6, 1996.
63. www.pwww.org/archives96/11-16-2/html.
64. "Racism at Texaco," editorial, *New York Times*, November 6, 1996.
65. Michael Kelly, "The Script," *New Republic*, December 9, 1996.
66. Ibid.
67. http://mbhs.bergtraum.k12.ny.us/cybereng/nyt/11-16-1.htm.
68. Vern E. Smith and Marc Peyser, "Terror in the Night Down South," *Newsweek*, June 3, 1996.
69. Michael Fumento, "Politics and Church Burnings: Racist Conspiracy Not Evident in Rash of Church Burnings," *Commentary*, October 1996.
70. Ibid.
71. Michael Kelly, "Playing with Fire," *New Yorker*, July 15, 1996.
72. Smith and Peyser, "Terror in the Night."
73. Kelly, "Playing with Fire."

74. Ibid.
75. Fumento, "Politics and Church Burnings."
76. Ibid.
77. Ibid.
78. Ibid.
79. http://archives.cjr.org/year/96/5/churches.asp.
80. Melissa Fay Greene, "Trial by Fire," *Washington Post*, July 1, 1996.
81. Al Sharpton, "The Fire This Time: A Rally for Our Churches," *Essence*, October 1996.
82. Deroy Murdoch, "Dems Need to Houseclean," *National Review* Online, January 6, 2003.
83. Ibid.
84. Ibid.
85. Kelly, "Playing with Fire."
86. Ibid.
87. James K. Glassman, "Hiding Behind the Smoke," *Washington Post*, June 18, 1996.
88. www.mediaresearch.org/BozellColumns~newscolumn/1996/col19961219.asp.
89. Fumento, "Politics and Church Burnings."
90. Ibid.
91. Ibid.
92. Michael Fumento, "*USA Today*'s Arson Artistry," *American Spectator*, December 1996.
93. Ibid.
94. Kelly, "Playing with Fire."
95. Jeremy Derfner, "The New Black Caucus," *American Prospect*, vol. 11, issue 10, March 27, 2000.
96. David Lublin, "Racial Redistricting and African-American Representation: A Critique of 'Do Majority-Minority Districts Maximize Substantive Black Representation in Congress?' " *American Political Science Review*, March 1999.
97. Tony Snow, "Democrat Campaigns Mirror Those They Criticized," *Washington Times*, November 2, 1998.
98. Matt Labash, "The New Race-Baiters," *Weekly Standard*, November 23, 1998.
99. Ibid.
100. Robert James Bindinotto, "Getting Away with Murder," *Reader's Digest*, July 1988.
101. Ibid.
102. Byron York, "Strange Justice: The Liberal Coalition that Killed the Pickering Nomination," *National Review*, April 8, 2002.
103. Stuart Taylor Jr., "Who's Worse? Race-Baiting Democrats or Class-Warring Republicans?" *National Journal*, January 18, 2003.
104. Carl Cannon, "The Judge and the Times," *Weekly Standard*, March 25, 2002.
105. Mona Charen, "McCarthyism," February 7, 2002.
106. Ibid.
107. "Judicial Selection After Trent Lott," editorial, *New York Times*, December 22, 2002.

108. Byron York, "The Next Big Fight," *National Review*, February 6, 2002.

109. Ibid.

110. Taylor, "Who's Worse?"

111. Ibid.

112. Cannon, "The Judge and the Times."

113. Taylor, "Who's Worse?"

114. Byron York, "Behind the Democrats' Attack," *National Review*, February 11, 2002.

115. Ibid.

116. Ibid.

117. Ibid.

118. Ibid.

119. Jesse J. Holland, "Bush Installs Federal Judge, Sidesteps Congress; Move Expected to Fuel Courts Battle," *Boston Globe*, January 17, 2004.

120. Paul Krugman, "Going for Broke," *New York Times*, January 20, 2004.

121. Byron York, "The Growing Fire Around Trent Lott," *National Review* Online, December 10, 2002.

122. Ibid.

123. Al Franken, *Lies and the Lying Liars Who Tell Them,* pp. 253–54.

124. www.nationalcenter.org/NVDavisBradley1299.html.

125. www.nationalcenter.org/P21NVDavisGore599.html.

126. www.frankenlies.com/civilrights.htm.

127. Gerard Alexander, "The Myth of the Racist Republicans," *Claremont Review of Books*, Spring 2004.

128. Mona Charen, "Republicans and the 'Race Card,' " December 19, 2002.

129. Alexander, "The Myth of the Racist Republicans."

130. Ibid.

131. Ibid.

132. Mark R. Levin, "Selective Moral Outrage," *National Review*, December 10, 2002.

133. abcnews.go.com/images/pdf/803alRace.pdf.

134. pollingreport.com/race.htm.

135. Ibid.

136. www.bet.comarticles/0,1048,clbg2082-2739-1,00.html#boardsAnchor.

137. Abigail and Stephen Thernstrom, *America in Black and White*, pp. 184–86.

138. John McWhorter, *Losing the Race*, p. 9.

139. Ibid., p. 191.

140. Ibid., p. 197.

141. Ibid., p. 10.

142. Personal interview with Stephen Thernstrom, May 2004.

**Chapter Three**

1. William Leuchtenberg, *Franklin D. Roosevelt and the New Deal*, pp. 2–3.

2. http://www.pbs.org/wgbh/amex/dustbowl/peopleevents/index.html.

3. Ibid.

4. Michael Tanner, *The End of Welfare*, p. 45.
5. Leuchtenberg, *Franklin D. Roosevelt*, p. 1.
6. Fred Siegel, *The Future Once Happened Here*, p. 48.
7. Michael B. Barket, "Reviving the Old Consensus," www.philanthropyround table.org/magazines/1998/september/rees.html.
8. Ibid.
9. Marvin Olasky, *The Tragedy of American Compassion*, p. 167.
10. Ibid.
11. Ibid., pp.168–69.
12. http://odur.let.rug.nl/~usa/P/lj36/speeches/su64lbj.htm.
13. John A. Andrew III, *Lyndon Johnson and the Great Society*, p. 81.
14. Olasky, *Tragedy of American Compassion*, p. 172.
15. Quoted in ibid., p. 175.
16. Vincent Cannato, *The Ungovernable City*, p. 540.
17. Felicia Kornbluh, "The Goals of the National Welfare Rights Movement: Why We Need Them Thirty Years Later," *Feminist Studies*, Spring 1998.
18. Heather MacDonald, "Billions of Dollars that Made Things Worse," *City Journal*, Autumn 1996.
19. Siegel, *The Future Once Happened Here*, p. 50.
20. Quoted in Charles Murray, *Losing Ground*, pp. 39, 40.
21. Cannato, *Ungovernable City*, p. 541.
22. Ibid., pp. 539, 540.
23. Siegel, *Future Once Happened Here*, pp. 57–58.
24. Ibid. p. 58.
25. Tanner, *End of Welfare,* p. 54.
26. *Goldberg v. Kelly*, 397 U.S. 254, 90 S.Ct, 1011.
27. Ibid.
28. Ibid.
29. Siegel, *Future Once Happened Here*, p. 51.
30. "Catholic Bishops Issue Letter on U.S. Economy; Call for Jobs Programs, Aid to Poor," *Facts on File World News Digest*, November 16, 1984.
31. Lawrence D. Maloney, "Catholic Prelates Are Once Again Taking Aim at Government Policies–and Stirring Some Bitter Debate," *U.S. News & World Report*, November 26, 1984.
32. John Greenwald, "Am I My Brother's Keeper?" *Time*, November 26, 1984.
33. Ibid.
34. Bill Moyers, "People Like Us," Public Broadcasting Service, June 20, 1988.
35. www.census.gov/Press-Release/www/2002/cb02-77.html.
36. Douglas J. Besharov, ed., *Family and Child Well-Being After Welfare Reform*, pp. 35–36.
37. "Capital Gang," CNN, March 25, 1995.
38. www.heritage.org/research/Welfare/WM126.
39. Kay S. Hymowitz, "The Children's Defense Fund: Not Part of the Solution," *City Journal*, Summer 2000.
40. Ibid.
41. Ibid.

42. Siegel, *Future Once Happened Here*, p. 53.
43. Lori Liebovich, "When Welfare Disappears," interview with William Julius Wilson, salon.com, and www.fumento.com/greatsociety.html.
44. Jonathan Rauch, "The Widening Marriage Gap: America's New Class Divide," *National Journal*, May 19, 2001.
45. Thernstrom, *America in Black and White*, p. 239.
46. Rauch, "The Widening Marriage Gap."
47. William Bennett, *Index of Leading Cultural Indicators*, p. 49.
48. Sol Stern, "Acorn's Nutty Regime for Cities," *City Journal*, Spring 2003.
49. Peter Jennings, *ABC World News Tonight*, June 20, 1991.
50. Ken Bode, "Washington Week in Review," PBS, January 13, 1995.
51. Thomas Sanction, "How to Get America Off the Dole," *Time*, May 25, 1992.
52. Rachel Wildavksy and Daniel R. Levine, "True Faces of Welfare," *Reader's Digest*, March 1999.
53. Tanner, *End of Welfare*, p. 19.
54. Mona Charen, "Soft-Headed 'Compassion' Harms More than Helps," *Augusta Chronicle*, June 24, 1996.
55. Mona Charen, "Dearth of Babies for Adoption," *Washington Times*, July 10, 2000.
56. Wildavksy and Levine, "True Faces of Welfare."
57. Tom Morganthau, "A Tough Winter," *Newsweek*, December 2, 1991.
58. Dan Rather, *CBS Evening News,* February 5, 1992.
59. John Cochran, *NBC News*, August 19, 1992.
60. David Bender and Bruno Leone, eds., *Welfare: Opposing Viewpoints*, p. 158.
61. Siegel, *Future Once Happened Here*, p. 61.
62. Paul Page, "Mother of 14 Says 'I'd Have 14 More,'" Associated Press, July 23, 1987.
63. Tom Sherwood, "Barry Helps Donahue Out on Welfare: Mayor, Mother of 14, Sociologist Wrestle with Urban Poverty," *Washington Post*, July 22, 1987.
64. Robert Rector, and Patrick Fagan, "The Continuing Good News on Welfare Reform," Heritage Foundation Backgrounder no. 1620, February 6, 2003.
65. www.reason.com/rauch/01_05_19.shtml.
66. Ibid.
67. Tanner, *End of Welfare*, p. 20.
68. Ibid.
69. Douglas Besharav and Peter Germanis, "Welfare Reform: Four Years Later," *Public Interest*, Summer 2000.
70. Valerie Polakow, "On a Tightrope Without a Net," *The Nation*, May 1, 1995.
71. Bob Herbert, "In America, the Mouths of Babes," *New York Times*, July 22, 1996.
72. "Look Ma! No Net," editorial, *The Nation*, December 11, 1995.
73. Judy Mann, "Let's Refrain From Attacking the Poor," *Washington Post*, November 23, 1994.
74. www.mediaresearch.org/oped/2002/noyes0802.asp.
75. Frances Fox Piven, "Poorhouse Politics, Welfare Reform," February 1995.
76. Andrew Hacker, "The Crackdown on African Americans," *The Nation*, July 10, 1995.

77. Rich Lowry, *Legacy*, p. 88.
78. Margot Hornblower, "Fixing the System: Los Angeles County Creates a Model Plan to Get Help into Troubled Homes," *Time*, December 11, 1995.
79. Tom Brokaw, "Interview with President Clinton," *Internight*, MSNBC, July 15, 1996.
80. Sam Donaldson, *This Week with David Brinkley*, ABC, August 4, 1996.
81. Dan Rather, *CBS Evening News*, August 25, 1996.
82. www.heritage.org/research/welfare/WM126.
83. Ibid.
84. www.senate.gov/~rpc/releases/1999/wf031902.htm.
85. Patrick J. Sloyan, "Convention 96/Welfare Legislation Is Likely to Draw Debate at Convention," *Newsday*, August 26, 1996.
86. Jeff Jacoby, "Welfare Catastrophe? No, It's a Modest Reform," *Boston Globe*, August 6, 1996.
87. www.mediaresearch.org/news/nq19960826.html.
88. www.heritage.org/research/welfare/WM126.
89. Michael Grunwald, "Is Kerry Really the Most Electable Democrat?" *New Republic*, February 2, 2004.
90. www.cnn.com/ALLPOLITICS/1996/news/9608/20/weld.kerry.debate/index.shtml.
91. slate.msn.com/id/20944399/.
92. CNN, *Inside Politics*, August 26, 1996.
93. ABC, *20/20*, September 20, 1996.
94. NBC, *Today*, September 23, 1996.
95. NBC, *Today*, April 28, 1997.
96. www.nrsc.org/nrscweb/daschel_watch/welfare_reform.pdf.
97. Ibid.
98. Ibid.
99. Peter Edelman, "The Worst Thing Bill Clinton Has Done," *Atlantic*, March 1997.
100. Ibid.
101. Jim Wallis, "The Issue Is Poverty," *Sojourners*, March/April 1997.
102. Rector and Fagan, "The Continuing Good News."
103. Besharov and Germanis, "Welfare Reform."
104. Ibid.
105. Kay Hymowitz, "More Good News About Welfare Reform," *City Journal*, Spring 2003.
106. Ibid.
107. National Center for Policy Analysis, www.ncpa.org/pi/congress/pd082201b.html.
108. Cheryl Wetzstein, "Welfare Rolls Down Despite Rise in Poverty, Census Bureau Says," *Washington Times*, September 4, 2003.
109. Kathy Kiely and William M. Welch, "Welfare Reform's Success Isn't Unquestioned," *USA Today*, August 22, 2001.
110. "Going for Broke?" *Uncommon Knowledge*, www.uncommonknowledge.org/01-02/625.html.
111. http://www.aecf.org/publications/advocasey/summer2002/.

112. Heather MacDonald, "Don't Mess with Welfare Reform's Success," *City Journal*, Winter 2002.
113. Mickey Kaus, "The Good Big News (That Nobody's Reporting)," www.slate.msn.com/id/1007879.
114. MacDonald, "Don't Mess with Welfare Reform's Success."


**Chapter Four**

1. Quoted in Anne Taylor Fleming, *Motherhood Deferred*, p. 24.
2. Betty Freidan, *The Feminine Mystique*, quoted in Fleming, *Motherhood Deferred*, p. 25.
3. Quoted in David Blankenhorn, *Fatherless America*, p. 32.
4. Marlene Dixon, "Why Women's Liberation? Racism and Male Supremacy," edweb.tusd.k12.az/us/USA/APUSH.
5. Quoted in Danielle Crittenden, *What Our Mothers Never Told Us*, p. 98.
6. Shulamith Firestone, *The Dialectic of Sex: The Case for Feminist Revolution*, p. 254.
7. Robin Morgan, *Sisterhood Is Powerful*, p. 537.
8. Germaine Greer, *The Female Eunuch*, p. 317.
9. Ibid., p. 233.
10. Kate Millet, *Sexual Politics*, p. 35.
11. www.spiritone.com/~law/hatequotes.html, September 20, 2002.
12. Jesse Bernard, *The Future of Marriage*, p. 51.
13. Christina Hoff Sommers, *Who Stole Feminism?* pp. 256–57.
14. Vivian Gornick, *The Daily Illini*, April 25, 1981.
15. gos.sbc.edu/d/dworkin2.html.
16. Andrea Dworkin, "Feminism: An Agenda," in *Letters from a War Zone*, p. 146.
17. Catherine MacKinnon, *Feminism Unmodified: Discourses on Life and Law*, p. 59.
18. *Trimble v. Gordon*, 430 U.S. 762 (1977).
19. Maggie Gallagher and David Blankenhorn, "Family Feud," *American Prospect*, July–August 1997.
20. Barbara DaFoe Whitehead, *The Divorce Culture*, p. 72.
21. Ibid., p. 79.
22. Ibid., p. 86.
23. Torrance Kelly, "Priestess Steinem Visits Her Flock," *Alberta Report*, December 15, 1997.
24. Gloria Norris and Jo Ann Miller, *The Working Mother's Complete Handbook*, p. 299, quoted in David Blankenhorn, *Fatherless America*, p. 79.
25. Judith Stacey, *In the Name of the Family*, p. 80.
26. Ibid., p. 51.
27. Crittenden, *What Our Mothers Never Told Us*, p. 106.
28. Barbara Ehrenreich, "Oh Those Family Values," *Time*, July 18, 1994.
29. Blankenhorn, *Fatherless America*, p. 80.
30. Gallagher and Blankenhorn, "Family Feud."
31. Ibid., pp. 80–81.
32. William Bennett, *Index of Leading Cultural Indicators*, p. 68.

33. Ibid., p. 72.
34. Ibid., pp. 48–49.
35. Stephanie Coontz, *The Way We Really Are: Coming to Terms with America's Changing Families*, p. 79.
36. Katha Pollitt and David Blankenhorn, "Divorce," *Slate*, February 22, 1997.
37. Ibid.
38. Stephen D. Sugarman, "Single Parent Families" in *All Our Families*, p. 13.
39. Quoted in Thernstrom, *America in Black and White*, p. 241.
40. Ibid., p. 137.
41. Blankenhorn, *Fatherless America*, p. 76.
42. *Washington Week in Review*, Public Broadcasting Service, May 22, 1992.
43. www.textfiles.com/politics/mbrown.txt.
44. Media Research Center, www.mrc.org.
45. www.thetruthmainly.tripod.com/1992/19920629.html.
46. www.textfiles.com/politics/mbrown.txt.
47. Bruce Morton, commentary, *CBS Evening News*, June 13, 1992.
48. Sari Horwitz, "Parents Skirted on Condoms in High School," *Washington Post*, September 4, 1992.
49. Shant R. Dube, "Childhood Abuse, Neglect, and Household Dysfunction and the Risk of Illicit Drug Use: The Adverse Experiences Study," *Pediatrics*, vol. 111, pp. 564–72.
50. Mona Charen, "Fresh Doubts on Divorce as Best Move," *Newsday*, February 13, 1989.
51. Mona Charen, "Time to Get Away from No-Fault Divorce," *Fort Worth Star-Telegram*, February, 15, 1996.
52. Whitehead, *The Divorce Culture*, p. 93.
53. Ibid., p. 197.
54. Ibid., p. 96.
55. Ibid., pp. 102–3.
56. Margo Wilson and Martin Daly, "The Risk of Maltreatment of Children Living with Stepparents," in Richard J. Gelles, and Jane B. Lancaster, eds., *Child Abuse and Neglect: Biosocial Dimensions, Foundations of Human Behavior*, p. 228.
57. www.heritage.org/research/features/familydatabase/deatil.cfm?ID1=5157.
58. www.heritage.org/Press/NewsReleases/NR060600.cfm.
59. www.ppl.org/ACSWP_Families_April2003.html.
60. Ibid.
61. Heritage Foundation Backgrounder no. 1732, "Marriage Still the Safest Place for Women and Children," March 9, 2004.
62. Bennett, *Index of Leading Cultural Indicators*, pp. 61-62.
63. Ibid., p. 67.
64. Patrick Fagan, Robert Rector, and Lauren R. Noyes, "Why Congress Should Ignore Radical Feminist Opposition to Marriage," Heritage Foundation Backgrounder no. 1662, June 16, 2003, p. 10.
65. Bennett, *Index*, p. 61.
66. Fagan, Rector, and Noyes, "Why Congress Should Ignore," p. 12.
67. www.thenation.com/doc.mhtml?i=20040315&c=1&s=Duggan.

68. Gwendolyn Mink and Anna Marie Smith, "Gay or Straight, Marriage May Not be Bliss," www.falcon.arts.cornell.edu/ams3/npmopedmar04.html.
69. www.legalmomentum.org/issues/wel/lookingforlove.pdf.
70. www.legalmomentum.org/issues/wel/MarriageBackgrounder.pdf.
71. www.progressive.org/0801issue/ehr0801.html.
72. Blankenhorn, *Fatherless America*, p. 183.
73. "Mrs. Clinton Faults 'Orphanage' Suggestion," *Baltimore Sun*, December 1, 1994.
74. William M. Welch, "Orphanage Talk Brings an Outcry," *USA Today*, December 6, 1994.
75. Cynthia Tucker, "The Good Newt and the Bad Newt," *New Orleans Times-Picayune*, January 9, 1995.
76. Charles V. Zehren, "Parting Shots: In a Farewell, Cuomo Rips the Republican Agenda," *Newsday*, December 17, 1994.
77. Richard B. McKenzie, ed., *Rethinking Orphanages for the 21st Century*, p. 89.
78. Leonard Greene, "Telling the Story of How Gingrich Stole Christmas," *Boston Herald*, December 5, 1994.
79. www.nolamarie.net/causes/mwe.
80. Myrna Blyth, *Spin Sisters*, p. 266.
81. Mary McGrory, "Newt's Orphanage Ideas Not as Odd as They Seem," *Buffalo News*, December 16, 1994.
82. Ellen Goodman, "Round Up the Ponies, Fellow Partisans," *Baltimore Sun*, January 13, 1995.
83. Richard J. Gelles, "Putting Children First," *The World and I*, February 1, 2000.
84. Rita Kramer, "In Foster Care, Children Come Last," *City Journal*, Autumn 1994.
85. Conna Craig and Derek Herbert, "The State of Child Welfare," in Richard B. McKenzie, ed., *Rethinking Orphanages for the 21st Century*, p. 24.
86. "Malnourished N.J. Boys Improve," cbsnews.com/2003/10/27/national.
87. Mona Charen, "Nationwide Amber Alert," August 22, 2002.
88. "Battered, Bruised, But Not Broken," *Geraldo*, March 14, 1996.
89. Daniel J. Lehmann, "Wallace Guilty of Hanging Son; Death Penalty Hearing Set for Next Month," *Chicago Sun-Times*, June 21, 1996.
90. R. Bruce Dold, "No Child Deserves This Boy's Pitiful Life," *Chicago Tribune*, May 24, 1996.
91. Mary McGrory, "Juvenile Justice Tastes the Whip," *Washington Post*, June 28, 2001.
92. "Children's Stories," *Washington Post*, September 12, 2001.
93. Ibid.
94. U.S. Department of Health and Human Services, Administration for Youth and Families, "Child Maltreatment 2002," www.acf.hhs.gov/programs/cb/publications/cm02/summary.htm.
95. Jason B. Johnson, "Foster Care Fails State Kids, U.S. Report Says," *San Francisco Chronicle*, January 14, 2003.
96. Mitch Lipka, "A Tug-of-War at N.J. Child-Care Agency," *Philadelphia Inquirer*, December 28, 2003.

97. Heather Vogell, "Deaths of Children in State System Rise," *Charlotte Observer*, January 27, 2002.
98. "Equip New DFCS Leader with Tools to Meet Goals," editorial, *Atlanta Journal-Constitution*, November 25, 2003.
99. Gelles, "Putting Children First."
100. Ibid.
101. Conna Craig, "What I Need Is a Mom," *Policy Review*, Summer 1995.
102. Statement of Shay Bilchik, president and CEO, Child Welfare League of America, www.cwla.org., February 4, 2004.
103. Adoption Factbook III, National Council for Adoption, 1999.
104. "National Association of Black Social Workers, Position Statement on Trans-Racial Adoption," September 1972, www.adoption@uoregon.edu.
105. Mona Charen, "Racial Identity Casualties," www.library.adoption.com.
106. www.childrensrights.org/Policy/policy_resources_raceculture_transracial.htm.
107. Rita Kramer, "In Foster Care, Children Come Last," *City Journal*, Autumn 1994.
108. Elizabeth Bartholet, *Nobody's Children*, p. 130.
109. www.nmsu.edu/~socwork/fpi/.
110. www.aecf.org/publications/data/insites_summer_00.pdf.
111. Robert Miller, "Junior League to Have a Ball," *Dallas Morning News*, February 6, 2004.
112. www.nccpr.org/reports/shadowsunshinestate.htm.
113. Patrick Murphy, "Family Preservation and Its Victims," *New York Times*, June 19, 1993.
114. Heather MacDonald, "The Ideology of Family Preservation," *Public Interest*, March 22, 1994.
115. Ibid.
116. Dennis Saffran, "Fatal Preservation," *City Journal,* Summer 1997.
117. Ibid.
118. MacDonald, "The Ideology of Family Preservation."
119. Saffran, "Fatal Preservation."
120. www.nccanch.acf.hhs.gov/topics/prevention/emerging/riskprotectivefactors.cfm.
121. www.preventchildabuse.org/help/remember_risk_factors.html.
122. Patrick Fagan and Kirk Johnson, "Marriage: The Safest Place for Women and Children," www.Heritage.org/Research/Family/BG1535.cfm.
123. www.cis.org.au/Media/OpEds/opeds1999/E091199.htm.
124. MacDonald, "The Ideology of Family Preservation."
125. "Protecting Children from Abuse and Neglect," www.futureofchildren.org.
126. MacDonald, "Ideology of Family Preservation."
127. www.pbs.org/wgbh/pages/frontline/shows/fostercare/inside/gelles.html.
128. National Conference of State Legislatures, http://www.ncsl.org/statefed/cf/asfasearch.htm.
129. www.pbs.org/wgbh/pages/frontline/shows/fostercare/inside/gelles.html.
130. "The Family Portrait," Family Research Council, Washington, D.C., www.frc.org.
131. The National Marriage Project of Rutgers University, quoted in *National Review* Online, June 15, 2001.

## Chapter Five

1. *Papachristou v. City of Jacksonville*, 405 U.S. 156, 92 S. Ct. 839.
2. Ibid.
3. Wesley R. Smith, "Don't Stand So Close to Me," *Policy Review*, Fall 1994.
4. Ibid.
5. E. Fuller Torrey, "Let's Stop Being Nutty About the Mentally Ill," *City Journal*, Summer 1997.
6. Willard Gaylin and Bruce Jennings, *The Perversion of Autonomy*, p. 209.
7. Myron Magnet, *The Dream and the Nightmare*, p. 93.
8. Ibid.
9. Ibid
10. Thomas Lueck, "Youths Set Homeless Man on Fire," *New York Times*, April 9, 2002.
11. Sally Satel, "Treating Insanity Reasonably," *City Journal*, Winter 1995.
12. Ibid.
13. Heather MacDonald, "What About the Children?" *City Journal*, Summer 1995.
14. Jonah Goldberg, "Lock 'Em Up," www.nationalreview.com/goldberg/goldberg1208899.
15. Jay Nordlinger, "Rosie O'Donnell, Political Activist," *National Review*, June 19, 2000.
16. David Brooks, "Mindlessness About Homelessness," December 20, 1999.
17. Magnet, *The Dream and the Nightmare*.
18. Ibid., pp. 108–9.
19. Heather MacDonald, "Have We Crossed the Line?" *City Journal*, Winter 1993.
20. George Kelling and Catherine M. Coles, *Fixing Broken Windows*, pp. 125–26.
21. "The Homeless: A Job But No Place to Live," *Time*, December 28, 1987.
22. Muriel Dobbin, "The Children of the Homeless," *U.S. News and World Report*, August 3, 1987.
23. Quoted in Brent Bozell, *Media Watch*, February 1996.
24. S. Robert Lichter, "Media's Typical Homeless Are Anything But," www.fortfreedom.org/n22.
25. Christopher Jencks, *The Homeless*, p. 2.
26. Jackie Judd, *ABC World News Tonight*, November 22, 1987.
27. Media Research Center, *CBS Evening News*, July 3, 2003.
28. Media Research Center, *Dateline*, July 4, 2003.
29. Quoted in Magnet, *The Dream and the Nightmare*, p. 80.
30. www.tech.mit.edu/V105/N52/hunger.html.
31. Kelly O'Donnell, Media Research Center, *Notable Quotables*, July 29, 1998.
32. Julia Soyer and Lula Guilbert, Teacher Handbook, www.giveusyourpoor.org/GUYPMiddleSchool.
33. Ibid.
34. Stephen Chapman, "Finding the Real Causes and Cures of Homelessness," *Chicago Tribune*, November 29, 1987.
35. Muriel Dobbin, "The Children of the Homeless."
36. Evan Thomas, "Coming in from the Cold," *Time*, February 4, 1985.

37. Chapman, "Finding the Causes and Cures of Homelessness."
38. Christopher Jencks, *The Homeless*, p. 22.
39. Patricia Zapf, et al, "An Examination of the Relationship of Homelessness to Mental Disorder," *Canadian Journal of Psychiatry*, vol. 41, September 1996.
40. Jencks, *The Homeless*, p. 96.
41. Ibid., pp. 96–97.
42. Andrew Peyton Thomas, "The Rise and Fall of the Homeless," *Weekly Standard*, April 8, 1996.
43. E. Fuller Torrey, "Leaving the Mentally Ill Out in the Cold," *City Journal*, Autumn 2003.
44. Testimony of Stanley J. Czerwinski, director, Physical Infrastructure Issues, Government Accounting Office, before Subcommittee on Housing and Transportation, U.S. Senate, March 6, 2002.
45. Heather MacDonald, "Holiday Homelessness Hype," *City Journal*, Winter 2003.
46. Brian Anderson and Matthew Robinson, "Willie Brown Shows How Not to Run a City," *City Journal*, Autumn 1988.
47. Ibid.
48. Joel Stein, "The Real Face of Homelessness," cnn.com/2003/allpolitics.
49. Lou Waters, *CNN Prime News*, August 8, 1989.
50. MacDonald, "Holiday Homelessness Hype."
51. Brooks, "Mindlessness About Homelessness."
52. MacDonald, "Have We Crossed the Line?"
53. Ibid.
54. Ibid.
55. Timothy Egan, "Racist Shootings Test Limits of System, and Laws," *New York Times*, August 14, 1999.
56. Robert Stacy McCain, "Homeless Population Poses Criminal Risk," *Washington Times*, March 18, 2003.
57. Ibid.
58. Richard Lezin Jones, "Suspect in Subway Attack Has a History of Violence," *New York Times*, November 17, 2001.
59. "We've Tried Mandatory Treatment–and It Works," *City Journal*, Summer 1999.
60. E. Fuller Torrey and Mary Zdanowicz, "A Right to Mental Illness?" *New York Post*, May 28, 1999.
61. "Who Let This Madman Walk?" editorial, *New York Post*, March 7, 2004.
62. Smith, "Don't Stand So Close to Me."

## Chapter Six

1. Charles J. Skyes, *Dumbing Down Our Kids*, p. 220.
2. Walter Mondale for President campaign, www.4president.org/brochures/mondale84.pdf.
3. Nancy Pelosi, letter to constituents, July 24, 2003, "Republican Head Start Bill Undermines the Aspirations of Hard Working Parents."
4. Presidential debates, 2000, www.debates.org/pages/trans2000.
5. Jay Mathews, "In Schools, a Battle on the WWII Learning Front," *Washington Post*, May 28, 2004.

6. Citizens Against Government Waste, Department of Education, www.cagw. org.
7. Bureau of the Census, Annual Survey of Local Government Finances, p. ix, www.census.gov/govs/www/school.
8. Deroy Murdoch, "Emancipation Proclamation," *National Review* Online, October 14, 2003.
9. Citizens Against Government Waste, www.cagw.org.
10. Christina Hoff Sommers, *The War Against Boys*, p. 53.
11. Ibid. p. 54.
12. Quoted in Abigail and Stephen Thernstrom, *No Excuses*, pp. 151–52.
13. Andrew Hacker, *Two Nations: Black and White, Separate, Hostile, Unequal*, p. 175.
14. www.nyclu.org/nassau/civil_liberties_1-03/kozol.html.
15. http://lincoln.senate.gov/leg_issue_edu.htm.
16. Emily Mitchell, "Do the Poor Deserve Bad Schools?" *Time,* October 14, 1991, p. 60.
17. www.pbs.org/newshour/bb/education//july-dec97/standards-9-18.html.
18. Thernstrom, *No Excuses*, pp. 154–55.
19. David Boaz, "The Public School Monopoly: America's Berlin Wall," in *Liberating Schools: Education in the Inner City*, Cato Institute, Washington, D.C., 1991.
20. Alan Bonsteel and Carlos A. Bonilla, *A Choice for the Children*, p. 69.
21. Quoted in Bonsteel and Bonilla, *A Choice for the Children*.
22. National Center for Education Statistics, nces.ed.gov/programs/quarterly/vol_1/1_3/3-esq13-c.asp.
23. Sol Stern, *Breaking Free*, pp. 179–80.
24. ——, "The Invisible Miracle of the Catholic Schools," *City Journal*, Summer 1996.
25. Nancy Pelosi, House speech, October 29, 2003.
26. Heritage Center for Data Analysis, data from U.S. Department of Education, 1998.
27. Senate New Democrat Coalition press release, 01-SNDC5, January 23, 2001.
28. "International Scorecard for U.S. Education: Big Spending, So-So Results," *School Reform News*, November 2003.
29. Ibid.
30. Sykes, *Dumbing Down Our Kids*, p. 17.
31. Ibid.
32. Hanna Skandera and Richard Sousa, *School Figures*, p. 135.
33. Paul E. Peterson, "Ticket to Nowhere," *Education Next*, www.education next.org/20032.
34. Casey J. Lartigue, "Politicizing Class Size," *Education Week*, September 29, 1999.
35. Organization for Economic Cooperation and Development, 1999, quoted in Peterson, "Ticket to Nowhere."
36. Blake Hurst, "End of an Illusion," *American Enterprise*, June 1, 2000, p. 44.
37. Quoted in Darcy Ann Olsen, "Benefits of Preschool Don't Last," Cato Institute. www.Cato.org.

38. John Boehner, "Making the Grade," *National Review*, April 6, 2001.
39. Thomas Sowell, *Inside American Education*, p. 80.
40. Remarks of Senator Patty Murray at LEAP Conference, February 20, 2004.
41. http://reid.senate.gov/~reid/press/01/05/2001516618.html.
42. Rosalie Pedalino Porter, "The Case Against Bilingual Education," *Atlantic Monthly*, May 1998.
43. Ibid.
44. Ibid.
45. V. Dion Haynes, "School Ends All Bilingual Classes; Test Scores Rise," *Chicago Tribune*, June 30, 1999.
46. Ibid.
47. Ibid.
48. Albert Shanker, "Where We Stand," March 21, 1993, www.aft.org.
49. Peterson, "Ticket to Nowhere."
50. Quoted in Rochester, J. Martin, *Class Warfare*, pp. 14–15.
51. Thomas Sowell, *Inside American Education*, p. 6.
52. "Pennsylvania's Major Employers Say Public Schools Are Failing to Make the Grade," Lincoln Institute, April 8, 1998, www.lincolninstitute.org/archives/newsrels/nr-kncs.htm.
53. www.ecs.org/clearinghouse/18/40/1840.htm.
54. "California Schools Fail While Spending Increases," www.heartland.org/archives/education/apr97/californ.htm.
55. "Twenty Troubling Facts About American Education," www.empower.org/stories/storyReader$236.
56. Ibid.
57. "Tests Reveal Students Unprepared for College," *School Reform News*, February 2004, p. 6.
58. Quoted in Diane Ravitch, "The Test of Time," www.findarticles.com/cf_dls/m0MJG.
59. Skandera and Sousa, *School Figures*, p. 145.
60. Martin Gross, *The Conspiracy of Ignorance*, pp. 78–79.
61. Quoted in Rochester, *Class Warfare*, p. 94.
62. Diane Ravitch, *Left Back: A Century of Battles Over School Reform*, p. 405.
63. www.educationrevolution.org/paulwellstone.html.
64. http://feingold.senate.gov/speeches/03/11/2003B24536.html.
65. Diane Ravitch, "It's Time to Test the Teachers," *Denver Post*, March 1, 1998.
66. Kerry A. White, "Eye on Performance," *Education Week*, www.edweek.org.
67. Anand Vaishnav, "State to Boost Teacher Training," *Boston Globe*, September 24, 2003.
68. Diane Ravitch, "Our School Problem and Its Solutions," *City Journal*, Winter 1999, p. 34.
69. Thernstrom, *No Excuses*, pp. 12–13.
70. Ibid., p. 13.
71. Ibid., p. 15.
72. Kay Hymowitz, "Philadelphia's Blackboard Jungle," *City Journal*, Winter 2001.

73. Skandera and Sousa, *School Figures,* p. 59.
74. Abigail Thernstrom, "Courting Disorder in the Schools," *Public Interest,* Summer, 1999.
75. Stuart Taylor, "How Courts and Congress Wrecked School Discipline," *National Journal,* November 15, 2003.
76. American Legislative Exchange Council, www.alec.org.
77. Quoted in Thernstrom, "Courting Disorder in the Schools."
78. Ibid.
79. *Tinker v. Des Moines School District,* www.supct.law.cornell.
80. Black Justice Hugo, dissent, *Tinker v. Des Moines School District,* www.supct.law.cornell.edu.
81. Kay Hymowitz, "Who Killed School Discipline?" *City Journal,* Spring 2000.
82. www.supct.law.cornell.edu.
83. Ibid.
84. Ibid.
85. Thernstrom, "Courting Disorder in the Public Schools."
86. Ibid.
87. "Teen Sues Over 'Lesbian Barbie' Shirt Ban," CNN.com/2003/education/06/20/life.barbie.reut/.
88. Adam Marcus, "How Liberals Put Teachers in the Line of Fire," *Washington Monthly,* June 1994.
89. Hymowitz, "Who Killed School Discipline?"
90. Marcus, "How Liberals Put Teachers in the Line of Fire."
91. Mary Pantazis, "Isn't My Child Special Too?" http://www.suite101.com/article.cfm/10060/71977.
92. Sol Stern, *Breaking Free,* p. 175.
93. Ibid.
94. Sol Stern, "The Invisible Miracle of the Catholic Schools," *City Journal,* Summer 1996.
95. Ibid., p. 176.
96. Ibid., p. 179.
97. Ibid., p. 177.
98. Interview with author, 1994.
99. "What Vouchers Can and Can't Solve," *Business Week,* May 10, 1999.
100. Sol Stern, "The Schools Vouchers Built," *City Journal,* Winter 1999.
101. Floyd H. Flake, "No Excuses for Failing Our Children," *Policy Review,* January–February 1999.
102. Ron Grossman, "Polly's Political Paradox," *Chicago Tribune,* August 20, 1993, p. 1.
103. "2000 Opinion Poll," www.jointcenter.org.
104. William J. Howell, et al, "Vouchers in New York, Dayton, and D.C.," *Education Next,* www.educationnext.org/20012/46howell.html.
105. Jennifer Hickey, "Reading, Writin' and Race," *Insight,* January 20, 2003.
106. Matthew Miller, "Education: A Bold Experiment to Fix City Schools," *Atlantic Monthly,* July 1, 1999.
107. "Symposium: Insight on the News: Is the President's Parental Choice Plan the Remedy for Failing Schools?" March 19, 2001.

108. Krista Kafer, "Opportunity for Me, Not for Thee," *Heritage Foundation*, September 24, 2003.
109. Jennifer Garrett, "School Choice: A Lesson in Hypocrisy," *Washington Times*, July 13, 2002.
110. Casey Lartigue, "School Choice Mood Swings," *Washington Times*, March 15, 2003.
111. David Boaz, *Liberating Schools: Education in the Inner City*, p. 9.
112. Pete Du Pont, "Liberals Against Choice," www.ncpa.org/abo/inthenews/Choice.html.
113. Ibid.
114. "NAACP 'No' to Choice," Organization Trends, Capital Research Center, September 2003.
115. Ibid.
116. "Candidates on the Issues," Associated Press, January 26, 2004.
117. "NAACP 'No' to Choice."
118. Peter Brimelow, *The Worm in the Apple*, p. 108.
119. Ibid.
120. Larry Margasak, "Labor Department Investigating National Education Association Reports," Associated Press, March 4, 2004.
121. Pennsylvania Education Association, quoted in Brimelow, *The Worm in the Apple*, p. 131.
122. www.pbs.org/newshour/bb/education/jan-june98/vouchers_4-29.
123. www.rethinkingschools.org, Spring 2002.
124. Mona Charen, "D.C. Vouchers," *Washington Times*, September 15, 2003.
125. Matthew Miller, "Education: A Bold Experiment," *Atlantic Monthly*, July 1, 1999.
126. Ibid.
127. www.goacta.org/publications/reports.html.
128. http://nces.ed.gov/coe.
129. Diane Ravitch, *The Language Police*, p. 142.
130. www.goa cta.org/Newsletter/a cta_2002_winter.pdf.
131. Ibid.
132. http://www.bartleby.com/124/press32.html.
133. Education Reporter, www.eagleforum.org/educate/2003/june03/history.shtml.

# Partial Bibliography

Andrew, John A. *Lyndon Johnson and the Great Society*. New York: Ivan R. Dee, 1988.

Arum, Richard. *Judging School Discipline*. Cambridge, MA: Harvard University Press, 2003.

Banfield, Edward C. *The Unheavenly City Revisited*. Prospect Heights, IL: Waveland Press, 1974.

Bartholet, Elizabeth. *Nobody's Children*. Boston: Beacon Press, 1999.

Bennett, William J. *The Index of Leading Cultural Indicators*. New York: Broadway Books, 1999.

Blankenhorn, David. *Fatherless America*. New York: Basic Books, 1995.

Boaz, David, ed. *Liberating Schools: Education in the Inner City*. Washington, D.C.: Cato Institute, 1991.

Bonsteel, Alan, and Carlos A. Bonilla. *A Choice for the Children*. San Francisco: Institute for Contemporary Studies Press, 1997.

Brimelow, Peter, *The Worm in the Apple*. New York: HarperCollins, 2003.

Cannato, Vincent J. *The Ungovernable City*. New York: Basic Books, 2001.

Coontz, Stephanie. *The Way We Really Are*. New York: Basic Books, 1997.

Crittenden, Danielle. *What Our Mothers Didn't Tell Us*. New York: Simon & Schuster, 1999.

D'Souza, Dinesh. *The End of Racism*. New York: The Free Press, 1995.

Fleming, Anne Taylor. *Motherhood Deferred*. New York: Random House, 1996.

Franken, Al. *Lies and the Lying Liars Who Tell Them*. New York: Dutton, 2003.

Frum, David. *How We Got Here*. New York: Basic Books, 2000.

Gaylin, Willard, and Bruce Jennings. *The Perversion of Autonomy*. New York: The Free Press, 1996.

Goldberg, Bernard. *Bias*. Washington, D.C.: Regnery Publishing, 2002.

Gross, Martin L. *The Conspiracy of Ignorance*. New York: Perennial, 1999.

Hacker, Andrew. *Two Nations: Black and White, Separate, Hostile, and Unequal*. New York: Ballantine Books, 1995.

Hirsch, E. D., Jr. *Cultural Literacy*. New York: Houghton Mifflin, 1988.

——. *The Schools We Need*. New York: Anchor Books, 1996.

Jencks, Christopher. *The Homeless*. Cambridge, MA: Harvard University Press, 1994.

——. *Rethinking Social Policy*. Cambridge, MA: Harvard University Press, 1992.

Kelling, George, and Catherine M. Coles. *Fixing Broken Windows*. New York: The Free Press, 1996.

Leming, James, Lucien Ellington, and Kathleen Porter. *Where Did Social Studies Go Wrong?* Washington, D.C.: Thomas B. Fordham Foundation, 2003.

Leuchtenberg, William E. *Franklin D. Roosevelt and the New Deal*. New York: Harper and Row, 1963.

——. *A Troubled Feast*. Boston: Little, Brown, and Co., 1973.

McGuigan, Patrick B., and Dawn M. Weyrich. *Ninth Justice,* Washington, D.C.: Free Congress Research and Education Foundation, 1990.

McKenzie, Richard B., ed. *Rethinking Orphanages for the 21st Century*. Thousand Oaks, CA: Sage Publications, 1999.

McWhorter, John H. *Losing the Race*. New York: The Free Press, 2000.

Magnet, Myron. *The Dream and the Nightmare*. New York: William Morrow and Company, 1993.

Magnet, Myron, ed. *The Millennial City*. Chicago: Ivan R. Dee, 2000.

Moore, Michael. *Stupid White Men*. New York: HarperCollins, 2001.

Murray, Charles. *Losing Ground*. New York: Basic Books, 1984.

Olasky, Marvin. *The Tragedy of American Compassion*. Washington, D.C.: Regnery Publishing, 1992.

Packer, Herbert L. *The Limits of the Criminal Sanction*. Stanford, CA: Stanford University Press, 1968.

Peterson, Jesse Lee. *Scam: How Black Leadership Exploits Black America*. Nashville, TN: WND Books, 2003.

Ravitch, Diane. *The Language Police*. New York: Alfred A. Knopf, 2003.

——. *Left Back*. New York: Simon & Schuster, 2000.

Ravitch, Diane, and Chester E. Finn, Jr. *What Do Our 17-Year-Olds Know?* New York: Harper and Row, 1987.

Rochester, J. Martin. *Class Warfare*. San Francisco: Encounter Books, 2002.

Siegel, Fred. *The Future Once Happened Here*. New York: The Free Press, 1997.

Simon, Rita J., Howard Alstein, and Marygold S. Melli. *The Case for Transracial Adoption*. Washington, D.C.: American University Press, 1994.

Skandera, Hanna, and Richard Sousa. *School Figures*. Stanford, CA: Hoover Institution Press, 2003.

Sommers, Christina Hoff. *The War Against Boys*. New York: Simon & Schuster, 2000.

——. *Who Stole Feminism?* New York: Simon & Schuster, 1994.

Sowell, Thomas. *Inside American Education*. New York: The Free Press, 1992.

Stacey, Judith. *In the Name of the Family*. Boston: Beacon Press, 1997.

Stern, Sol. *Breaking Free*. San Francisco: Encounter Books, 2003.

Sykes, Charles J. *Dumbing Down Our Kids*. New York: St. Martin's Griffin, 1995.

Tanner, Michael. *The End of Welfare*. Washington, D.C.: Cato Institute, 1996.

Thernstrom, Abigail and Stephen. *America in Black and White*. New York: Simon & Schuster, 1997.

——. *No Excuses*. New York: Simon & Schuster, 2003.

Whitehead, Barbara DaFoe. *The Divorce Culture*. New York: Vintage Books, 1998.

# Index